DR. ATKINS' SUPERENERGY DIET

DR.ATKINS' SUPERENERGY DIET

by **ROBERT C. ATKINS, M.D.**
and **SHIRLEY LINDE**

The diet revolution answer to fatigue and depression

CROWN PUBLISHERS, INC., NEW YORK

This book
is dedicated to
those
open-minded physicians
who are so concerned
with their patients'
well-being
that they are willing
to reject
medical orthodoxy
in order to explore
the advantages
that nutrition medicine
offers

© 1977 by Robert C. Atkins, M.D., and Shirley Linde

Printed in the United States of America

Published simultaneously in Canada by General Publishing Company Limited

Library of Congress Cataloging in Publication Data

Atkins, Robert C
    Dr. Atkins' superenergy diet.

    1. Low-carbohydrate diet. I. Linde, Shirley Motter, joint author.
II. Title.
RM222.2.A85   1976   613.2   76-27687
ISBN 0-517-52538-0

Third Printing, March, 1977

Contents

Preface

This is a book about your energy, or lack of it. Specifically, it will help you learn whether a change in your diet will provide a new level of energy and well-being. If you read this book carefully and follow its recommendations, you may soon experience health benefits you hadn't expected—chronic symptoms and fatigue fading away, as if by magic.

At the same time, you may read or hear discussions of the "Atkins diet." The Atkins diet is referred to as though it were a single set of recommendations for all to follow by rote. It is not, nor was it ever meant to be a single diet. Rather, it is a guide to nutrition, based on thousands of successful applications, permitting each individual to find his own best lifetime diet.

In fact, any physician with an open, exploring mind and a desire to find the single best diet for a patient would, no matter what his preconception, finally prescribe the very same set of dietary recommendations as I. Painstaking trial-and-error examination to determine the diet most perfectly suited to an individual's metabolic response, lifestyle, and preferences must inevitably produce the same result, no matter how it is approached.

This book will provide you with the guidelines to enable you to find the best nutritional recommendations possible for *you*.

Because the nutritional approach eliminates some foods, we

can expect criticism either directly from the affected industries or their spokesmen. Should this happen, bear one fact in mind: the dietary recommendations this book offers have been tested and proven effective in thousands of individuals like you, and by many knowledgeable physicians other than myself. When a diet works and proves safe, no honest scientist can report that it does not. The safety record of these diets, under proper supervision, is unexcelled.

I hope that more than merely reading this book you will try to follow its recommendations as they apply to you. You should experience what thousands before you have learned—that the benefits of nutritional changes can be felt in just a few weeks. This, more than all the words in this book, will convince you that its message is true.

ROBERT C. ATKINS, M.D.

Preface

I know this book will be controversial. There is a great deal of risk in our saying the things that we do. But since we believe in personal integrity, freedom of speech, truth, and the need to stand up for what one knows to be the truth, we write this book. We bring you the facts; some people agree with them, some do not. The truth will be borne out by the public and the test of time.

I have the reputation of being a science writer who probes deeply into any subject. When Bob Atkins and I talked about doing this book together, I questioned other doctors; I researched the literature; I talked to other people who went on the diet. And most importantly, I went on the diet myself, to test its effectiveness.

The diet changed my life. In the past, despite being a fairly bubbly and energetic person, I was usually utterly drained and exhausted by late afternoon. And in the past, I never really felt right unless I had nine hours' sleep. Now my energy level is sustained through the day. I need less sleep. And I no longer leave good company and good times because I'm tired.

It took a year to write this book, and a lifetime to prepare for it. The book is finished, but I'm staying on the diet . . . and I plan to stay on it for another, say, seventy-five years or so.

SHIRLEY LINDE

A Note of Explanation

Nutrition medicine is the science which will enable your doctor to treat and prevent illness and symptoms by using the techniques of nutrition, rather than drugs.

Good nutrition involves more than administering the right vitamins and minerals; it also requires that each individual find the best mixture of fuel to supply his unique metabolic needs.

Since this book deals largely with helping you find that combination of metabolic fuels best suited for your particular needs, we must, at the outset, define the terms we will be using.

There are three major fuels of metabolism—protein, fat, and carbohydrate. For many of us, there is a fourth—alcohol, for which a definition is unnecessary.

Proteins are the nitrogen-containing fuels whose principal function is to provide essential building blocks to vital organs, muscular tissue, and body chemicals. Protein taken in beyond these needs converts into either carbohydrates or fat. Proteins are aggregations of amino acids, some of which the body can manufacture itself (nonessential amino acids) and others which can be derived only from dietary sources (essential amino acids). Any long-term diet must contain these proteins.

Fats are the major storage form of metabolic fuel. Storage fat (triglyceride) provides two major metabolic fuels, free fatty acids and ketone bodies. These fuels are liberated when fat stores break down for the purpose of providing energy. Some fats, too, must be provided by the diet; they are called essential fatty acids, since man cannot manufacture them.

Proteins and fats occur together as constituents of animal products—the meat, fish, fowl, eggs, and cheese that we eat. Thus, it would be nearly impossible to devise a palatable high protein diet that is very low in fat.

Carbohydrates, on the other hand, derived mainly from the vegetable, rather than the animal, kingdom, provide a large share of the metabolic fuel in our westernized diets. The fuel is delivered readily because carbohydrates break down directly to form glucose, the major fuel of metabolism. But since the body has mechanisms that produce glucose, or fuels that perform the same functions, carbohydrate is the one nutrient that need not be provided by the diet.

This nonessentiality of carbohydrate is one of the biologic principles that makes these carbohydrate-restricted diets feasible, safe, and effective.

The diets in this book contain foods which are primarily protein and fat. You may have been told to avoid diets containing fats for fear that your level of cholesterol will increase and subject you to greater risk of heart disease. The diets in this book have been extensively tested on over twelve thousand patients and the opposite result takes place much more often than not. Chapter 22 will tell you why.

I've found these diets to be quite free from dangerous consequences, but then, all my patients had the safeguard of working with a concerned physician. You, too, can safely follow these diets with the same safeguard—use them in conjunction with medical supervision.

1

What this book will reveal to you

Chances are you are reading this book because either you or someone you know read my first book, *Dr. Atkins' Diet Revolution,* and said: "I don't care what anybody says, I feel better than ever before."

To hear my patients utter these golden words, "I feel better than ever before," is my greatest satisfaction in medicine. And in just a short time I hope to have the great satisfaction of knowing that you too will be uttering these very words.

THE SUPERENERGY DIET. This book will show you how you personally can develop a diet that will provide these advantages: more energy, less fatigue, less depression, and the correction of a host of symptoms which you may have been disabled by, or have become accustomed to and have taken for granted.

Chances are that if you felt absolutely perfect, you would not be reading this book. I would imagine that you are reading this book because you believe there is room for improvement. Perhaps you don't feel as great as you think you could. And chances are that you're right.

TOO MANY OF US HAVE SYMPTOMS THAT WE TAKE FOR GRANTED. If we're a little tired, we believe it's natural because we're not as young as we used to be, or we work too hard, or we're under so much stress.

1

If we feel depressed, it's because we have problems, or our loved ones have problems, or the outlook for the future is filled with uncertainty, or frustration, or boredom.

And so we don't seek help for these everyday problems.

WE'RE NOT EVEN AWARE THAT THEY EXIST UNTIL THEY GO AWAY. And then we begin to realize that something really was causing us to be more tired than we need be, or more depressed than we need be.

I believe that as you read this book and change your dietary habits, you will have feelings of well-being, both physical and emotional, that will make you realize only in retrospect that you weren't operating at your best.

OR, YOU MAY ALREADY BE AWARE THAT THERE IS A PROBLEM. Perhaps you feel tired all the time, too listless to do any of the things you want to. Or, perhaps you're only tired some of the time, with spells that come on at certain times of the day, spells of fatigue, or irritability, or crankiness.

Perhaps you have periods of depression that just don't seem to go away.

Or you may have spells that seem for all the world as though you have a serious illness, as when your heart suddenly begins to pound and race, or you break into a cold sweat, or you feel dizzy, or you faint.

Or you may have headaches or allergies.

Or you may have insomnia and be unable to fall asleep, or you may wake up in the middle of the night for no good reason. Or you may have the opposite problem: falling asleep when you don't want to, when you're attending a class or a lecture, or watching a movie.

Or, you may have sexual disabilities like impotency or frigidity, or you may just feel as though you're getting old, even though your logic tells you that you're really not.

But if you are like most of my patients, the symptom that you are most likely to experience is that of just not feeling right, just feeling tired and weak. TV commercials call it the blahs. All are different ways of saying the same thing, that your body is not working perfectly.

IT'S NOT JUST YOUR NERVES. If I felt that way, I would consult a doctor, as I'm sure that most of you have. But I wonder if he has been able to help you. So often a doctor does his examinations and then tells you, "I'm sorry but I don't find anything wrong. It must be your nerves, or tension."

He fails to find a physical reason for your complaints and concludes that it must be something mental—a psychosomatic illness.

One of the problems with medical thinking is falling into the trap that says: "If I can't find it, then it doesn't exist." Perhaps we make this mistake too often. If the doctor does not find something physical, he all too frequently concludes that it is something mental.

But suppose that it's not in your head, but in your body?

IN FACT, I HAVE COME TO THE CONCLUSION THAT IN THE GREAT MAJORITY OF CASES, IT CAN ALL BE IN YOUR DIET. Those of you who read the first Diet Revolution book and went on the diet know what I mean. You remember how much better you felt. Or a friend of yours who went on our diet may have reported that he was struck by how much better he felt. You can probably remember some time when you were at the peak of health and felt vibrant, alive. That's how you should feel all the time.

SYMPTOMS IMPROVE WHEN THE DIET CHANGES. Most of my own seventeen years in the private practice of medicine have been involved primarily in changing and modifying the diets of twelve thousand patients. And in changing these people's diets, I have over and over again been told of symptoms which improved when the diet changed.

Of course it didn't happen in every case. Fatigue and depression can be caused by things other than diet, but in an astounding number of cases, when the patients' diets were changed, they readily noticed the difference in the way they felt.

I have written this book to pass on to you the results of these years of asking myself: "What can I do for this person to make him feel his very best?"

You probably have realized that, in order to write this book for you, there are two things I must believe. One is that a doctor *can* pass on his knowledge and experience through the medium of a book addressed to an unseen audience, and through it improve the quality of the reader's life. The other is that people *are* willing to change their eating habits and to give up their old indulgences, if it means feeling better and being healthier.

AND SO THIS BOOK WILL TELL YOU MANY THINGS, THINGS THAT WILL MAKE YOU <u>FEEL</u> SO MUCH BETTER YOU WILL KNOW THAT AN IMPROVEMENT IS TAKING PLACE WITHIN YOUR BODY. You will learn how to evaluate your own fatigue and depression or other symptoms, how to uncover hidden causes for them, how to take your own case history, how to find your own best diet, and just as important, how to work with your own doctor to determine your best diet. I will show you the evidence that the sugar in your diet may be more dangerous than the fats or the cholesterol, that amounts and kinds of carbohydrates may be more significant than calories, and that vitamin and mineral supplements can be used the way medications have been used before. The book will tell you what you must do before starting the diet, how to do your own diet experiment to learn which type and level of four basic diets is best for you, and how to follow that diet step by step as you develop your own eating regimen. There will be special advice on proper diets for children, for women at menopause, or those on birth control pills, and for people who have trouble losing weight or gaining it.

The book will help you understand your metabolism and the metabolism of others. It will tell you why your present eating pattern may be the culprit that causes fatigue and how a new diet can lead to Superenergy.

I will tell you all the specific things you need to know: what to avoid, what vitamins and minerals to take in exactly what doses, all the things in detail that have been so beneficial to the patients in my practice.

I WILL PROVIDE YOU NOT JUST A DIET, BUT A DIET PLAN. It will not be just a diet for fat people, or skinny people, or people with low blood sugar, but a diet program for every individual. The program of custom-made diets makes it possible for you to find the best diet for *your* type of metabolism so you can have *your* best figure and experience *your* best health.

Although this book can help you gain weight, lose weight, or stay the same weight, it is aimed much more against fatigue, anxiety, depression, and a host of symptoms. There are several diets, since there are many different reasons for dieting, but all maintain the benefits of eliminating most carbohydrates as did the first Diet Revolution book. Certain kinds of carbohydrates often leave you with fatigue; you will learn which ones, and which alternatives will work best.

I'M CONVINCED THAT NO ONE HAS TO BE TIRED. This book will show you *a diet way to renewed energy*. It is a how-to-feel-better book for both overweight people and those who are not.

This antifatigue diet evolved from my treatment of overweight patients, as I kept finding that the same low-carbohydrate diet that made them slim again also gave them renewed energy. Time after time they returned to the office saying they felt better than ever before. My readers confirmed this too, as letters poured in by the thousands reporting that the diet was working the same "miracles" for them.

SUGAR AND FATIGUE. From my own clinical research, and that of others, I learned that a great percentage of overweight people have abnormalities in the specific areas of sugar metabolism. Sometimes, this was slight, sometimes, severe. Particularly unexpected was the large number of people suffering fatigue and anxiety who showed blood sugar findings that were abnormal. There seemed to be a definite relationship between fatigue and these abnormalities of sugar metabolism. And the low-carbohydrate diet was able to improve or correct the condition.

Thus far I've alluded to the benefits of the low-carbohydrate diet in obesity, fatigue, and depression. But the low-carbohydrate diet has many more applications, some of which may be very important in your life, because the type and quantity of carbohydrates, especially sugar, that twentieth-century people eat have been found to play a major role in heart disease, high blood pressure, ulcers, diseases of the colon, allergies, alcoholism, behavior disorders, diabetes, migraine headache, Ménière's syndrome, schizophrenia, and other mental illnesses.

When the matter has been evaluated by careful medical studies, the low-carbohydrate diet has been found often to have a remarkable and significant influence on these illnesses.

These are rather astounding findings and have far-reaching implications.

But what is even more astounding is the evidence pointing to sugar . . . the plain old sugar that most everyone heaps into his coffee, eats in cookies and candy and soft drinks . . . as being one of the major factors in high blood pressure, heart disease, fatigue, and a host of common chronic complaints.

You will learn how to get this hidden hazard out of your diet.

THE DIET IS A SUPERVITAMIN DIET. At present the official recommended daily allowances for vitamins and minerals is-sued by the FDA are proving to be too low for many people. I'll show you why many people need more than these amounts. And I'll make specific recommendations of the doses of vitamins and minerals that should be taken.

YOU WILL DO THE TEST. Sometimes I think many doctors fail to give their patients much credit for intelligence. I think most of you have excellent judgment, especially when it comes to what is best for your own body.

Now I have made a rather powerful claim: that this diet can make you feel better. I want you to make the test and be the judge. If you're not feeling at your best, if you have fatigue or insomnia or mood swings or depression, and if I can show you a way you can eat to make these symptoms go away, that will be the proof. Then you will be able to judge who is really right: the person who says, "If you improve your nutrition you will feel better," or the person who says, "Changing your diet cannot possibly make you feel better."

If you do everything I recommend in this book, and do not feel better, the diet will not be right for you, and I will have failed to make a convincing case. But if you, like the over-whelming majority, feel better than you ever have before, I know I will have proved my point to you.

VITAMINS AND MINERALS ARE DEFINITELY NEEDED. The American Medical Association, the Food and Drug Adminis-tration, and many others contend that vitamin supplements are unnecessary. Their stand negates the work done on vitamin C in the prevention of the common cold, or the use of vitamin E in circulatory conditions, or the success of niacin, pyridoxine, folic acid, and other vitamins and trace minerals in nervous and mental disorders. Yet my own practice experience definitely corroborates the usefulness of these vitamins and minerals in these very conditions and in a host of others.

The AMA and FDA say vitamin preparations should be administered only if there has been an undue stress and then only until the person is able to resume his regular eating pattern. They maintain that our "regular eating pattern" is proper. I maintain—and so do many other leading nutritionists—that we can also have borderline deficiencies that lead to measurable losses of energy and vitality. And a surprising number of people have specific defects of metabolism that can be overcome only by massive doses of specific vitamins. From questioning patients I've learned that it is a rare person today whose regular eating pattern is nutritionally satisfactory.

Many organizations also deny that hypoglycemia . . . low blood sugar . . . is a common problem. Again I disagree. I maintain it affects millions of unsuspecting persons in one degree or another.

WHEN YOU GO IN FOR A PHYSICAL EXAMINATION HOW MANY PHYSICIANS EVER ASK YOU ANYTHING ABOUT YOUR DIET? Think about the last time you had a complete medical checkup. I'll bet the doctor asked you many questions, but did he ask you what you ate? Did he ask how much of your diet consisted of sweets or alcohol or flour or junk food? How can a doctor practice good medicine if he does not know what his patient customarily eats?

American doctors are just not yet geared to test routinely for nutritional deficiencies, partly because the doctor still mistakenly believes that nothing can be wrong with the American diet, that in this wealthiest of countries nutritional deficiencies are most unlikely.

One of my greatest frustrations in the practice of medicine has been observing the reluctant physician, the doctor reluctant to consider nutritional deficiencies among his patients.

The reluctant physician still believes that the American

diet is adequate, that we don't need nutritional supplements, that we need not modify our basic diet. These attitudes prevail despite data from the government's own surveys showing the widespread existence of malnutrition.

HOW MANY ILLNESSES THERE ARE WHOSE COURSE MIGHT BE MODIFIED BY CHANGES IN DIET! One recent patient of mine typifies this. She came to me with a variety of symptoms including dizziness, fatigue, and a depression so severe that she felt every hour might be her last. And because she was troubled with many phobias and "weird thoughts" she went to a psychiatrist who administered drugs and counseled her for months.

Out of desperation she came to me, hoping that nutrition would help. I ordered a glucose tolerance test and found that she had low blood sugar, which I felt was responsible for *all* the symptoms. She told this to her psychiatrist, who said simply, "Atkins is a quack." But, by the time he told her that, we had already started a new diet, and her symptoms were beginning to clear. The key to her case had been that her previous diet consisted of about 80 percent sugar, mainly Coca-Cola, which she guzzled to the exclusion of all other food. And the doctor who called *me* a quack had never even bothered to find out what she ate!

The outcome of the case: the depression lifted; her energy level is normal again; and the depression and "weird thoughts" are gone. Occasionally she has a setback, but these can be correlated with going off the diet. She no longer needs the psychiatrist. She merely needs to look after her nutrition.

IMAGINARY HEALTH. The lack of knowledge about nutrition is appalling. As Dr. Willis A. Gortner, former professor of biochemistry at Cornell University and director of the U.S. Department of Agriculture's Human Nutrition Division in Maryland, said at a science writers' seminar: "We can tell the farmer more about feeding his livestock than about feeding his family."

Many is the time, Dr. Gortner said, that patients go to a physician with symptoms and are told that they are not really sick but that they have an imaginary sickness. The real problem says Gortner is just the opposite. Many of us have "imaginary health." "We think we're well when we're not . . . because we have never really known what it feels like to be superhealthy! We suffer from nutritional deficiencies that we don't even know about. We think the way we feel is natural, or that we're just getting a little older, and it isn't true."

Dr. Gortner calls nutrition "internal environmental protection," and maintains that if subtle, or sometimes not so subtle, nutrition problems could be recognized at a very early stage, we might be able not only to counteract common fatigue and depression, but even to prevent or delay symptoms of obesity, anemia, heart disease, diabetes, and other health problems, probably starting from birth.

MALNUTRITION IS BEING IGNORED. Other scientists have also cried out against present nutrition practices, or lack of them, by physicians.

Dr. Alfred D. Klinger, of the department of preventive medicine at Rush Medical College in Chicago, says malnutrition in this country is responsible in large degree for many of our present-day illnesses. Yet, he says, "There is little or no teaching or even interest in nutrition in most medical schools. . . . There are those in high circles of medicine who are agape at such a thing as malnutrition in the U.S.

"As a consequence, hardly any doctors know about nutrition. Few take interest in a dietary history or understand how to prescribe a proper one or correct one that's improper. Yet nutrition is the cornerstone of life. Its proper application sustains body and mind."

IT'S TIME FOR A REVOLUTION IN NUTRITION. I'm happy that voices like those of Dr. Gortner and Dr. Klinger are being raised and heard. I would like this book to be a rallying point for the change so sorely needed.

AND I WANT YOU TO BE PART OF THE CHANGE. I want you to read in the next chapters about the thoughtless ways by which we have arrived at our twentieth-century diet, so you will understand the background of your new diet. Then I want you to test the diet yourself to see how it makes you feel.

And then I want you to be part of a bigger test . . . the first of its kind . . . by filling in the questionnaire in this book. Your answers plus those of tens of thousands of other people across the nation will give us unprecedented statistics about nutrition that we have never had before.

IF YOU READ THE DIET REVOLUTION, YOU KNOW WHAT HAPPENED—YOU KNOW HOW IT CHANGED YOUR LIFE. Now read this book and see how this diet plan can give you new energy.

2

The hypoglycemia hypothesis

Yesterday, in my medical practice, not unlike any other day in my office, I saw an interesting group of patients.

One patient was a secretary who complained of feeling exhausted every day about four o'clock and who collapsed by the time she got home from work. Another was a usually self-confident advertising executive who complained of spells of "nervous anxiety" with cold clammy sweats and a racing pulse.

Another was a housewife who had become edgy and found herself screaming at her children. Then there was a pharmacist who complained of headaches which seemed to be worse when he was hungry and sometimes would clear up when he ate.

After that, I saw a fashion model who complained of dizzy spells and light-headedness, a man who averaged ten hours of sleep but was tired the next day, a man who had become impotent, and a mother with a hyperactive child. A diverse group of patients? Yes. But all of them had the same condition . . . a condition known as hypoglycemia, or low blood sugar. These are all types of cases which I have been called upon to treat on many occasions. I treated them primarily by a diet, the diet in this book, and in each case, despite the wide variety and range of these symptoms, when these people went on the diet I am about to describe, the symptoms cleared up.

A UNIVERSAL CURE? Your first thought must be that I am

11

making the outrageous claim that my diet is good for everything. Well it's not. There is no panacea in medicine, and I am
certainly not offering this diet as one. Actually the diet is good
only for a few things, but one of these in turn affects many other
conditions. That one thing is hypoglycemia, low blood sugar.

Now I am not stating that low blood sugar *invariably*
causes this wide and diverse list of symptoms, but I do state that
the dietary regimen that you are about to learn of has in all
these cases cleared up the symptoms for patients whom I have
treated personally.

THE SYMPTOM COMPLEX. Authorities have recited an extremely long list of symptoms due to low blood sugar, all of
which I, too, have seen in my practice. The list is headed by
fatigue, depression, anxiety, and tension. If you have hypoglycemia, those may be your only symptoms.

Or you may have attacks of sweating, weakness, tremor,
light-headedness, rapid beating of the heart, and inner trem-
bling. Or you may always feel hungry, even sometimes after a
meal. Or thirsty. Or you may have unexplainable physical symptoms that come and go; symptoms like headache, blurred vision, mental confusion, incoherent speech, sudden phobias,
sometimes even fainting or convulsions. Or you may go through
mood swings, outbursts of temper, forgetfulness, inability to
concentrate or work under pressure, indecision, crying spells,
prolonged sleepiness or the converse—tossing and turning with
insomnia, sudden awakening or nightmares. You may be over-
whelmed by worry and fear, feel insecure, unable to cope. You
may have cold hands and feet, cramps in your legs or in other
muscles. You may feel like eating at all the wrong times, such as
in the middle of the night. You may have an ulcer, heartburn, or
hiatal hernia. Or you may be prone to allergies.

IS THIS YOU? You frequently feel tired, and feeling tired
always seems to happen at the wrong time. When there's a
movie you want to see, or a party you want to go to or some work
you have to get done, that's just when it seems to crop up.

Your family may think you are weak-willed, antisocial,
shrewish, hostile, hysterical, unpredictable, unstable, flighty,
tearful, argumentative, bored, lazy, a drag, a crank, a com-

plainer, a hypochondriac, or a neurotic. You wonder where your *joie de vivre* went, or why you don't feel as good as you know you should.

OTHER PROBLEMS. Low blood sugar can also exaggerate or even falsely mimic symptoms of migraine, ulcers, heart disease, hysteria, epilepsy, schizophrenia, manic-depression, or the brain deterioration of old age. Or it may contribute to a child's learning disability or hyperactivity.

MORE SUGAR NEEDED? The most important rule to bear in mind is that low blood sugar is not what it seems by its name. It is not merely the absence of sufficient sugar in the blood, to be treated by taking in more sugar. Just the opposite holds true; low blood sugar is really a term describing an intolerance to sugar or to other similar carbohydrates. It really is better described by the term *hyperinsulinism*, which means that the body puts out too much insulin in response to the ingestion of sugar or similar carbohydrate. The excessive insulin in turn drives the blood sugar down farther than it had been before the sugar was taken.

The implication of this fact is clear: *sugar or any other simple carbohydrate makes low blood sugar worse* by exaggerating the already imbalanced insulin mechanism.

Further, when experts studied this phenomenon of low blood sugar, they found that the symptoms correlate better with the rapidity of fall of the blood sugar level than with the absolute level of sugar in the subject's bloodstream at any given single moment. In fact, the symptoms of low blood sugar often occur when the blood sugar level is in the normal range, but falling.

THIS RAPIDLY FALLING BLOOD SUGAR LEVEL CAN AFFECT BOTH THE MIND AND THE BODY. The brain, which uses glucose as fuel, may be affected, and the person may notice an inability to think clearly or to concentrate, and perhaps may be emotionally upset. From this, we see schoolchildren become underachievers, or depression-prone people becoming more depressed, or the paranoid person becoming more paranoid, or the anxiety-prone person becoming more anxious.

THE ADRENALIN CONNECTION. The lack of sugar delivered to the brain and to the body provides one mechanism whereby low blood sugar causes symptoms. But there is another mechanism. When the sugar level falls, the body can quickly compensate, raising it again by pouring out adrenalin from the adrenal glands. The response is seen in a sudden fright or in a typical anxiety reaction. The heart begins to beat harder; the mouth becomes dry; the breathing is rapid; there is a tendency to shake and be extremely tense. Think of the phrase: "My adrenalin was flowing" and you'll know what it means.

Adrenalin is a very rapid acting hormone that can change the physiology of the body in less than a minute's time. In fact, the reaction is so fast that commonly during a glucose tolerance test, the doctor does not even have time to collect a blood specimen before the blood sugar has shot up much higher than it was just a moment earlier . . . before the adrenalin release took place.

Many systems of the body can be made to malfunction suddenly in the presence of this sudden adrenalin release, and, because of this backfiring, hypoglycemia can be the triggering mechanism of a variety of conditions—sudden changes in heart rate or heart rhythm, sudden attacks of fainting or dizzy spells, sudden onset of headaches or ringing in the ears, an outpouring of hydrochloric acid and pepsin in the stomach, and even the cardiac pain called angina pectoris.

SO YOU SEE, LOW BLOOD SUGAR CAN CAUSE SYMPTOMS IN SEVERAL WAYS. One is by the direct lowering of the level of glucose as a fuel for metabolism of the brain and the other vital tissues. The second way is from the adrenalin which may be suddenly released when signaled by the dropping blood sugar. The third mechanism involves the effects that are set off by the sudden change in the balance of the body's chemistry.

THAT'S ME. Mind you, I said that all of these symptoms *may* occur as a result of low blood sugar. I know that many of you will read this list and notice the presence of a symptom that has been troubling you, and say, "Aha! I have it, I have low blood sugar."

Well, that would be just as big a mistake as the mistake of

automatically saying that you don't have it. There is more than merely identifying a symptom to establishing the correct diagnosis of low blood sugar.

THE HEATED DEBATE. As a matter of fact, hypoglycemia is the focal point of perhaps the hottest medical debate of the decade. The debate centers on whether it is a very common or a very rare condition. Now because this debate has such important ramifications in *your* life and reflects so directly on the management of *your* health, it is very important that we scrutinize the conflict here and now.

I am by no means the first author to state that hypoglycemia is a very common condition. Dr. Sam Roberts, Dr. J. Frank Hurdle, Carlton Fredericks, Dr. E. M. Abrahamson, just to mention a few, have all informed us that it is a very common condition, estimating that from 20 to 80 percent of the population of our country are victims of hypoglycemia.

MY EXPERIENCE. In my own practice, I have collected a rather large series of glucose tolerance tests (the test which uncovers low blood sugar). Over the past ten years, my office has performed twelve thousand glucose tolerance tests on patients. My tabulations indicate certainly that the majority of these patients had findings suggestive of the diagnosis of low blood sugar. More importantly, there was a solid 20 percent of these people who carried an *unequivocal* diagnosis, a diagnosis which I could present to the most stubborn skeptic who would thereupon be forced to concede, "Well, yes, this would be a case of hypoglycemia."

I have attended medical meetings among physicians who are interested in metabolic problems. They too are roughly divided into those who feel as I do that it is indeed very common, and those who do not. The significant point is that those who feel that low blood sugar is not common are invariably physicians who do not routinely do glucose tolerance tests—the best way to test for low blood sugar.

HE WHO LOOKS, FINDS. *Those physicians who regularly perform glucose tolerance tests find low blood sugar to be quite common.*

A review of the scientific literature portrays the same picture. For instance Dr. Georgina Faludi and her associates, in performing glucose tolerance tests on 238 obese patients at Hahnemann Hospital in Philadelphia, diagnosed hypoglycemia in 101 patients, 42 percent.

And when United Airlines tested 177 pilots, forty-four had it. That's one out of four.

Unpublished data from the 1966/67 National Health Interview Survey conducted by the U.S. Department of Health, Education and Welfare showed of about 42,000 households (approximately 134,000 persons), some 66,000 persons reported having hypoglycemia. That's almost one out of two.

You probably know of someone yourself who has had it and has treated it effectively with diet.

Dr. Sam E. Roberts says in his book *Exhaustion: Causes and Treatment:* "Hypoglycemia is probably the most common disease in the United States. . . . I would estimate that at least fifty per cent of the work in this country is done by people who are extremely tired or exhausted—and don't know it. Often they do not mention fatigue or exhaustion as a chief complaint. They have accepted it as a part of life!"

THE OPPOSING VIEW. But despite this overwhelming scientific evidence that hypoglycemia is indeed a common condition, a powerful and vocal group of "scientists" in our country seem determined to convince us that low blood sugar is almost nonexistent. One nutritional leader has even stated that hypoglycemia is "pretty largely a figment of the imagination."

WHAT WAS YOUR DOCTOR TOLD? You should know that your own doctor probably read in his medical journals the combined position statement by the American Medical Association, the American Diabetes Association, and the Endocrine Society that "hypoglycemia is quite rare and does not constitute an important health problem . . . and that there is no good evidence that hypoglycemia causes depression, chronic fatigue, allergies, nervous breakdowns, alcoholism, juvenile delinquency, childhood behavior problems, drug addiction or inadequate sexual performance."

You must know this background to understand why your

own doctor may seem a little slow in agreeing that it is worth looking into your prospects of having low blood sugar.

A COMPLETE TURNABOUT. How times have changed since 1949 when the American Medical Association gave its highest scientific award, the Distinguished Service Medal, to Dr. Seale Harris for the first description of hypoglycemia and the implication that diet was to blame for the symptoms!

THE REVELATION. Somebody wants our doctors to believe that hypoglycemia is rare. But these statements lead to inadequate, improper, and ineffective patient care. The person who suffers is the patient. He cannot possibly get proper medical care if his doctor is not treating him for the condition he has.

Millions of people have already learned that they, in fact, do have hypoglycemia, yet these medical groups continue to publicize the legend that the condition is rare.

A SCIENTIST'S DRAMATIC PERSONAL EXPERIENCE. One scientist who took exception to this attitude, Dr. Herman Kraybill, of the National Cancer Institute, spoke out at a National Academy of Sciences meeting (March 1975). The audience applauded as he gave his own story. "Hypoglycemia is brushed under the rug too often. I've been diagnosed as a relative hypoglycemic. This is not hogwash.

"When a person gets relief by mere dietary management, when by just reducing your sucrose [sugar] markedly, and upping the protein and eating a cheese snack at ten thirty in the morning and two thirty in the afternoon, and you start feeling great, then this is more than psychosomatic medicine."

WHO HAS IT? One of the reasons for the debate is that there are no hard and fast criteria as to where hypoglycemia really begins and normalcy ends.

Obviously, the stricter the criteria for hypoglycemia, the smaller the percentage of people who would fulfill those criteria and fit the diagnosis. If the criteria are very liberal, a larger segment of the population would be considered hypoglycemic.

Hypoglycemia is not like rabies, where you either have it or you do not. Low blood sugar is rather like height; everybody has some, it is just a matter of how much. Who has not felt a sense of fatigue or letdown when the effects of too much alcohol or too many sugar desserts wore off? On the other end of the continuum are some of our more sensitive cases who might have a severe reaction upon taking in food containing so little sugar that it cannot even be tasted.

Most people fall somewhere in the middle between hypoglycemic and normal. There is no way that we can truly draw a dividing line and say that A and B have it and C and D don't have it. What would be more accurate is to say that A and B have it under ordinary circumstances and C and D do not usually respond that way except under unusual conditions. Jane may be somewhat hypoglycemic, John is more hypoglycemic, Helen is extremely hypoglycemic. Bearing this distinction in mind, for it is a most important one, we can go on with the business of helping you, who may be a little hypoglycemic, or your friend, who may be more hypoglycemic.

To establish the diagnosis of hypoglycemia *with certainty,* several criteria must be present. Not only should there be laboratory confirmation by a glucose tolerance test, but also *symptoms should be present at the time of the drop in blood sugar,* and these symptoms should be temporarily correctable by food or sugar. I even use a fourth criterion: that the treatment known to be effective against low blood sugar, the dietary and nutritional regimen that this book will outline, be shown to be effective as well.

For no matter what the laboratory tests show, the important thing is whether the treatment with a new diet works to eliminate the symptoms.

OUR NATIONAL DIET CAUSES HYPOGLYCEMIA. We in twentieth-century America have been exposed to a diet which is historically unique. We now, for the first time in history, eat most of our carbohydrates in a refined form. This means that the food supply which provides our carbohydrate has in large part been partitioned, and essential parts of the nutritional makeup of these foods have been removed and denied us.

THE HYPOGLYCEMIA HYPOTHESIS. A hypothesis is a tentative theory, a working explanation of facts that is used to build a course of action. If the course of action works, it tends to prove the hypothesis.

I believe hypoglycemia is very common and that hypoglycemia, along with specific deficiencies of essential vitamins and minerals, causes millions of cases of fatigue, depression, anxiety, and the many symptoms which I have described.

The hypothesis that particular symptoms and complaints may be caused by your hypoglycemia certainly warrants an effort to find out whether this is so. In most instances, the testing of the hypothesis involves nothing more than changing your diet.

If the new diet works for a person and he feels better, then for him the objective has been accomplished and the hypothesis confirmed.

Your diet can affect your energy level, can change your emotional responses, can, in fact, completely transform your personality. I continually see this, and I never cease to be amazed. People come in tired, depressed, defeated, looking years older than their age. Change their diet and in a few weeks they are energetic, youthful and buoyant.

THERE ARE MANY DIFFERENT CAUSES OF HYPOGLYCEMIA. Some represent serious conditions. But this book really is addressing itself to the commonest type of low blood sugar, which goes by the name of functional hypoglycemia, reactive hypoglycemia, or alimentary hypoglycemia. The more serious types involve blood sugar readings which are usually low *before* glucose is administered, which are classified as fasting hypoglycemia. This type can indeed be caused by tumors of the pancreas, disorders of the liver, malignancies, defects in enzymes, or disorders of the pituitary and adrenal glands. There is no question that these conditions should be ruled out by your doctor.

But from this point on let us assume that when we are talking about hypoglycemia we are talking about the functional type.

Should every case of hypoglycemia be investigated by an exhaustive search for tumor of the pancreas or other serious cause? Ordinarily, such a search is indicated only if on the laboratory test the fasting blood sugar (the one before glucose is given) is well below the normal range, or if the blood sugar drops to extremely low levels, or if it remains depressed for a long time.

HOW TO RECOGNIZE THE COMMONEST TYPE OF HYPO-GLYCEMIA. The functional type of low blood sugar in its most usual form reacts something like this: If you take in some sugar, you can expect your blood sugar to be raised for a half hour or several hours, during which time you would have adequate energy and mental acuity. But then as the blood sugar level starts dropping, sometimes within the first hour but most commonly at the end of three or four hours, you get a letdown. The symptoms of fatigue or dizziness or tension or drowsiness usually correlate with the time in which the blood sugar is dropping.

If the symptoms don't follow this pattern, then the diagnosis of hypoglycemia is less likely. For instance, chronic relentless fatigue which never seems to let up is not as likely to be caused by low blood sugar. Neither is a chronic depression which never lifts. They are more likely due to some underlying disease condition, or to a vitamin deficiency or trace mineral imbalance. But spells of fatigue or depression that come at a relatively fixed time following a meal are much more certain to be related to blood sugar.

So ask yourself what happens in the hours after a meal.

The time of letdown will also depend on what you had to eat. Protein and fat will buffer the response more than will straight sugar or carbohydrate. This buffering delays the effects so that a person may have a letdown four to five hours after a typical full dinner. This often occurs in the middle of the night and can cause symptoms which awaken you from a sound sleep.

This midnight awakening is one of the most specific examples of low blood sugar. I would estimate that nine out of ten people who awaken in the middle of the night to raid the refrigerator or think about eating, are not, as legend would have it, compulsive, gluttonous people, but rather people who have that common condition called nocturnal hypoglycemia.

In examining your own responses, pay attention to the amount of sugar that you have taken in. You are more likely to get symptoms when your meals are higher in sugar, so that cake and sugared coffee would provide a more accelerated and stronger reaction than a typical sandwich, which is protein and starch. Sometimes two meals might overlap in effect. A person who has a sandwich at twelve o'clock and a piece of candy at three o'clock may experience low blood sugar at four, a combination of the four-hour delay after the sandwich and a one-hour delay after the candy.

WHAT IF THE HYPOGLYCEMIA HYPOTHESIS IS WRONG? What if those who say hypoglycemia is nearly nonexistent are really correct? There would still be one unassailable point, and that is: if we were to place a group of people with these symptoms on a diet devised for the purpose of controlling hypoglycemia, as the diets in this book are, the overwhelming majority of the people would feel better. Even if the hypothesis were to be proven wrong, no one can deny the clinical results. No one can deny the results my patients or the patients of other doctors who work with hypoglycemia get, and the results you will get as well. The real bottom line is the final result—and that's what proves the hypothesis.

THE IMPORTANT THING: THE DIET WORKS. Perhaps it would be better if we avoided arguments over definitions, and circumvented labels. If a person comes to my office with fatigue, I can speak to him of hypoglycemia, or I can leave out telling him he has hypoglycemia and simply tell him what he should eat; and he would feel better anyway.

You may never know whether hypoglycemia was really the major problem. But the point is, no matter what you call it, you will feel better.

And the reason you will feel better is that this diet is different. It attacks *every* aspect of fatigue. Just as there was a need for a new diet to treat obesity, so there is a need for a new diet to treat fatigue.

The diet we will tell you about in this book is the diet to meet that need.

3

The world's most dangerous food additive

This book originates from the lessons I learned practicing medicine on people just like you, people who were tired, depressed, overweight, or suffering from one or another rather common medical condition.

One lesson I learned is that many of my patients are addicts. Not drug addicts, but addicts of a substance in the diet.

Not only do they have cravings which cannot be diverted easily, but they find immediate relief of symptoms when the substance is taken in, and a renewal of the cravings when the substance wears off. They can have a difficult withdrawal period when it is stopped, which gradually diminishes if withdrawal persists.

That substance is sugar.

OUR MOST COMMON ADDICTION. Sugar addiction is, in my view, probably our most common addiction, even more common than alcoholism. It is far and away the most common cause of relapse in my own group of patients, responsible for that all-too-frequent dieter who does fantastically well, seemingly achieving the goal of health and slimness, only to be seen at a later date having regained all the lost weight, and then some. How many people do you know just like that? People who would be slim and vibrant today were it not for their addiction to sweets?

WHAT COULD BE BAD? Because so many of us consider our desserts and sweets to be the high spot of our day's eating

22

enjoyment, we are all more than willing to listen to the sugar industry's propaganda and believe such misleading statements as "our brains can't function without sugar." These are the same voices who during the next decade will be telling us, "It has not been proven that sugar is a cause of heart disease, or of diabetes, or of hypoglycemia."

But, despite these powerful voices with the powerful financial support behind them, the truth about sugar is so apparent that warning voices from within scientific ranks are being raised and are being heard.

SCIENTISTS SPEAK OUT. For instance, at a symposium held in Washington by the National Academy of Sciences in March 1975, Joan Gussow, a nutritionist at Columbia University, stated: "I want to know about added sugar in processed foods. I want the public to know so that they at least have a choice. . . . Sugar is in almost everything . . . but we don't know how much. . . . I think the fact that one has no choice on how much sugar one takes in is a very important issue!

"Anyone who wants to put anything in the food supply at all whether it has any nutritive value or not may do so as long as it's made with FDA certified chemicals. There is no requirement that there is any need for such a product, that it will do anyone good, or even that it will not do them harm. . . . We are all simply defenseless."

At the same meeting various speakers stressed that we are now consuming, on the average, over 150 grams of sugar a day in the United States. That's a pound every three days. And since that's an average, many of us consume even more than that.

Sugar provides nearly 25 percent of the calories in a typical diet.

SUGAR'S ROLE IN DISEASE. Several speakers at that meeting pointed to sugar as possibly serving a role in all of these areas: contributing to obesity, causing dental caries, causing high blood pressure, raising serum triglycerides and cholesterol, decreasing longevity, and being a factor in allergies, kidney disease, and carbohydrate intolerance.

Dr. Richard Ahrens of the University of Maryland stated that he found that sugar caused high blood pressure in animals, and when he tested human subjects, he found that all of them had higher blood pressure when they ate large amounts of sugar, some people more than others. From Dr. Ahrens's data, it appears that about 25 percent of people are particularly sugar sensitive, recording dangerously high levels of blood pressure.

So the hue and cry about the dangers of refined sugar that began with the pioneers of the health food movement two generations ago is beginning to take hold upon mainstream medical thinking.

SUGAR WAS NOT A PART OF MANKIND'S DIET UNTIL RATHER RECENTLY. Man used to get a little natural sugar in the berries and fruits he picked, or occasionally a cache of honey scooped from a tree.

Even when refined sugar was produced in Asia and brought back to Europe by the returning Crusaders, it was used only occasionally by the wealthy who bought it in small amounts from apothecary shops. Columbus brought sugarcane to the West Indies in 1493. And later U.S. ships plied their well-known three-way traffic of slaves, molasses, and rum, all based on trade with the sugarcane plantations of the West Indies.

But white sugar didn't become important until the nineteenth century, when Napoleon set up sugar factories in Europe. In 1815 the average Englishman was consuming only about 7½ pounds of sugar a year. By 1850, total world sugar production was about 1.5 million tons per year.

TODAY THE WORLD SUGAR PRODUCTION IS 70 MILLION TONS, AND STILL GROWING. We consume not 10 pounds a year, but 120 pounds per person—a twelvefold increase in a few generations.

LAST YEAR THE AVERAGE PERSON IN THE UNITED STATES ATE 20 POUNDS OF CANDY, CHEWED 135 STICKS OF CHEWING GUM, AND DRANK 450 CANS OF CARBONATED DRINKS. The average American twelve-year-old boy drinks three cans of soda pop a day, and one out of twelve of them drinks *eight or more* cans a day! But this doesn't hold back the National Soft Drink Association from trying to place soda pop vending machines in school hallways to increase consumption even more!

In addition, you and your children eat sugar in cakes, pies, cookies, donuts, and, probably without realizing it, in many brands of canned vegetables and fruit bought off the grocery shelf. In manufacturing today, sugar is even added to fruits that are already sweet, and to sweet potatoes, and . . . the biggest crime of all . . . to baby food, starting early to build up the desire for sugar in children who never have a chance to develop appreciation for natural food flavors.

There is so much hidden sugar in the food you buy that you probably get seventy-five pounds of it this way in a year . . . whether you want it or not. At the latest count, in the United States, food processors used twelve billion pounds of sugar a year just as a food additive. This is an added dietary constituent that has no nutritional value except its bare calories, but which may rot your teeth, put on fat, irritate the digestive tract, and cause diabetes, high blood pressure, ulcers, heart disease, skin infections, headaches, allergies, and the fatigue and depression of hypoglycemia as well as decreasing the availability of essential vitamins and minerals.

One study of teen-agers in Iowa showed that the average sugar intake for girls was fifty-five teaspoons per day, and for boys was seventy-eight teaspoons. Many of them were consuming more than *one hundred teaspoons* per day, amounting to four hundred pounds per year.

This huge jump in sugar consumption is probably the most drastic dietary change man has made in his whole fifty million years of existence!

"PURE, WHITE AND DEADLY." That's what Dr. John Yudkin, internationally recognized nutritionist at Queen Elizabeth College in London, calls sugar.

And it may well be one of the biggest criminals of our time, robbing us of energy and of joy, causing us to commit acts of anger and rage because of metabolic imbalance, maiming us by causing ulcers and infections and rotten teeth, and helping kill us through diabetes, high blood pressure, and heart disease.

WHAT IS THE EVIDENCE CITED BY THE SCIENTISTS WHO BELIEVE SUGAR IS A KILLER? There are hundreds of studies. Here are some of the most important ones.

First, there are tremendous statistical correlations between sugar consumption and diabetes, between sugar consumption and heart disease, and between sugar consumption and decreased life-span.

I don't believe there is any exception to the statement that every time sugar is significantly increased in a population, diabetes and deaths from heart disease increase.

As Drs. Cleave and Campbell, in their very important book *The Saccharine Disease* pointed out, it takes twenty years after refined carbohydrates are brought into a diet for diabetes and heart disease to become epidemic. One such example was seen in Iceland where, in the early 1930s, diabetes was exceedingly rare. At that point, the diet became Westernized and sugar consumption rose dramatically. Twenty years later, diabetes became a common condition.

In our country, sugar consumption escalated most rapidly between the years 1890 and 1925. Between 1910 and 1945, there was a parallel increase in the prevalence of diabetes and of heart disease.

And conversely, diabetes largely disappears in times of sugar scarcity. This was seen during both World War I and World War II when sugar consumption dropped and saccharine was used instead. Then after each war, sugar use increased again and so did obesity, arteriosclerosis, heart attacks, and diabetes.

Dr. Richard A. Ahrens says, "The most carefully designed studies have consistently shown that heart disease victims consume more sucrose." And he adds that the epidemic of arteriosclerotic and degenerative heart disease "continues to increase on a worldwide scale in rough proportion to the increase in sucrose consumption."

THE SUGAR HEARINGS. Senator George McGovern, chairman of the Senate Select Committee on Nutrition and Human Needs, investigated the role of sugar in diabetes and heart disease and raised many questions at the sugar hearings regarding dangers of high sugar consumption in the United States.

Senator Richard S. Schweicker of the same committee echoed his fear of the disturbing implications. "There is concern that this tremendous consumption of refined sugar is related to some of the nation's most serious health problems," Schweicker said at the hearings. "We have produced one of the most economically sufficient societies in history and yet the net result, nutritionally, seems to be going backwards."

Some astounding facts on sugar dangers have been unearthed by Dr. George Campbell who came all the way from South Africa to the committee hearings in Washington to report them. When social conditions change anywhere, said Dr. Campbell, the very first thing that changes significantly is the food that people eat. "There is at once an addictive and often irreversible move toward massive intake of highly refined carbohydrate foods, of which white and brown sugar, white bread and the various spectrums of the sugar-sweetened foods figure largely.

"Wherever we have solicited information from experts on every corner of the globe, the pattern has been an identical one," Campbell told the committee, "whether we are dealing with red Indians, East Indians, Papuans, Zulus, Polynesians, Eskimos, West Indians, Yemeni Jews, Zambians, Kurds, or any other of a host of other ethnic groups."

When the intake of sugar or other refined carbohydrate increases dramatically within any culture, the same disease pattern emerges. He lists these conditions as diabetes, obesity, coronary thrombosis, gallstones, peptic ulcer, diverticulosis, varicose veins, hemorrhoids, E. coli infections, dental caries, and, in part, cancer of the colon, hypertension, hiatal hernia, and gout.

Throw in the psychiatric disturbances, hypoglycemia, alcoholism, behavior disturbances in children, arthritis, and other forms of cancer that others have implicated as probably diet-related, and you may conclude that most of modern medicine is involved in treating what may be the consequences of our twentieth-century diet!

SUGAR AND DEATH. We are led to believe that saturated animal fat is the number one dietary correlate with death rates, particularly those from heart disease.

But, if you take all the available statistics from different countries as to sugar intake, fat consumption, and other dietary factors, you find that deaths from heart disease are specifically related more to sugar intake than to any other factor! The countries highest in sugar consumption have the most heart disease deaths.

And if you look at the heart attack statistics for most countries now as compared to just one generation ago, you see the same correlation. In Poland for example the death rates went up alarmingly. Almost four to one! If you look at the dietary factors over approximately the same ten-year period for Poland, you will see that the intake of saturated fat actually went down by 22 percent, whereas the intake of sugar went up a very significant 366 percent. The sugar intake quadrupled and the death rate quadrupled.

In Yugoslavia, exactly the same thing occurred. The use of saturated fat went down more than in any other country, but the sugar intake went up almost three to one, directly correlated with a threefold increase in the death rate.

And if you look at twenty-three other countries studied by the World Health Organization itself, the strongest correlation of any diet factor with death rate is the correlation with sucrose intake.

Drs. Alfredo Lopez, Robert E. Hodges, and Willard A. Krehl of the University of Iowa College of Medicine did a similar study comparing serum cholesterol levels with diet in sixteen countries. They found no correlation between fat in the diet and cholesterol in the blood, but again there was a highly significant correlation with the consumption of sugar.

Evidence like this, as it continues to mount, certainly portrays the devastating effect sugar can have upon your health and your children's health.

But these are only statistical correlations, some people say.

ANIMAL STUDIES CONFIRM THE FINDINGS! As far back as 1924, Dr. A. A. Gigon showed in a dramatic group of experiments that adding large quantities of sugar to an otherwise good diet causes sickness and death in a variety of animals. And, ever since then, more experiments have shown the same results.

Medical reports have shown the following effects: sugar shortens the life-span of animals by one-fourth; reduces the growth rate; increases deposition of fat; and increases the concentration in the blood of cholesterol, triglycerides, insulin, corticosteroid, and cortisol. It reduces glucose tolerance and so produces diabetes; it increases the size of the liver and kidneys and causes changes in their cells; it causes gallstones, causes dental decay, and produces atherosclerosis. It produces disturbed actions of blood platelets and blood clotting; changes the activity of several enzymes; increases acidity of gastric juice; causes a vitamin B deficit; and causes blindness, kidney failure, and sterility by producing thickened blocked capillaries serving vital organs.

DR. COHEN AND THE YEMENITES. This is a classic experiment that scientists often refer to because it was so beautifully designed and so dramatic in its conclusions. Dr. A. M. Cohen in Israel in performing a large-scale diabetes study took urine samples of sixteen thousand people, including one special ethnic group of five thousand people who had just come to Israel from Yemen. Almost none of the Yemenites had diabetes. The dietary analysis of the nomadic Yemenite culture indicated their sugar intake was one of the lowest in the world. But when Dr. Cohen examined the Yemenites living in Jerusalem, those who had been there a long time and had adapted to the food and diet habits of the Western World, including heavy sugar intake, he found they had as high a level of diabetes as the rest of the city population.

At the same time there was another new group coming to Israel: one thousand people from Kurdistan. These newcomers too had almost no diabetes. Dr. Cohen located people from Kurdistan who had lived in Israel for twenty-five years or more and, yes, they had diabetes.

Next Dr. Cohen went to the laboratory, giving "old-country" diets with no sugar to one group of animals and a "civilized" diet with typical high sugar to another group of animals. The same results were found as in the humans.

His next step was on human volunteers, where he confirmed that sugar has a greater cholesterol-elevating potential than other carbohydrates.

After doing both animal and human studies, Dr. Cohen says, "Until we find a way to identify those who are genetically sensitive to sucrose and those who are not, we recommend cutting down to a minimum the use of sucrose and other refined sugars to about 5 percent of the carbohydrate intake." And he adds, "This curtailment of sucrose consumption should be applied from birth, since the noxious effect is cumulative and takes a long time to become apparent."

Impressed with the fact that this susceptibility to sugar was greater in some persons than in others and tended to be genetically determined insofar as it seemed to run in families, Dr. Cohen went back to his animal studies. He fed a high sugar diet to a group of laboratory rats and selected those in whom sugar produced the greatest increase in blood sugar levels and those that showed the least. He bred the high responders and studied their offspring; he did the same with the low responders, repeating this, generation by generation, until at the end of three or four generations he had developed a line of rats who became diabetic when exposed to dietary sugar.

Thus Dr. Cohen created a laboratory situation that embodies the theory that diabetes is produced by feeding sugar to the genetically susceptible individual.

SUGAR, CHOLESTEROL, AND TRIGLYCERIDES. Since 1961 many investigators have shown that diets high in sugar will raise the level of cholesterol and triglycerides in the blood of both normal people and people who have too much blood fat to begin with.

There have been numerous reports to prove the hypothesis that when sugar is cut out of the diet, these levels of blood fats will drop significantly.

I have tabulated my own results on just such a no-sugar diet and have observed that the triglyceride-lowering effect of such a diet is far more potent than the most effective drug yet devised for that purpose.

Other investigators have reported that people who have arterial disease eat almost twice as much sugar as do people without arterial disease, and that patients who have just had their first heart attack were eating significantly more sugar than a group of control patients.

So the facts we learn from both research and from observing various cultures around the globe provide strong support to the statement that man simply does not have the metabolic machinery to handle the deluge of sugar that we now consider to be a normal intake. From all this evidence many physician-scientists now feel that too much sugar is a major factor in causing diabetes, high blood pressure, and heart disease. Not the *only* factor, because there are many, but a very major factor.

Yet how many of my patients, when I see them for the first time, look at me incredulously when I tell them that sugar does not even belong in their household. If I succeed with you in no other way, let me, at least, convince you that sugar is a killer, not only for you, but for your family.

THE AMERICAN POPULATION IS A DISEASED POPULATION. The typical "healthy" American who is considered normal has spent twenty years consuming candy, cookies, and cola. If our theory that the increased consumption of sugar and other refined carbohydrates has led to an epidemic of abnormal glucose tolerance is correct, then the very people we're using as norms are *not* norms. In one study on women, a very high percentage had low blood sugar on the glucose tolerance test. The conclusion was that, since it occurred so frequently, it was not abnormal. The proper conclusion should be that most American people are eating a totally unhealthy diet and have been eating so poorly all their lives that we accept poor health as the norm, unaware of how well we really can function. Yet there are several other cultures, where many people live to be a hundred, vigorous, working, sexually active, smiling, and full of energy. Natives of Hunza, Abkhasia, and Vilcabamba, Peru, are well-known examples. The average person in the United States and other "civilized" countries has been subjected to an unnatural diet for so long he doesn't know what being "normal" really is.

HOW LONG ARE WE GOING TO WAIT? How long before our medical leaders realize we're in the throes of an epidemic? When will education point to the dangers of sugar?

EVENTUALLY THE TRUTH IS GOING TO COME OUT ABOUT SUGAR. How the nice white scrumptious sugar that you put on your table every morning is a threat to your health. More documentation will be needed . . . there will be a tremendous fight

. . . but the explosion is coming, perhaps years away, but it is coming.

Already in 1972 an international scientific convention in West Germany, attended by world-recognized experts on diabetes, obesity, metabolism, and arteriosclerosis, recommended officially that people stop eating sugar.

Dr. Cohen, Dr. Yudkin, I, and many other scientists have crossed sugar off our menus. We simply won't touch it any more than cyanide or cigarettes.

MEANWHILE YOU WILL HAVE TO MAKE YOUR OWN DECISION, for you and your children. You have to look at the evidence and decide whether it makes sense for you to eat sugar. One good way to do it would be to go on one of these diets and, among other things, eliminate sugar and see how it makes you feel.

I'll wager that after you've been on the diet for only a few weeks, you will experience a sense of well-being you had forgotten was possible.

4

Who says we're well nourished?

Have you noticed how many more statements there are lately from "responsible" nutritionists telling us that vitamins are not only unnecessary, but possibly dangerous? But at the same time you've probably also noticed that more and more of your friends are telling you about "curing" themselves of a great variety of medical conditions by taking a large doses of these same vitamins.

There's a story behind the paradox. The giants of the food industry do not want the public to believe there is anything improper about the way they are fulfilling their obligation to provide us adequate nutrition. Remember the great efforts the leaders of the tobacco industry made to convince us that there was no real menace to cigarette smoking?

THE FOOD INDUSTRY'S SUCCESS. The food industry has succeeded in governing our attitudes. Most of us believe about nutrition what these economic interests want us to believe. And they have succeeded in gaining ideologic harmony with the government's powerful Food and Drug Administration (FDA), which has unflinchingly backed their interest in nearly all areas of nutrition controversy.

THE COURAGEOUS SENATOR. But some have challenged this alignment. One of these is Wisconsin's Senator William

Proxmire, who denounced the FDA's low recommended daily allowances on vitamins.

In providing some insights into the FDA's militant attempt to dictate to consumers how many vitamins they can buy, the senator points out that the FDA accepts recommendations given it by the National Academy of Sciences, "which is influenced, dominated and financed in part by the . . . food industry.

"It represents one of the most scandalous conflicts of interest in the federal government," he says.

Thus the FDA's official position is that "vitamin and mineral supplements are unnecessary for nutrition and useless to prevent illness."

THE AMA POSITION. And, in case you think that the nation's physicians would take the side of their patients' welfare in this confrontation with the food industry, think again. The official position of the AMA is that, unless you're actually sick, there is no place for vitamin and mineral supplements if you eat the usual American diet.

Just how deeply entrenched their attitude is was brought home to me during my own day at the Senate hearings when Senator McGovern asked Dr. C. E. Butterworth, Jr., who is chairman of the AMA Council on Foods and Nutrition, just what it was that he objected to regarding my diet. My jaw dropped a foot when out came the reply, "It's all those vitamins."

But just what is known about our nutritional status? Are the AMA and the FDA correct? or are the Rodales, Adelle Davis, I, and a host of others correct when we say vitamin deficiencies are very real and very significant?

WHAT OFFICIAL GOVERNMENT SURVEYS SHOW. Much of what we know is based upon a comprehensive government national nutrition survey. Published in 1972, it took four years of work with a maze of field studies, laboratory and computer analysis, all evaluating eighty-six thousand people as to what they ate, and whether they had any clinical or chemical signs of nutritional ill health.

The survey found a shocking degree of malnutrition, with deficiencies in vitamin A, riboflavin, thiamine, niacin, vitamin D, vitamin C, iron, and sometimes even protein. The most shocking and disconcerting figures were found in the children. Huge numbers of children were found too short for their age, stunted in growth by their deficiencies.

Those who read the report were shaken by its dangerous implications. Dr. Alfred Klinger of Rush Medical College in Chicago wrote that the survey confirmed that the number one health problem of the United States is inadequate nutrition, and he added, "The ramifications are enormous for the young in terms of learning ability, healthy emotional development, ability to perform a muscular task, to reproduce and bring forth healthy offspring without complication, to withstand infection, to become creative and to attain a decent life-span.

"What in effect our nation has created with this bargain-basement approach to nutrition are bargain-basement individuals," he says.

A few years later another follow-up survey was done. This one on some thirty thousand people in sixty-five areas across the country. The findings were no better. And recently, a very comprehensive Canadian study showed essentially the same conclusions there.

Other nutritional surveys have the same grim statistics: brain damage, anemia, skin infection, stunted growth, all because of lack of proper food.

In Memphis children, 16 percent were clinically stunted in growth and 90 percent of those under age three were anemic, causing them to be weak, drowsy, and slow to respond. As many as 15 percent of the children had severely stunted brain growth.

Several studies showed that two-thirds of the pregnant women in this country have below normal levels of folic acid; and women taking birth control pills or anticonvulsant drugs also are frequently deficient in folic acid. Another study discovered that 75 *percent* of women using birth control pills had a deficiency of Vitamin B_6.

Our national nutritional status is on shaky grounds indeed. If this were an epidemic of infectious disease, we would all be up in arms; but when it's malnutrition, it is merely glossed over.

To me the most alarming aspect of the surveys was that only a small percentage of essential nutrients was looked for. Others, such as the trace minerals, were not even tested for.

And these are the very areas where nutrition therapy gets the most exciting results. They, too, must be presumed to be present in insufficient amounts.

THESE SURVEYS HAVE LOOKED ONLY FOR THE LARGE AND OBVIOUS DEFICIENCIES. If that many of us have easily observable deficiencies in so many vitamins and minerals, isn't it logical to assume that many of us may have minor or borderline deficiencies or deficiencies in other essential nutrients? Millions of us must be experiencing hidden forms of malnutrition that affect us in dozens of ways day by day, our hungry cells crying out for vitamins and minerals they vitally need but are not getting.

We may not have rickets or scurvy or beriberi or pellagra, but it's a good bet that many chronic ailments that we consider to be part of "normal" aging may be related to this less obvious type of malnutrition.

IF WE CORRECTED THESE SUBTLE DEFICIENCIES. If we had a totally well-nourished society without these missing nutrients, in other words, if we achieved supernutrition, we could have the very best of health and well-being. Children would be given a better chance at life both intellectually and physically; many older people who are victims of "senility" would be helped; many "patients" not responding to orthodox therapies would get better; and many "normal" people would find day-to-day living more satisfying.

NUTRITION THERAPY. A perfect example is in the treatment of a psychiatric condition . . . schizophrenia. There are hundreds of nutrition-oriented doctors across the continent who have been getting remarkably reproducible results using megadoses of niacinamide, Vitamin C, pyridoxine, and other vitamins and minerals.

These same vitamins and minerals could be important in managing our number one killer, heart disease. For instance, there are twice as many heart deaths reported among men in nine north Georgia counties compared to similar men in nine southern Georgia counties. In the nine northern counties there are thirteen trace elements missing that are present in ample amounts in the nine southern counties. Perhaps some of these are important in avoiding heart disease.

Many women find when they take Vitamin E or folic acid, a number of the side effects of menopause disappear. Yet menopause is thought to be part of aging, and women are either put on estrogens or told to live with their symptoms.

We have now learned that many "mental" patients have high copper levels and low levels of zinc. Zinc therapy can correct both these abnormalities.

Dozens of these medical-nutritional interrelationships have been discovered; hundreds remain to be discovered. I would like to propose the term "Nutritional Pharmacology" to describe the new science that is developing to provide the background for this most rapidly advancing area in medicine.

NUTRITION—A YOUNG SCIENCE. The study of vitamins and trace minerals is an infant science barely past the stage now that penicillin was in when Fleming first discovered that a mold in his laboratory inhibited the growth of some bacteria. Many scientists believe there are probably dozens of vitamins and trace minerals that we haven't yet identified that are vital to the body.

For example, in one classic experiment on laboratory rats, the time they could swim until fatigued was measured after they were given all *known* nutrients and then again after liver extract was added. They were able to swim much longer with the added liver. The most probable conclusion was that the liver contains a nutrient (or nutrients) we do not yet know about. Yet too many responsible "nutritionists" talk as if no new vitamins can possibly be discovered.

MORE JUNK FOOD. Our usage of nutritious foods is going down steadily while our consumption of junk foods is going up dramatically. Since the end of World War II, consumption of soft drinks is up 80 percent; pies, cookies, and desserts are up about 70 percent; and snack foods like potato chips are up 85 percent.

EVIDENCES OF MALNUTRITION EXTEND ACROSS ALL SOCIO-ECONOMIC CLASSES, INCLUDING THOSE THAT CAN AFFORD THE BEST IN NUTRITION. The Department of Agriculture and the

Department of Health, Education and Welfare classify the diets of 50 percent of us as only fair or poor.

The payoff is that our life expectancy, despite all the recent advances in medical science, is getting shorter, rather than longer. Now fourteen major nations surpass us in life expectancy, even though our health expenditures total more than $70 billion a year. But, as Senator Richard Schweicker points out, "Most of this expenditure is going toward *curing* rather than *preventing* diseases."

There are many of us whose knowledge of nutrition is not much greater than the listings we read on our breakfast cereal cartons. We note the eight or ten nutrients that they mention (those synthetics that are restored to the nutritionally barren cereal). We trust that these must be the only *really* important nutrients. (If other nutrients were important, would not they, too, be included?) Sometimes we trust that these nutrients represent only a sampling of the remarkable nutritional value of the product, not fully comprehending that they are only present because they were added by the manufacturer, and that the other important nutrients register nearly zero.

The first rule of thumb of the careful consumer should be: *Those nutrients which are not mentioned on the boxtop are not there.* But the probability is that these unlisted nutrients are the ones we are most likely to be deficient in and they are the ones most likely to correct our nutrition-based health problems.

NATIONWIDE DEFICIENCIES. Dr. Walter Mertz, chairman of the Human Nutrition Institute of the U.S. Department of Agriculture, says Americans have many marginal deficiencies, even those on supposedly optimal diets. He believes we are not getting enough of many micronutrients, particularly zinc, chromium, folic acid, iron, and Vitamin B_6.

With today's typical diet, we simply are not getting all the nutrients we need. The nutritionists aligned with the food industry say we don't need supplements. But supplements do make a difference. For example, we get such very good effects from increasing the zinc intake of people with problems of fatigue or emotional disturbances, that we cannot help but conclude that the majority of people must not be getting enough zinc.

Dr. Carl Pfeiffer, the director of the Brain Bio Center of Princeton, New Jersey, and one of the world's foremost authorities on the biochemical abnormalities of schizophrenia and related conditions, finds that the majority of his patients respond both biochemically and clinically to significant supplements of zinc. What's more important to you is the fact that this response can be noted in the majority of "normal" people, as well.

And Dr. Henry Schroeder, after a comprehensive analysis of all segments of our food supply, has concluded that we cannot possibly replenish our losses of the essential trace mineral chromium on any variation of the American diet unless we gorge on brewer's yeast, molasses, and oysters.

THE MYTH OF THE BALANCED DIET. Dr. Schroeder pointed out that in the past our foods . . . unprocessed, unrefined . . . contained the micronutrients and essential elements necessary for their own metabolism. If they hadn't, man and other animals dependent upon those foods probably could not have survived.

Wild animals don't need a carefully varied diet. They automatically get it because every natural food they eat contains within itself all the nutrients necessary to be processed through the animal's body. Can you imagine a wild animal, or a primate forerunner of man, running around looking for food every day to represent the four main food groups to make sure it has a balanced diet? Nature provided for that by seeing to it that the nutrients necessary for metabolizing the food were contained within the food being consumed.

It is no surprise that sugarcane is high in chromium, which is a substance necessary to metabolize sugar. It is not a passing curiosity that wheat contains vitamin B factors which are necessary for the body to metabolize the carbohydrate of wheat. It is the one thing necessary for us to use the wheat completely.

THE NUTRITIONALLY MISLED. Now we consume processed foods with all these necessary ingredients taken out. Cereal products are nearly stripped of nutrients, then a few nutrients are restored, but some, an important "some," are not returned. The natural product has been made so barren that the synthetic additions stand almost alone. We are misled into thinking that they are nutritious products. The multimillion dollar advertising campaigns dedicated to promoting these products have left in their wake a nation of the nutritionally misled.

Consider that our wheat flour and the cereals made of it have suffered a loss of 75 to 85 percent of many of the nutrients that nature's original whole wheat contains.

EVEN THE PRESIDENT OF THE AMERICAN INSTITUTE OF BAKING HAS CALLED FOR CHANGES. Dr. William B. Bradley urges members of the industry to stop stripping wheat of all of its nutrients. "Today's bakery flour," he said, "in its highly milled state retains only about 10 percent of vitamin B6, 20 percent of the thiamine of the wheat, and none of the vitamin E.

"All of this can be changed," he said, "by using 80 percent extraction flour to produce good quality bread that retains all of these vitamins."

But, so far, his voice and the voices of others have been unheeded.

Why should we need vitamin supplements? It is because we polish our rice, degerm the wheat, refine the sugarcane, and throw away the nutrients essential to the metabolizing of the very foods we're eating. Sugar does have the chromium and other trace minerals necessary for it to be metabolized, except that they happen to be in the part that we throw away.

WHO IS RESPONSIBLE FOR THE PERPETUATION OF OUR COURSE TOWARD NUTRITIONAL BANKRUPTCY? Is it our governmental agencies that have historically served as "yes men" to the very food and drug industries that they are supposed to be policing? Is it the leaders of medical organizations who have disregarded the truth about nutrition research's disclosures? Is it the food industry whose advertisers have bombarded us with a campaign designed to turn junk food into a nutritional wonder in our minds?

There can be no question that all of these factors have been and are taking place with predictable regularity.

And it has been easy to hoodwink most of us because there are so few people who have an intimate knowledge of science and who have been able to see what is going on. The average person says, "I'm not a scientist or a doctor, how can I judge? If the AMA says vitamin C is no good, then vitamin C must be no good. If the FDA says we can't use folic acid in the dose that other countries consider to be quite proper, they must know what they're doing." Not only does the man in the street not know, but even the average writer for a magazine, newspaper, or television show depends on these agencies for "expert" opinion. Thus, the myths are established and grow even in the press.

The saddest thing is that doctors have been brainwashed more than anyone. I went through it myself, and I can tell you I knew practically nothing about nutrition when I was graduated from medical school or even when I finished my residency and was supposedly ready to begin my practice. I was perfectly willing to accept what I had been taught, which is that we don't need vitamins unless we have been under an unusual physical stress. Judging from the AMA statement of August 11, 1975 . . . that megavitamins are "pharmacological lunacy" . . . today's doctors are getting the same message. Their patients are the victims.

THE AMA AND THE FDA. Despite the clear evidence that taking vitamins and minerals may well be the easiest and best avenue toward being healthy, the American Medical Association and the Food and Drug Administration both do their utmost to fight the use of vitamin and mineral supplements. This is despite the fact that tens of thousands of people who have used vitamins know otherwise.

The stand of the Food and Drug Administration is very hard to swallow. While they spend very little time or money on getting rid of the rat feces and other contaminants in our food or the dangerous additives that constantly appear, they spend millions of dollars of our tax money in everything from Gestapo-like harassment, including armed breaking and entering into doctors' offices, to sophisticated hiring of Madison Avenue advertising executives to prepare brochures, films, news releases, and other "educational" means of convincing the American public that they really don't want to use vitamins and minerals. And now after ten years of study, using your money, they have come up with recommended regulations on the sale and promotion of vitamins and minerals that seem designed to guarantee the ineffectiveness of nutrition. Their latest proposal is that if any vitamin preparation contains more than 1½ times their recommended daily allowance *then you cannot buy it yourself as an over-the-counter product.*

Later I'll help you develop a vitamin and mineral regimen to accompany your diet. And I'll give you some specifics, vitamin by vitamin, and mineral by mineral, about the results the scientists who have used megadoses against various diseases have achieved. And I'll tell you about their side effects, as well. You see, I can't agree with the FDA that the public is too stupid to figure out what makes them feel good and what doesn't. I'll give you as much information as I can and leave the choices up to you.

5

The antifatigue superenergy diet

I could not have been so critical of your present eating pattern if I hadn't felt confident that I could offer you something far better. If fatigue is your problem, this book will provide not just a single diet, but an entire program of diets, so that you can select the diet that meets your needs.

But before we start, may I lay down certain ground rules, just as I do for all my patients? Dieting, for health purposes, as well as for weight reduction, involves a very special attitude on your part. It's really a new set of values. Isn't it true that for most of your life you chose your food on the basis of what you liked or enjoyed? Oh, occasionally, you would "go on a diet" to improve your weight or your vitality. But, like a book or a movie, that diet would have a beginning and an end. Then you would return to your usual philosophy of eating what pleases your palate the most.

YOUR NEW VALUES. But with the new values I am asking you to adopt, I would hope you will choose your food on the basis of what is best, not for your taste buds, but for your health and your feeling of well-being. Sweets, for example, are something that is good for your pleasure, but not for your health. When your values change, it won't make any difference how delicious some things taste; because you'll be selecting a diet for a much more meaningful purpose—to achieve permanent good health.

43

And your new way of eating won't be a short-lived experience, but will be a part of all the rest of your life.

Since there are different objectives for different people, it is obviously necessary to have a variety of diets. This book will present four of them, each with a different purpose.

Diet #1. The Superenergy Weight-Reducing Diet. This really is an updated version of the ketogenic low-carbohydrate diet of my first book *Diet Revolution*. It is still the number one diet for those who want to lose weight as well as gain energy. But it is improved because four years have passed since I wrote the book, four years of learning more about the nutritional approach to overweight.

Diet #2. The Superenergy Weight-Gaining Diet. This is for the underweight person who must gain weight as well as energy.

Diet #3. The Superenergy Weight-Maintenance Diet. This is an intermediate diet for those whose weight is at or near the ideal, who don't have to lose or gain, but who are seeking to end fatigue.

Diet #4. The Special Situation Diet. This is a special situation diet for those who have a complicating factor, such as pregnancy, a yet to be diagnosed problem, or a condition requiring certain kinds of medication. It's a diet for marking time, building up general nutrition, awaiting the proper time to start one of the other diets.

Analyze your objectives—what you would like a diet to do for you—and it should be easy to learn which diet you will be working with. There is no such thing as one diet that's good for everyone. Find the one diet that is most suitable for *your* ideal weight, *your* metabolism, *your* health, *your* energy, and *your* outlook.

Although the diets differ, there are certain health features common to all of them. They are:

You avoid the biggest health hazard of all—sugar.

You avoid the second great hazard—refined flour.

You cut down on quantities of carbohydrates, finding your best level according to tests I will show you how to conduct upon yourselves.

You eat frequently, not just two or three times a day.

You take supplementary vitamins and minerals according to guidelines I will provide.

YOU MAY NOT KNOW YOU'RE TIRED. People who are fat all know they're fat, but people who are tired often don't even know that they're tired. In the past, people who were tired had not even thought of going on a diet, whereas the person who is fat is *always* thinking about going on a diet.

MY PRACTICE HAS TAUGHT ME ONE BASIC THING. If a person is tired, and you then take away his sugar, give him minerals and vitamins, and cut down carbohydrates, you can usually get him to feel better. It works for almost everybody.

Whether the person has hypoglycemia or whether he has a vitamin or mineral deficiency, or a food allergy, or a need for something to relate to can be argued all day. The fact of the matter is he will feel better.

DIET VERSUS NUTRITION. I once appeared on a TV program, and then a year later went back. The first time I talked about my diet. The second time I told the interviewer that my subject was to be nutrition. The interviewer seemed astounded, asking, "Isn't that a switch—from diet to nutrition?"

Too many people fail to see the connection between diet and nutrition. They think only the overweight person has to be on a diet. If there is one message that this book should deliver, it is that *everybody* should be on a diet. Everyone should try to provide himself the best possible nutrition for his body.

Many people consider "diet" to be synonymous with a reducing regimen, but it is not. "Diet" is really another word for eating pattern—referring merely to what you eat.

There are good diets and bad diets; there are diets that can make you lose weight, or gain weight; there are special diets for certain diseases like heart disease and diabetes, and other diets that cause these conditions.

If there is one diet that is antinutritious, it's the twentieth-century American diet. We have come to process all our foods to the point where *nutrients are discarded.*

Refined carbohydrates, now everywhere, are added to

salad dressings, luncheon meats, frozen vegetables, TV dinners, convenience foods.

It's no wonder that you stand to benefit from a change in your diet.

It doesn't take very much intelligence to realize that the person who wakes up to have a jelly donut and a cup of coffee with two lumps of sugar, then a hamburger with french fries and a Coke for lunch, plus candy morning and afternoon and night might well be jeopardizing his health. But even the person drinking juice and having a corn muffin for breakfast, perhaps a bowl of vegetable soup for lunch, and a four-course dinner at night can still have symptoms of fatigue or anxiety, and may be suffering from imaginary health—and all because of his diet.

THE QUEST FOR YOUR BEST DIET. This book does not feature one diet; it features a different diet for each of you. It presents basic principles which each individual will then be able to apply himself to whatever degree is best for him.

The guidelines will enable you to find the diet that will make you feel, and be, your best.

If I believed in long, boring titles, I would call this book *The Search for the Proper Metabolic Fuel for Your Optimum Feeling of Well-Being.* This is exactly what is involved when I see a patient, and that is what is involved as you, the reader, work with me to find the diet which is best for you.

EVEN IF YOU THINK YOU FEEL PERFECTLY FINE, YOU MIGHT FEEL EVEN BETTER ON ONE OF THESE DIETS. I ask my patients "Do you feel fantastically well, really perfect?" Unless they say yes to that, I know there's room for improvement.

Or many will feel rather well some of the time, but experience fatigue, emotional problems, depression, and irritability just in spells. It's not rare for patients to come in with spells of rapid heartbeat, migraines, dizzy spells, seizures, or free-floating anxiety attacks. Or sometimes they will have periods of blurred speech or inability to concentrate. These are all evidences of not functioning well. These are *not* necessarily psychosomatic and *not* necessarily due to "your nerves." Symptoms like these may all derive from the way in which the fuel of metabolism is being provided to your body and your brain.

MY OWN ENERGY CHANGE. I initially went on this diet searching for a solution to my own ever-increasing weight problem. Then after I was on it, I began to be more alert, to feel less fatigued, to require less sleep at night, and to give up daytime naps I had previously needed. But I attributed the change, as almost anyone who loses weight does, to the fact that I was not carrying around so much extra weight. Just as later when I heard patients tell me, "Doc, I feel better than ever before," I just thought, "Isn't weight loss wonderful?"

It took years really before the full significance hit me. When I woke up early, it wasn't just because I was thinner and was exhilarated over it. It was actually the beginning of a new sleep pattern. Never again did I require the nine hours sleep I did before. From that point forward I needed only six or seven hours, and that's all I need now despite the fact that I usually work an eleven-hour day with office hours starting at 7:30 A.M. Now I always ask patients what time they go to bed, what time they wake up, how much sleep they require. Because one of the most measurable things which a proper diet can do for you is to change an excessive sleep requirement.

THE KNOWLEDGE I PRESENT TO YOU IN THIS BOOK HAS COME GRADUALLY. I began with an interest in obesity, but I was soon forced into an awareness of the importance of carbohydrate metabolism, which then became my principal medical specialization. I made it a rule that every patient would have a glucose tolerance test. At first it was only a three-hour test to look for diabetes, because I believed what I had been told—that low blood sugar practically doesn't exist.

But even in this three-hour test I began to notice that the blood sugars of some patients started off by going much higher than the acceptable limits of normality and then dropped very rapidly. When I began ordering four-hour glucose tolerance tests, the number of people who showed this curve was much greater. Many people showed their lowest reading just at four hours. Later we extended the test to five hours, and found even more who had this combination of high and low blood sugar.

I wanted to find out what caused the abnormal sugar curve. What conditions that were associated with the curve did the patients have in common? It was amazing how many conditions were found that were correlated—diabetes, angina pectoris, hypertension, congestive heart failure, disturbances of heart rhythm, depression, irritability, fatigue, anxiety, migraine, Ménière's syndrome, peptic ulcer, hiatal hernia, gallbladder disease, and senility. There was an increased frequency of the abnormal curve in all of these conditions—some more than others. The curve was extremely common in excessive coffee drinkers or those with a significant alcohol intake. And it was extremely common among those requiring psychiatric attention.

And these conditions, I found, could be modified by regulating the rise and fall of the blood sugar levels by changing the diet.

I also found a correlation between the abnormal curve and certain medications. The exaggerated sugar curve was seen more often in women on birth control pills or on estrogen therapy, and in patients on diuretics or patients with a history of taking diet pills over a long time. These diet-pill victims are some of the worst cases I have ever seen, in fact.

The effort to solve this question brought me to the next phase of my education, which of necessity meant learning more about nutrition. This came gradually, because you must remember I was a very "proper" doctor. Even though I was taught that vitamins are no good and that our "balanced" American diet gives us all the nutrition we need, there were many cases where I felt that the new diet and the vitamins had convincingly turned the tide and made a stubborn and difficult clinical "problem case" a resounding success. So rather tentatively at first, and then with the ever increasing confidence bred by success, I began to experiment with large dosages of various vitamins. Much to my surprise and my great satisfaction I found that the introduction of large doses of vitamins and minerals did make a difference. The patients who had felt well felt even better, and the patients who did not feel well often had their problem corrected quickly.

I avidly studied the research papers on vitamin therapy, ever seeking the lead that would help the different types of problem patients with whom I was struggling—those patients who had as yet not uttered those magic words, "I feel better than ever before."

Certain vitamins for which claims have been made were disappointing; others have been a great satisfaction and benefit to the patients.

One result of these discoveries was that I no longer considered that my specialty was limited to obesity (bariatric medicine), or to carbohydrate metabolism, but rather to the specialty of nutrition medicine.

Those of you who remember my first book may recall that, although I was interested in megavitamins, in truth, I only recommended moderate supplements. It has been since the book came out that I really began to comprehend the true value of vitamin therapy.

Occasionally, in the past I had to use blood-sugar-regulating hormones or medications in addition to diet to help the problem patient. With a more vigorous usage of vitamins, the problem is usually solved so that resorting to medications becomes unnecessary.

EVERY DIETER SHOULD ALSO BE TAKING SUPPLEMENTARY VITAMINS AND MINERALS. Each plan has two major factors: the diet, and the vitamin and mineral supplements. The diet may work without the vitamin supplements, but just as likely it won't. And the vitamins without the diet aren't enough. As a matter of fact, most of the "negative" results of vitamin therapy have occurred because little or no effort was made to provide for an effective diet to go with them.

DON'T I GET ENOUGH VITAMINS AND MINERALS IN MY REGULAR DIET? People may have in the past. But despite what you sometimes hear, the average person no longer can be assured of getting enough vitamins and minerals naturally in his diet. Now that we have so many refined foods such as those made of milled wheat and polished rice and sugar, essential nutrients are missing in epidemic proportions. There is no question that there are cultures such as those of the Hunzas and the Abkhasians in which people live life-spans far exceeding ours and without vitamin supplements. But they don't have refined foods in their diets.

We in the Western World have been eating sugar and other refined foods for a lifetime. If, as the mounting evidence suggests, this surfeit of refined carbohydrates uses up our vital nutrients without replacing them, then we have a lot of catching up to do with our nutritional deficiencies. There might come a time when, having caught up with our deficiencies, we could go on a diet of all natural and unrefined foods and do very well. But if you are reading this book because you are tired, or depressed, or overweight, you may well suspect that, at least for now, you may need some catching up on your vitamin reserves.

WHAT WE ARE DOING IS SEARCHING FOR THE BEST FUEL FORMULA FOR YOUR BODY. Choosing how much protein, fat, and carbohydrates you will eat is like designing the gas formula best for your car—finding how much high test should be mixed in with the basic fuel for smooth running. The vitamins and minerals are the catalysts, the no-knock additives, the oil or the antifreeze that are necessary to the best utilization of that fuel.

There is a proper fuel mixture for everybody. The people with no symptoms can function well on a variety of fuel mixtures. They might need no help at all, or might just need a general tune-up. But the greater the symptoms, the more carefully planned out the fuel mixture has to be. The people who are having problems, who have a tough time feeling well, need a fuel mixture that's just exactly right.

To find your best fuel—the best diet for you—there are several things you must do. The next four chapters deal with what every dieter should do before starting the diet.

6

How to take your own case history

It's hard to practice medicine on somebody through a book. I can't see you, listen to your problems, examine you, do your lab work, and find your response to various treatments. But there is something I, as a physician-author, can do: get you started in the right direction.

The first thing that you and I will have to do is to find out just what is bothering you most. We cannot make much progress if I am treating you for one thing, and you're suffering from another. So the first order of business is to find out just what it is that you would like this book to help you with. Is it fatigue? Is it an emotional problem such as depression? Is it a specific symptom, a pain, a discomfort, a dizzy spell, a series of headaches, a problem in your digestive tract, a sleeping problem, a problem in adjusting to others?

The lead-off question that a doctor asks when he sees a new patient for the first time is "What is your chief complaint, the primary reason that you are here?

PERHAPS YOU HAVE A SERIES OF PROBLEMS. What I would like you to do is to list your complaints in order of importance to you. Let's put it this way. If you had five medical wishes to clear up, for which symptom would you use your first wish, for which the second, for which your third? Once you have listed these complaints, we will try to attack them one by one.

Suppose you are the type of person who wakes up in the

51

morning not quite ready to face the day. You finally get yourself together for a few good hours of work, but by late morning you feel tired, but you keep going, and by late afternoon you're irritable, your attention keeps wandering. You have wasted the day but by the end of it you're exhausted. You feel vaguely discontented or else tense and anxious, snapping at your family. After dinner you're too tired to go out, and you can't even manage to watch television without feeling drowsy. If this sounds like you, you may be one of those people with imaginary health who can be helped with this book.

If you were a patient in my office complaining of fatigue, there are many questions that I would ask you. I would want to know "How long have you had it, under what circumstances did it begin, did it begin suddenly or gradually?" If it did begin suddenly, the events which surrounded that sudden onset are important because they may tip me off as to what is really behind this complaint. I would want to know "What seems to make it better, and what seems to make it worse?" "Does some food or drink make it better or worse?" Then, of course, I must know just how severe the fatigue is.

I WANT YOU TO TAKE PART IN A GREAT EXPERIMENT. I am going to ask you to fill out a questionnaire about your symptoms and whether your new diet changes them. I hope every person who purchases this book will take the time to submit his responses. There are many important questions about the effects of nutrition that need answering. You will have a chance to participate and help contribute to the results. Your personal experiences will provide the case material that medical experts will use to form tentative, but important conclusions about what diets such as those in this book can do for fatigue and other important everyday symptoms.

To do this we need a yardstick to measure symptoms objectively, and I would like to propose a way in which you can actually quantify a symptom, and give it a number. Then, after you have been on the diet for one week, or one month, you can measure this symptom again to see if the diet made a difference.

YOUR FATIGUE CHART. So, let's make a chart with nine time periods.

Energy Quotient

1. When you first get up.	1. ————
2. Immediately after breakfast.	2. ————
3. Before lunch.	3. ————
4. After lunch.	4. ————
5. The middle of the afternoon.	5. ————
6. Before dinner.	6. ————
7. After dinner.	7. ————
8. Before bedtime.	8. ————
9. Sleeping.	9. ————

Total

SCORING YOUR FATIGUE. Suppose fatigue is the symptom you are scoring. You will do it with a Superenergy score. Three days of observation will provide your base line.

At each of the nine times ask yourself how much energy (or fatigue) you seem to have, using the following scoring system.

Perfect; feeling especially great, even after strenuous exercise . . . Superenergy itself. . . . 10 points.

Feeling great doing ordinary everyday activities. . . . 9 points.

Feeling everyday good, or feeling normally tired after effective exercise. . . . 8 points.

Neutral . . . unremarkable, neither supergood nor superbad. . . . 7 points.

A tinge of fatigue, not quite at your best, a little cranky, or you make mistakes at routine jobs. . . . 6 points.

Your fatigue is discernible enough that you say, "I'm tired but I'll keep going." . . . 5 points.

You must rest or eat or drink something to keep your energy going. . . . 4 points.

Fatigue so great you take a nap, or fall asleep at a lecture, in a theatre, or watching television. . . . 3 points.

Fatigue so great you feel muscular pains, a discomfort in your chest, back, or head. . . . 2 points.

Prostrated, unable to get out of bed. . . . 1 point.

In the bottom row for your sleeping period you will enter points for the amount of sleep that you required that night.

If you needed only five hours, give yourself 20 points. If it was six hours, 18 points. Seven hours, 16 points. Eight hours,

14 points. Nine hours, 12 points. Ten hours, 10 points. Eleven hours, 8 points.

Add up your points to get your energy score for the day. Your maximum score would be a hundred points.

Your three-day average will show your typical degree of energy. Now for the first time you have a number which you can use to compare with scores in the future.

You might compare your score with passing grades in school. A score of 70 would be barely passable, an 80 good, and a 90 excellent. Less than 70, the clinical problem of fatigue truly would demand attention.

It will be interesting to see how this number will change after you have been on the diet and vitamin regimen for a few days, for a week, for a month, for a year. You will be able to determine whether your fatigue is lessening or worsening. Having this number you can make objective observations. Women can determine whether their fatigue is related to their menstrual cycle. You can determine when a viral illness has stopped exerting its effect. You can determine the effect of a change in diet or an exercise program, or a new vitamin dosage.

FINDING THE CAUSE. We now begin the fascinating clinical problem of finding the causes of your fatigue. I don't want to mislead you into thinking that fatigue is always a matter of improper diet. There are many causes of fatigue: anemias and other blood disturbances, metabolic defects, sluggishness of the thyroid, imbalances of other endocrine glands, chronic infections, allergies, environmental poisonings, insufficiencies of certain organs such as the kidneys and liver, serious diseases, both malignant and nonmalignant, reactions from past or present medications (even aspirin or birth control pills), smoking or drinking to excess, recent surgery, overwork. But eliminate these and there are millions of unexplained cases, cases that may be due to a wrong diet. And there are some who suffer from one or more of the above conditions, as well as an improper diet. These are the people who may not have to be tired at all if they follow the right diet.

When I first started my practice of internal medicine, fatigue was, as it is now, the most common symptom that patients mentioned. In those days I was lucky to be able to reduce the fatigue of more than one patient out of five. But now that I have some ability to use nutritional techniques, four out of five patients with fatigue report improvement.

DEPRESSION. A new diet often can solve the other frequent complaint that is the first cousin of fatigue—depression.

Many people suffer from depression without realizing it. In fact the World Health Organization calls depression the "major mental health problem in the world today." In the United States probably one out of every seven people will have symptoms of depression this year.

But few of them will receive the treatment they should have, or will even realize that they have a condition that *can* be treated.

Depression can be serious enough to cause suicide or it can be mild, simply taking the joy from each day. The person who feels no pleasure in life, the person who is always tired, and the underachiever are often really suffering from depression, and the older person diagnosed as senile may really be depressed.

PILLS VERSUS DIET. For just one category of antidepressant drugs, some twenty-five *million* prescriptions were written last year. Pills are necessary to treat many depressions, of course, and often bring about dramatic recovery. But they don't always work and they often cause side effects. In fact, psychotropic drugs sometimes make people even worse without their realizing it!

Many tranquilizer and antidepressant drugs have the effect of increasing insulin output and leading to weight gain and hypoglycemia.

Since hypoglycemia is often the *cause* of symptoms such as depression and anxiety, when the person's problem is really hypoglycemia, the medicines can do more harm than good.

What they may need most is *correction* of the hypoglycemia.

As in the case of fatigue, depression can be caused by other things besides diet:

The symptoms of depression often begin so slowly that the person may not be sure when they started. He may feel or look melancholy or there may be tears . . . a lack of feeling or meaning . . . there may be a diminished interest or an apathy toward work . . . there may be a feeling of failure, self-reproach, or self-pity . . . there may be increased anxiety or irritability, heavy intake of alcohol, neglect of hair or clothes, difficulty in reaching a decision or in starting something new, sleep disturbances or bad dreams. To me, the clearest symptom is the loss of a sense of humor.

The depression may be steady and unrelenting or may come and go.

YOUR MOOD SCORE. If you would like to evaluate the symptom of depression to see whether it may be altered by good nutrition, you may use a scale similar to the energy-fatigue scale. Make the same kind of chart for times of day and number of days. Score yourself as follows:

Euphoric, with total joy or elation, unable to stop smiling. . . . 10 points.

Happy, contented, quietly joyous, easily responding with laughter. . . . 9 points.

Serene, somewhat more happy than sad. . . . 8 points.

The neutral point, neither happy nor sad, unaware of any mood. . . . 7 points.

Ever so slightly down or troubled, somewhat more sad than happy. . . . 6 points.

Down in the dumps, but no real impairment of performance. . . . 5 points.

Depressed, apathetic, lethargic, unable to concentrate or perform your job well. . . . 4 points.

Barely able to function, or to function only with medication. . . . 3 points.

Crying easily or being near tears, feeling hopeless, unable to carry out your day's work. . . . 2 points.

Hopelessness, despair and futility, questioning whether your life is even worth continuing. . . . 1 point.

To score yourself for the sleeping period, evaluate your thoughts while falling asleep, or your mood while dreaming. Double your sleeping time score. Add your points.

Your score may range between 10 and 100.

KEEP THIS, ALONG WITH YOUR FATIGUE SCORE, FOR FUTURE REFERENCE. You will be comparing it with your later score after you have been on the diet. You will soon learn whether changing your diet will change your mood.

ANXIETY. Using this simple scorekeeping technique, where ten is perfect, seven is neutral, and one is the most severe example of the symptom, you can evaluate just about any chronic symptom: tension, anxiety, nervousness, inability to concentrate, shakiness, sweating, indigestion, headache, allergy. For example, if anxiety attacks are a major problem, determine your serenity-calmness score using the nine time periods. Remember that anxiety may involve apprehension, panic, palpitation of the heart, racing pulse, dry mouth, shakiness, rapid shallow breathing, pallor, and sweating. Rate the symptoms; chart them out.

These anxiety symptoms can be emotional reactions to something in your life situation or they can be brought on by diet. Charting them out may help you determine the role that diet plays in your case.

The possibilities of using this scoring system are limitless. Whatever your particular problem is, keep a chart to provide a base line to evaluate future therapies.

TAKING YOUR DIET CASE HISTORY. Before you see your doctor you should take your diet case history. Start with your family history. Were your mother and father fat or thin? What about your grandparents, your brothers and sisters?

Did any of your relatives have problems with alcoholism, sugar cravings, allergies, ulcers, or diabetes?

What is your own history? Have you always been overweight or underweight? If you have gained or lost weight recently when did the change start and how rapidly did it happen? (Sudden unexplained weight loss can be a signal of something serious. It should *always* be reported to your doctor immediately. If you had the flu for two weeks and ate nothing but tea and chicken soup, it's understandable. But if there's not an obvious reason, make an appointment with your doctor now.)

YOUR DIET PROFILE. You may think you eat a fairly balanced diet, but you will probably be amazed when you analyze it objectively to see how much empty carbohydrate you eat, even though you don't particularly have a sweet tooth.

It is not at all rare in the United States to find people who are getting 50 percent of their calories as refined sugar! The national *average* is more than 137 grams per day, and it matches up to an equal amount of flour. And that amounts to 1,100 empty calories a day of just the two foods—sugar and flour.

For at least three days (a week would be better), eat and drink just as you usually do. Carry a notebook or paper with you at all times, and just as soon as you've had anything to eat or drink write it down with the amount. Later, look up the grams of carbohydrates you took in, from the list in the back of the book. Tabulate all items in your diet and add the total. Do it for three days to secure an accurate estimate of your daily carbohydrate intake.

Keep this record for your own information and for your doctor to see.

WHEN YOUR SYMPTOMS HAPPEN IS IMPORTANT TOO. There is one other thing I want you to do to help determine if diet is causing your fatigue, depression, anxiety, or tension. And that is to check the time of your symptoms in relation to your diet.

When you chart your symptoms for severity, mark also when you eat and drink and what you eat and drink. Study your charts. See if you can find any connection between the eating and the symptoms. Is your fatigue relieved by eating? Or is it made worse and, if so, how many hours later?

If your problem is depression, or irritability, or crankiness, or emotional instability, chart it on the scale, then see if it comes between meals or is relieved by eating.

Sometimes this will be enough of a clue to tell you there is a connection between your symptoms and your diet. But even so, you should take the glucose tolerance test I'll describe later. Sometimes even though diet may be the cause, symptoms may not vary with meals. Often a bout of prolonged sweets consumption produces a sugar hangover that continues right into the next day, and longer.

THE VALUE OF SCORING. The true test of whether diet is the cause of your symptoms is whether changing your diet will get rid of them. You know your problem was caused by diet if the new diet makes the symptoms go away. Having done these

charts to get your symptom scores will provide you the objective measurement for comparing any change, or for evaluating future medications or comparing diets. For instance, if
you have a favorite "balanced" diet and you want to compare it
with these, you might go on it and check your energy level,
then compare the results with what you find on the diet that
I am suggesting.

With this chart, no matter what you try and what you test,
you can see what makes symptoms better and what makes them
worse.

Once you have identified the symptoms, you have taken
one giant step in the direction of correcting those symptoms.

7

The hyperinsulin connection—how fatigue, overweight, and blood sugar may fit together

Fatigue, the single most common chronic *symptom* today, is often related to obesity, the single most common *physical* abnormality.

In this chapter, I propose to show you what that connection might be.

WHAT IS THE REAL CAUSE OF OBESITY? We have all been taught that obesity comes from overeating. It is implied that people are as uniform as assembly-line Fords, all getting approximately the same miles to the gallon, or in this case to the calories, and those who take in too much fuel get fat. But it just ain't so.

MANY DIET SURVEYS HAVE BEEN DONE. Most of them show that overweight people actually consume fewer calories than people of normal weight. In my own practice I find that most fat people tell the truth when they say, "Doctor, I don't eat that much." And don't all of us know overweight people who always seem to be eating less than we do?

IS IT UNDEREXERCISING? That is true to an extent. Yet how many people do we know who work out strenuously and often, but won't lose an ounce until their diets are changed?

OR IS IT PSYCHOLOGICAL? Do we eat too much to make up for a lack of love or to seek solace? There are many who do; I see them in my practice. But can these psychological factors explain away the woman who diets with great motivation but *gains* weight on a 1200-calorie diet, or else experiences unbearable hunger when she tries to cut down to 900 calories? I see many more from this latter group than the former.

HEREDITY, THEN? Certainly, heredity is an important causative factor. If both your parents are overweight, chances are four out of five that you will be too. If neither parent is overweight, chances are more like one in ten. But for heredity to play a role, there must be a mechanism. Through what means does heredity work?

ONE MECHANISM WILL EXPLAIN ALL THESE THEORIES. It is our metabolism—our body chemistry—that is responsible for overweight. There are specific areas or pathways of metabolism that can and do go awry, that cause our body fuel to be used abnormally and cause us to be fat.

THE MOST COMMON METABOLIC UPSET INVOLVES CARBO-HYDRATE METABOLISM. Studies on sugar and insulin levels, studies of hereditary factors, as well as the exciting results on low-carbohydrate diets, strongly indicate that the nutritional-chemical defect in most overweight people involves carbohydrate metabolism. The heredity factor is thus explained. Carbohydrate intolerance is the commonest hereditary defect in metabolism; it can be bred into mice in just a few generations by feeding them sugar.

FINDING OF EXCESS INSULIN. In 1959 Drs. Rosalyn Yalow and Solomon Berson perfected a technique for determining the actual levels of insulin in our blood. The discoveries that followed led scientists to revamp their thinking about several subjects. Up to that time, we still considered low blood sugar to be the opposite of diabetes. And we tended to think that overweight individuals were no different metabolically from those of normal weight.

But reports showing otherwise began to come in from the

scientific community. The new data showed the diabetic person in the early and middle stages puts out not less, but *more* insulin than normal people, and so did very fat people! There it was—a metabolic difference that could truly explain why fat people are fat, and thin people thin.

INSULIN IS THE FATTENING HORMONE. You see, insulin is the one hormone in the body that promotes storage of fuel. Most of you know it lowers the blood sugar, but did you know it does this by converting the sugar to a storage form of carbohydrate, called glycogen (animal starch), and into fat, which is called triglyceride? Insulin also converts the other major fuels—the fatty acids and the ketone bodies—back to stored fat.

So, the primary actions of insulin are all directed toward making us fat. It's no wonder that those of us who tend to have higher than normal insulin levels tend to get fat.

The most consistently found biochemical abnormality associated with obesity is an excessively high level of insulin. And the very same high level of insulin is found in hypoglycemia (a major cause of fatigue) and in early diabetes.

THE MOST EFFECTIVE TREATMENT. The therapeutic principle that my theories are based on is: *In managing these conditions, all therapy should be directed toward eliminating every stimulus to the insulin overresponse.*

In other words, if excessive insulin promotes fatigue and diabetes and obesity, then the correction of it would logically involve cutting out those factors which promote the release of insulin. And that's the most of what this book and this diet is all about.

WHAT ABOUT DIET AS A CAUSE OF OBESITY? How does this metabolic theory fit in with my oft-repeated accusation that obesity is really caused by our improper twentieth-century Western World diet? It fits quite well, because it is this diet that *leads* to these metabolic imbalances. Most of the steps leading to this inescapable conclusion have been demonstrated. For instance, Drs. Cleave and Campbell, in their brilliant book, have shown that in cultures where there are no refined carbohydrates in the diet, there is no diabetes. And it has often been observed that where there is no diabetes, there is virtually no obesity.

And we will learn of other illnesses, common in our society, but rare in cultures where the diet is not dominated by refined carbohydrates, as is ours.

Refined carbohydrates, hypoglycemia, diabetes, hunger, fatigue, obesity, and high levels of insulin are unquestionably interrelated.

HERE'S HOW IT SEEMS TO WORK. If you take in a large amount of sugar often enough, your body begins to overreact, and an increased amount of insulin is secreted in the blood, which lowers your blood sugar level below its starting point. At this point, you experience hunger and will probably eat more than your body can use, so that obesity is the outcome.

Dr. A. M. Cohen was able to demonstrate the same sequence in laboratory animals. He described the cycle of "the more you eat, the more you need, until you get obese . . . a chain reaction."

The fat person actually gets hooked into a hyperinsulin-hypoglycemia-diabetes cycle. The first part of the triad is too much insulin, which causes low blood sugar. The three-way cycle leads to getting fat because the low blood sugar induces hunger. So, too, it produces your low energy level.

THAT'S WHY THE SUPERENERGY DIET IS SO EFFECTIVE. Much of the diet's success comes because it attacks these causes. It counteracts the carbohydrate intolerance, the excessive insulin levels, the hypoglycemia, and the adrenalin reaction triggered by hypoglycemia. Also, it eliminates antinutrients and counteracts deficiencies of vitamins and minerals.

So several avenues are merging to produce the great feeling you will have of renewed energy and well-being.

THE SECOND PART OF THE TRIAD: HYPOGLYCEMIA. As Chapter 3 discussed, there is good reason to relate fatigue to hypoglycemia, or at least to situations where the blood sugar is falling. And when actual testing of insulin levels is done on people with low blood sugar, an excessive release of insulin is found in many cases of hypoglycemia. Further, whenever large numbers of obese subjects were given glucose tolerance tests, results of the studies show that the majority of the overweight have hypoglycemia.

It is no wonder that they both respond best to the ketogenic diet.

AND THE THIRD PART: DIABETES. Most of my patients are quite comfortable discussing with me their fatigue or their weight problems, but they are often put off when I mention to them the possibility of diabetes. Perhaps that's because people are not frightened when they talk about *symptoms,* but they are when you force them to think about *illness.*

But if we are to accept that today's improper diet can lead to the metabolic disturbance of hyperinsulinism, which in turn leads to obesity and hypoglycemia, then we must accept that this diet can lead to the further consequence of hyper-insulinism—diabetes in its various stages.

COULD I REALLY HAVE DIABETES? Anyone who does have hypoglycemia could, indeed, develop diabetes, since low blood sugar must be considered a possible forerunner of diabetes.

Many cases are hidden. In my practice only one in ten patients who show diabetes on a glucose tolerance test previously knew they had this condition. This fits with the textbook statement that the potential for this disease exists in up to 20 percent of the population. Or, as Dr. Leonard J. Kryston states in his textbook *Endocrinology and Diabetes,* "Diabetes should be suspected in every patient who walks into the physician's office."

IF YOU'RE SIGNIFICANTLY OVERWEIGHT. Your chances of being diabetic can go up to one in two, according to separate studies by Dr. Garfield Duncan and Dr. Irving Perlstein. My own series of twelve thousand tests places the incidence of diabetes from the earliest stage on as closer to one out of three, but in the case of men over forty-five who are more than seventy-five pounds overweight, the chances can go to three out of five.

Other factors that indicate you might be particularly at risk of diabetes: family history, complications during pregnancy, and high birth weight of babies you have.

DIABETES AND HYPOGLYCEMIA ARE DEFINITELY RELATED. Many authorities used to consider diabetes to be the opposite of low blood sugar; the average layman still believes this. But it is not. Rather, it is the same illness—diabetes is merely a further advanced stage than hypoglycemia. The common denominator is the excessive level of insulin—the common cause is the continued consumption of refined carbohydrates.

These facts are still considered controversial, but *all* scientific evidence confirms them. There have been many studies since three professors with the University of Michigan Medical School in Ann Arbor, Drs. Holbrooke Seltzer, Stefan S. Fajans, and Jerome W. Conn, reported on a large number of patients with complaints of "weakness, nervousness, tremor, hunger and sweating" several hours after eating. When the doctors did glucose tolerance tests on them, they not only found hypoglycemia, but also mild unrecognized diabetes.

They studied 110 patients over a six-year period and concluded that "symptoms of hypoglycemia occurring three to five hours after meals represent the earliest clinical manifestation of diabetes in many cases."

PREDIABETES. Other scientists made the case stronger when they studied the offspring of two diabetic parents, individuals who were, by definition, prediabetic. They found that the first abnormality these subjects showed was hypoglycemia; the next deviation, sometimes years later, was still hypoglycemia, but with elevations of the early blood sugar reading within an hour after glucose was administered. The next stage that showed up was the classic findings representing early diabetes.

THIS IS EXACTLY WHAT I WAS FINDING IN MY PRACTICE. Further, I found that many people, as their tests were repeated under different circumstances, would shift back and forth between hypoglycemia and diabetes. Hypoglycemic people who continued their consumption of sweets and starches would return a few years later as diabetics, and diabetics who had successfully dieted by restricting their carbohydrates would retest only hypoglycemic. The overwhelming majority of these patients, however, displayed variations of the curve, where both diabetes and hypoglycemia coexisted—the very combination that Dr. Seale Harris first described over half a century ago.

Some theorists have stated that *all* cases of diabetes probably first pass through the stage of hypoglycemia. Indeed, the fact that the person with hypoglycemia is often a prediabetic is used by some physicians as an early warning sign to look out for the full-blown symptoms of diabetes in the future.

CHANGING THE DIET CAN SOMETIMES PREVENT DIABETES COMPLETELY. Dr. Leon S. Smelo, of the Medical College of Alabama, who at first disagreed with the hypoglycemia-diabetes connection, later reported in a scientific paper that in his own practice he had indeed confirmed this.

And in this report, Dr. Smelo points out that treatment of this disease in its hypoglycemic stage by diet can arrest the course of the diabetes so it never reaches its overt stage, never reaches the stage of causing diabetic symptoms or the dreaded complications. *Changing the diet can prevent the expected diabetes!*

HERE'S HOW IT IS BELIEVED THIS STRANGE PARADOX OCCURS. When a person eats refined carbohydrate with no vitamins and minerals necessary for its metabolism, the body attempts to compensate by signaling the pancreas to release more insulin to process the sugar. The pancreas, sooner or later, begins to overreact and insulin is released in excess. This extra insulin is what causes the hypoglycemia and its symptoms. The body begins to compensate for this insulin excess by putting out an insulin antagonist, so that we usually find both high levels of sugar and high levels of insulin in the early stages of diabetes.

IF YOU KEEP EXCESS SUGAR OUT OF THE BODY, YOU PREVENT THE WHOLE SERIES! Or as Dr. Smelo says, "Avoidance of hypoglycemia is the key to prevention in diabetes mellitus. It is also the key to successful therapy in the management of its hypoglycemic phase. The overwhelmingly favorable probability should be made clear that adherence to therapy will arrest the downhill course of the diabetes and will forestall the future obligatory need for insulin or even for oral hypoglycemic agents."

THE TIE-IN WITH OBESITY. In 1968, Drs. Georgina Faludi, Gordon Bendersky, and Philip Gerber, of Hahnemann Medical College and Hospital in Philadelphia, not only confirmed hypoglycemia as a first sign of diabetes, but also theorized that this was the cause of obesity and diabetes so often being found together.

These three doctors studied 238 obese patients, aged fifteen to seventy-two, and found 83 percent had some abnormality in their glucose tolerance test.

Their theory: that the hypoglycemia (the symptoms of which are relieved by eating, remember) causes a greater food intake, which in turn causes obesity.

This, they said, can be the explanation of the three-way interrelationship often found between diabetes, obesity, and hypoglycemia and can explain the well-known observation that obesity often precedes the development of diabetes.

THE LOW CARBOHYDRATE DIET CAN STOP ALL THREE! The effectiveness of a very low carbohydrate diet in preventing excess insulin production has been reported by many, including Drs. W. A. Miller, G. R. Faloona, and R. H. Unger, who wrote of their results in the *New England Journal of Medicine* in 1970, and by Drs. E. F. Pfeiffer and H. Laube of Ulm, West Germany, who reported their data at the International Symposium on Lipid Metabolism, Obesity and Diabetes Mellitus in 1974.

When Dr. Pfeiffer described their work at the International Symposium in Stuttgart, Germany, he blasted starch and sugar for their effects on insulin and speculated that diabetes might not occur at all without them.

If all of these theories are correct, then the longer a person is exposed to today's national diet, containing well over a thousand calories a day of sugar and flour, the more diabetic he will become. And that is exactly what we find. Blood sugar levels increase so much, decade by decade, that a person in his seventies is considered normal if his sugar levels equal those we would call diabetic in a young adult.

Diabetes is of special importance, then, not because it is a complication of obesity or of hypoglycemia, but because it is the basic disturbance of which these other conditions are early manifestations.

This is one reason it is so important that a glucose tolerance test be performed, and it should be done before you start the diet. One of the big mistakes many of my readers might make would be to do things in the wrong sequence. Having read this book, the inescapable urge is to try the diet, to see what it does. The reader is going to say, well, I can skip the glucose tolerance test for now and just go right into the diet manipulation.

There's really nothing wrong with that except the diet does such a good job of correcting upsets in metabolism that the diagnosis of diabetes will be masked and a false sense of security could be the result.

When a person who has been eating improperly, suddenly begins to eat sensibly and then goes for a glucose tolerance test, he may well find that his test will be normal. Should he be a person who relapses into bad eating habits, which so many of us do, he will not realize the danger that diabetes may be developing. I've seen it too often—patients with early diabetes who spend a few weeks on a low-carbohydrate diet and find that their test comes out normal. Reassuring? Yes . . . but falsely so, since an important illness is missed.

In the next chapter, I will tell you about the most important test you may ever take in your life.

8

The most important test you may ever take in your life

I don't know how I was ever able to practice proper medicine on a patient whose glucose tolerance tests I didn't know. The glucose tolerance test (the GTT) is a simple, inexpensive office procedure which has become in my view the most important laboratory test in clinical medicine.

THE GLUCOSE TOLERANCE TEST IS CAPABLE OF MAKING TWO DIAGNOSES. It can prove the presence of hypoglycemia, and it can prove the presence of diabetes. And it can serve to predict the likelihood of your developing either of these two conditions.

To me, its great contribution has been the way it demonstrates that these two seemingly opposite conditions of hypoglycemia and diabetes coexist so often that they must, in fact, be considered two facets of the very same condition. This two-faceted condition is often called the hypoglycemia of early diabetes, or diabetic reactive hypoglycemia.

Many nutritionists and physicians still insist that hypoglycemia is a rare condition. Yet, when large numbers of patients have been studied, it has been found to be anything but rare. The test which shows this is the glucose tolerance test.

GOING TO THE DOCTOR. I have no doubt that most of you will read this book, recognize in yourself some of the symptoms

69

this book will describe, and even recognize the relationships between these symptoms and the food and beverage that you take in each day. So you will probably eagerly and innocently walk into your doctor's office and say, "I believe that I may have hypoglycemia, I have all the symptoms." When you do, be prepared to encounter the first of many obstacles that will be placed in your way because chances are your doctor will say, "I don't believe in hypoglycemia, that is a fad. I won't be a party to it; if you want your glucose tolerance done, you'll have to have it done elsewhere."

I do hope your doctor is more reasonable than that, but I have learned that such an attitude is all too common. More likely, your doctor may decide to do the test, and upon reviewing the results, will say it is normal, even though that conclusion is at variance with the interpretation this book will offer you.

YOU ARE NOW LEARNING THE SECOND LESSON ABOUT GLUCOSE TOLERANCE TESTS. Namely, there is no unanimity of agreement on how to interpret them. Two doctors looking at the same set of test results can come to opposite conclusions, one saying, "Yes, this is a classic case of low blood sugar," and the other one saying, "There is no sign of it."

There are no hard and fast criteria that have been generally accepted to separate low blood sugar from the norm. (Fortunately, this is not so much the case when we are dealing with diabetes.)

No one has ever issued an official position statement as to how to interpret a glucose tolerance test for low blood sugar. The authoritative organizations merely state that it is a low level of sugar in the blood, but they don't state how low.

HISTORICAL BACKGROUND. Efforts have been made by scholars in the field beginning with Dr. Seale Harris's first description of hypoglycemia in 1924 to define and delineate this condition, but the early workers were content merely to describe the syndrome when it was in its classic, more obvious form.

Dr. Harris himself offered the criterion that the diagnosis could be made when the blood sugar fell below 70 milligram (mg) percent (the measure of sugar in 100 milligrams of blood), but his final diagnoses were really based on the reproduction of the clinical signs and symptoms, rather than the glucose tolerance test. The wiser practitioners of the art still use the clinical symptoms as the final criteria.

In the 1930s, '40s and '50s, Dr. Jerome W. Conn of the University of Michigan Medical School wrote many papers categorizing hypoglycemia and its treatment. His writings became widely quoted and, perhaps more than anyone else, he influenced the mainstream of medical thinking. His work was instrumental in convincing the profession that a high-protein, low-carbohydrate diet is the best treatment for functional hypoglycemia; but unfortunately in 1955, he stated, somewhat arbitrarily, that unless levels below 40 mg percent of blood sugar can be demonstrated, the test should not be regarded as diagnostic.

The impact was that hundreds of thousands of patients, whose lives were being plagued by disabling symptoms, whose blood sugars would drop only into the 40 to 60 range, were being told "you are normal, you are fine, you don't have hypoglycemia." They were told it was their "nerves," were given tranquilizers or pep pills, and left to continue their suffering.

THE COUNTERPROPOSAL—RELATIVE HYPOGLYCEMIA. But in the fifties, several researchers were openly dissatisfied with these criteria, which in their minds excluded too many patients who obviously had all the symptoms and responses of hypoglycemia. Drs. Sidney Portis, Maximilian Fabrykant, Stephen Gyland, Harry M. Salzer, Martin Buehler, all working independently, stressed in their writings that hypoglycemia was prevalent and symptom provoking, even when the sugar levels failed to drop below 50 mg percent. These clinicians developed the concept of *relative* hypoglycemia.

I have gone into the history of the glucose tolerance test in some detail simply because I do not want it said that the guidelines for interpreting your GTT that I'm about to offer you are arbitrary or mine alone.

GETTING THE TEST DONE. One of the important things to remember is that you are not to be on a low-carbohydrate diet immediately before you are tested; in fact, you actually will be consuming some of the foods you may later find out you shouldn't be eating, such as bread and sweets. You should have at least 150 grams of carbohydrate daily for three days or more; so for at least three days, you eat plenty of bread, fruit, juice, and starchy vegetables. Those of you who normally eat a lot of carbohydrates need not change your diet at all. If a person is tested during a low-carbohydrate diet, there is a tendency to exaggerate the response, particularly that of elevating the early blood sugar readings. After supper the night before the chosen day, you don't eat or drink anything other than water or tea with no sugar or milk in it.

When you go to your doctor's office the next morning, you will have a blood specimen taken. This will be used to test the fasting blood sugar (FBS), which is the level of sugar after a period of no food. Then you will immediately be given a bottle of sweet drink, a flavored glucose (sugar) solution, which contains a measured amount of glucose. In a half hour, the doctor or technician will come back to take another quick blood test, and again another half hour later, and again every hour on the hour for five or six hours. At about the time of each blood test you will leave a urine specimen and will report to the doctor or technician whether you are experiencing any symptoms. That's all there is to your part. The lab does a very simple analysis on each specimen for glucose.

After the test your doctor will go over the results with you. I hope you will ask him not just for his conclusions, but for the actual numbers, which I would like you to write down in order to compare them with the numbers we will talk about.

A two-hour or three-hour test is not sufficient. A five- or six-hour test is needed, because any low readings usually occur at the third, fourth, or fifth hour. If a test is too brief, the diagnosis will be missed in altogether too many cases, and the test would have to be done all over again. And make sure that a fasting blood sugar alone is not done. It is almost valueless for hypoglycemia or early diabetes.

Pay attention during the test and note whether the symptoms of which you are complaining take place. This usually correlates with the dropping blood sugar levels.

GOING OVER THE RESULTS. There is great disagreement about how the results of the GTT should be interpreted. That's why you should always ask for a copy of the numbers so that you personally can see whether there could be a question about the findings.

The criteria I am providing are based on an analysis of twelve thousand GTTs done in my private practice. They represent an effort to answer the question: Which findings correlate best with the symptoms, the family history, and later repeat testings?

When your results come back, they will appear as a list that looks like this example of a perfectly normal curve:

FBS	80
½ hour	140
1 hour	130
2 hour	85
3 hour	70
4 hour	75
5 hour	80

Or it may be on a graph, which looks like this:

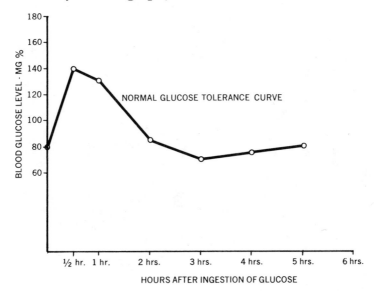

NORMAL GLUCOSE TOLERANCE CURVE

BLOOD GLUCOSE LEVEL · MG %

HOURS AFTER INGESTION OF GLUCOSE

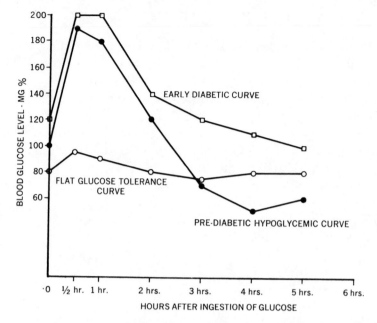

EARLY INSULIN HYPOGLYCEMIC CURVE

Types of glucose tolerance curves encountered clinically. The typical curve in the hypoglycemic patient has a drop of 20 mg% or more below the initial value. The prediabetic curve goes much higher and drops 60 mg% or more in the third and fourth hour. The flat type of curve still indicates hypoglycemia. Other factors to be seriously considered are the occurrence of typical symptoms during the test, such as sweating, impaired perceptions, nausea, and tremor. Relief of symptoms with a low starch and sugar diet also indicates functional hypoglycemia. These patients have a return of their initial symptoms when they eat sugar.

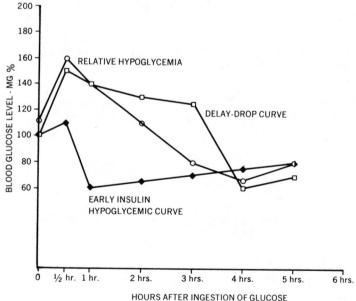

To be a strictly normal curve, the fasting blood sugar (FBS) should be between 70 and 110, the high reading should be no more than a 70 mg percent increase above this base line, and the low reading should be very similar to the base line. The difference between the highest and the lowest readings is usually 50 to 80 mg percent. The extent to which this difference is exceeded is the extent to which the curve obtained is abnormal.

If your results fall within these ranges, then you have a normal curve. If you are one of those fortunate people who has none of the symptoms this book discusses, or whose symptoms are not relieved or aggravated by food intake, then this confirms that your carbohydrate metabolism is probably normal. If, however, you do have symptoms relieved by food and brought on by excessive intake of "junk" foods, remember this: A normal curve does not rule out hypoglycemia, it merely fails to substantiate it.

HOW TO ANALYZE YOUR CURVE. If your curve is not normal, you should identify the type and extent of the abnormality. First, evaluate for the diabetic component. If the fasting blood sugar (FBS) level is over 110 mg percent, if the one-hour reading is over 170 or the two-hour reading over 130, diabetes should be suspected.

To differentiate normal (nondiabetic) from a diagnosis of diabetes, many criteria have been proposed. One of the most accurate is that proposed by Dr. Thaddeus Danowski of Pittsburgh: Add up the four sets of numbers represented by the fasting, the thirty-minute specimen, the one-hour and the two-hour samples. This represents the Glucose Tolerance Sum (GTS).

If your GTS is less than 500, you do not have diabetes. If your GTS is over 800, you do have it. If it falls between 651 and 800, there is a 95 percent probability that you have it. If it falls between 501 and 650, there is a distinct possibility that you have it. (These are the ones we would classify as borderline diabetics.) The higher the GTS, the more probable the diagnosis of diabetes.

This is why you do not want your doctor to give you just a yes, no, or "you're all right" answer, but rather the exact readings at each measurement. This will tell you your own GTS number and show you how close to diabetes you might be.

The second thing you will analyze is how much of a *drop* you have, which will tell you how close you are to being hypoglycemic.

GETTING THE TERMINOLOGY STRAIGHT. You may have heard the terms "latent diabetes," "early diabetes," "prediabetes," and "chemical diabetes." They are approximately the same thing, but there are differences. The term *chemical diabetes* describes the curve where the fasting level of sugar is normal, but the blood sugar is elevated after a load of glucose or food has been administered. This is a stage of diabetes diagnosable by laboratory means, but is not yet overt full-fledged diabetes. The term *latent diabetic* refers to a person who has shown a diabetic curve on glucose testing under a stressful situation such as a pregnancy or following an illness or a period of grossly improper eating, but who when tested later was found normal. *Prediabetic* is the term given to a person who is an offspring of two diabetic parents and does not show diabetes yet, but is expected to later. *Borderline diabetes* refers to a curve that falls within a few points of the established criteria for normality, some readings being a few points over and some readings a few points under. *Early diabetes* is just a little bit beyond that, where the blood sugar readings are really elevated, but not to a great degree.

In analyzing for diabetes, two individual readings are more important than the others. One is the fasting blood sugar (FBS) because it differentiates *overt diabetes* (when the FBS is elevated) from *chemical diabetes* (when the FBS is normal). It also helps differentiate fasting hypoglycemia (the more serious, possibly organic variation) from reactive hypoglycemia, the dietary type we have been discussing.

The other is the two-hour reading, because it picks up the characteristic diabetic response of the *delay* in the fall of the sugar level. Thus a two-hour reading over 130 is suspicious for diabetes, even when there are not elevated readings high enough to produce sugar in the urine.

The criteria for the diagnosis of diabetes are generally agreed upon by most doctors.

You should also keep in mind that sometimes after the

taking of some medication or some unusual stress there can be blood sugar elevations.

HOW TO ANALYZE THE HYPOGLYCEMIA PHASE. To get the most accurate interpretation possible, there are ten questions to ask yourself.

1. What is the very lowest level of sugar found during the test?

2. What is the number of points between the fasting level and the lowest recorded level?

3. *When* is the greatest drop, and the lowest reading?

4. How great is the *rate* of fall during the test, as seen by the steepness of the curve?

5. What is the maximum difference between the highest and the lowest readings?

6. What is the shape of the curve?

7. Is the sugar falling or rising during the last hour of the test?

8. Is the fasting level below 60 or 70 and does the low reading persist?

9. Was there sugar in any of the urine specimens collected during the test?

10. What symptoms, if any, did you experience during the test, and when?

The following may help you understand why all these questions may be important. Here are the explanations for each question.

1. Most medical textbooks say hypoglycemia occurs when the blood glucose level on the test falls below 50 mg percent. Others demand that it fall below 40 mg percent; some diagnose hypoglycemia at 60 mg. But this single criterion is not necessarily accurate. When it is low, it misses too many who are hypoglycemic and, when it is higher, includes too many non-hypoglycemics.

2. The doctors who proposed the concept of relative hypoglycemia have suggested that a diagnosis could be made when the low reading is 20 percent below the fasting level. I consider

a drop of 30 percent necessary to make hypoglycemia a probable diagnosis.

3. The timing of the fall is very important. If the sugar has not fallen below 130 after two hours, this can be interpreted as a delay, which makes it suspicious for diabetes. On the other hand, if the lowest reading occurs as early as two hours and especially after one hour, this implies an *early* overproduction of insulin, a rather difficult-to-treat variant of hypoglycemia.

4. The rate of fall is the feature which has the greatest correlation with the symptom complex of hypoglycemia. There is at present no general agreement as to how to measure this. Dr. Richard Cole devised a formula involving the rate of fall in the 90 minutes immediately preceding the low. My criteria involve finding any portion of the curve after the first hour in which the sugar level falls at the rate of a point a minute or more.

5. This comparison of highest and lowest points (peak to nadir) is the most characteristic of all. Approximately four out of five hypoglycemics have high sugar readings early in the test; conversely, approximately four out of five *early* diabetics will display a hypoglycemic drop. Therefore, a common abnormality includes both high and low readings. I believe a difference of 100 points between the highest and the lowest readings is definitely abnormal, and 80 points would be suspicious of hypoglycemia, and/or diabetes.

6. The normal curve goes up following the glucose, then drops, then returns toward the base line. If there is a second peak, it is considered abnormal. However, this variation can also occur due to laboratory error. One feature that should be looked for is the "delay-drop curve" when the rate of fall, having been rather slow, suddenly accelerates, usually in the third or fourth hour, very indicative of hypoglycemia.

7. This feature is important only insofar as a still falling glucose indicates that the low had not been located and this, in a sense, constitutes an incomplete test.

8. If the fasting level is low, or if the low reading persists, then this would be considered fasting hypoglycemia. That has a more serious clinical implication than the functional or reactive hypoglycemia we have been talking about. It might represent, for example, an insulin-producing tumor of the pancreas and would be deserving of a complete medical evaluation. Abnor-

mal curves can also be caused by liver disease, enzyme deficiencies, and other conditions, but they are all rather rare.

9. The presence of sugar in the urine during a glucose tolerance test is definitely *not* normal. It implies that somewhere during the test the blood sugar level exceeded the threshold of the kidneys. It is usually seen in diabetes, but almost as frequently is seen in hypoglycemia when there is a high initial elevation of blood sugar followed by the low readings. There is a condition called renal glycosuria in which sugar appears in the urine while blood sugars are not elevated. Often when these patients undergo a repeat GTT years later, elevations of the blood sugar readings are found.

10. This consideration is perhaps the most important because if the symptoms that have been troubling you were duplicated during the glucose tolerance test and if they correspond to the point in the test where the blood sugar was falling at its greatest rate, you have confirmed the connection between your low blood sugar and your symptoms. It is possible for a person to have a low blood sugar curve and have symptoms, and yet the two might just be unrelated; but when the symptoms coincide, it is extremely unlikely that they are unrelated.

SO THERE IS MORE THAN ONE WAY TO DIAGNOSE LOW BLOOD SUGAR FROM A GLUCOSE TOLERANCE TEST. If any *one* of these criteria is applicable, you and your doctor should consider the possibility that hypoglycemia really stands behind your fatigue and the cluster of everyday symptoms that have been troubling you.

The reason we have gone to such lengths to describe the glucose tolerance test and all its vagaries is that this is an area of unsettled controversy and honest difference of opinion among medical practitioners. Sometimes your own physician may be so certain of his own conclusion that he may neglect to point out to you that another physician may interpret the same data in a different way. I would like you to be aware of those areas where the difference of opinion may affect you.

A DO-IT-YOURSELF TEST. If you cannot get a glucose tolerance test done by your doctor, you can perform a do-it-yourself glucose tolerance test that can provide some medical information.

To do a home glucose tolerance test, eat nothing after supper, and in the morning take a bottle of glucola which you can get from the drugstore. Or take cola syrup diluted in water, using one tablespoon of syrup for every 20 pounds you weigh. Drink the solution down quickly. Do not eat or drink anything (except water) for six hours. Then observe every hour for the next five or six hours exactly how you feel and whether any of the symptoms that often plague you are duplicated. If any of these symptoms takes place, it would strongly suggest, but not prove, that you have low blood sugar.

As part of this test, you should test your urine. Have on hand some urine glucose testing strips (also available at your drugstore; no prescription necessary). Collect a urine sample every hour or two and test it with the strips. (Keep drinking lots of water.) If there is sugar in your urine, Test-Tape will turn green, and Clinistix will turn blue.

If you have found either sugar in your urine or have reproduced your symptoms during this home glucose tolerance test, I think you could go with some certainty to your physician at this point, and armed with this information, convince even the most resistant skeptic that a laboratory glucose tolerance test is worth doing.

I CANNOT OVERSTRESS JUST HOW FAR-REACHING IS THE APPLICABILITY OF THE GLUCOSE TOLERANCE TEST IN CLINICAL MEDICINE. For instance, if you have symptoms which might lead you to a psychiatrist or psychologist, you should know that there is general agreement among the nutrition-oriented psychiatrists who routinely do glucose tolerance tests that the majority of their patients do show abnormalities.

If you have headaches, you should know that 50 percent of people with recurrent headaches show abnormalities in a glucose tolerance test.

If your complaint is heartburn or stomach cramps or peptic ulcer, you should know that the majority of those so afflicted show an abnormal glucose tolerance test.

In addition, heart disease, arrhythmias, allergies, alcoholism, addiction, and the usage of many medications are all conditions which are associated with a higher-than-normal distribution of abnormal GTTs.

Conditions which affect the GTT results are so prevalent

that I must conclude: Everyone in our culture should have at least one properly performed GTT done in his life.

THERE IS A COMPELLING REASON THAT A GLUCOSE TOLERANCE TEST BE PERFORMED <u>BEFORE</u> YOU START THE DIET. Let me repeat that one of the big mistakes many of my readers might make would be to do things in the wrong sequence. Having read this book, the inescapable urge is to try the diet, to see what it does. The reader is going to say, well, I can skip the glucose tolerance test for now and just go right into the diet and vitamin recommendations. Don't, you could mask a case of diabetes as we mentioned before.

LAURA G.'S STORY IS ALL TOO COMMON. She complained of a relentless fatigue and inability to concentrate, to the point where after reading the newspaper, she couldn't tell you a word that she had read. Since she had been a very good student in high school and knew this was not her usual self, she sought help. She went to her doctor, convinced him that she should have a glucose tolerance test, and when the results came back, he said her test was normal. She then put aside the possibility that she might have low blood sugar, and her symptoms continued for another three years, until finally she consulted me. Her glucose tolerance test showed the presence of a relative hypoglycemia such as we discussed in criterion 2. I placed her on a diet in this book, and her symptoms began to clear up in a week. At the end of three weeks she uttered the magic words, "I feel better than ever before." Out of curiosity I asked her previous physician to send her earlier record, her so-called normal glucose tolerance curve. There it was . . . exactly the same findings showing a relative hypoglycemia three years before. Laura had been subjected to three years of unnecessary suffering, because she did not ask the doctor for the numbers and apply these criteria herself.

Make sure you are armed with the knowledge in this chapter before you go back to talk to your doctor about his interpretation of your glucose tolerance test results. If your test is abnormal by any of the criteria outlined, it certainly would be worthwhile for you to try the appropriate diet in this book to see to what extent you will respond. The response to the diet is one way of proving that the glucose tolerance test was, in fact, significant.

9

How to prepare to visit your doctor, and how to manage him when you get there

How many times have you heard of a medical book being criticized because it supposedly encourages self-medication and treatment? Such an accusation *cannot* be made about this book because my dietary recommendations are made only to be followed in conjunction with your doctor's management.

My goal is to improve your state of health, and that includes not just *feeling* healthy, but also *testing out* as physically healthy. I have had many patients who came to me feeling just fine, but on examination I found they had things like high blood pressure, or a spot on the lung, or high serum triglycerides. Without your doctor, how can you be sure that you have none of these insidious conditions?

So, before you start this, or *any* other serious diet, you should see your doctor. You should get a clear picture of what, in addition to your desire to feel better, your new health restoration program must accomplish, and whether anything other than wrong diet is responsible for your fatigue, or depression, or other symptoms. A thorough checkup is the only way to find that out.

YOUR CHECKUP SHOULD BE DONE FIRST, NOT AS AN AFTERTHOUGHT. There are several reasons. First, the new diet, as I have mentioned, can provide such a great feeling of well-being that it could mask a hidden condition that might otherwise be apparent. Second, an accurate base line of medical data should be obtained to avoid such unnecessary speculations as "did the new diet raise or lower my cholesterol level?" Third, it may avoid incorrect self-treatment. For example, an anemia may be due to a nutritional deficiency, or a blood loss, or some other reason; the type of treatment depends on the diagnosis.

WHERE DO I FIND A DOCTOR WHO WILL GO ALONG WITH YOUR THEORIES? Many of you, experienced in the ways of the medical profession, know that may not be easy. But most doctors want to see you feeling better and will be willing to help you pursue your self-improvement efforts. Your doctor will usually listen to you if you approach him properly.

If you know you have a condition, such as gout, hypertension, kidney trouble, and so on, it is doubly essential that your doctor evaluate you not only before but after a few weeks on the diet.

IF YOU TAKE MEDICINES REGULARLY. These diets modify many conditions and change the dosage requirements of the medications you may be taking for such conditions as allergy, diabetes, hypertension, edema, depression and anxiety, to mention just a few.

For example, the diet has a strong diuretic effect and so enhances the action of diuretic pills, given for high blood pressure or other conditions, sometimes even to the point of causing muscle cramps and weakness. The person who needs diuretics usually improves greatly on this diet, but he must work with his physician to go off the diuretic pills or reduce the dosage. The problem is that the physician may feel that his authority is being challenged by a layman professing medical knowledge. But the matter is worth perseverance. People on diuretics stand to benefit a great deal from this diet because it can provide the same result as the diuretic pills without any of their hazards.

If you are on medication, work closely with your doctor, make the adjustments under his supervision, and let him see just how well the diet works. If you are one who goes on and off the diet, you must also tell him, so that he can see for himself just how much your symptoms and dosage requirements are changed by changes in your diet.

THE DOCTOR TAKES YOUR HISTORY. Many of you will be fortunate enough to find that your physician, knowledgeable and open-minded, is happy that you are willing to cut the junk foods out of your diet and embark upon a self-improvement campaign.

He may recommend that you begin with a complete check-up or a partial one. In either case he will start by questioning you about your symptoms. He will particularly want to know when they first began and how often they recur, and what seems to affect them. He will try to relate them chronologically to other events in your past life, changes in lifestyle, crises in your life, childbirth, illnesses, other medications, and, if he is nutrition-oriented, to changes in your eating pattern.

When I interview my first-time patients, I often notice certain relationships such as symptoms beginning after a pregnancy, or after going on The Pill, or as a rebound reaction to a prolonged course of diet pills. Symptoms often date back to the high school years, and the diet history usually reveals that even people who eat carefully now, certainly did not when they were teen-agers. Many patients date their onset of symptoms to a psychiatric "breakdown" and the prolonged period of drug therapy during their recovery. With others, it might date to the beginning of a sedentary lifestyle and the curtailment of school athletics. To others, it might relate to the start of the less-structured, hectic lifestyle of a young, living-alone career person.

Even though no two cases are alike, it's fascinating how an orientation to nutrition will lead in so many cases to a plausible hypothesis as to how these symptoms came about.

THE GENETIC LINK. Another important and often overlooked facet of medical history-taking is the family history. In my view, the gene which is responsible for the inheritance of diabetes seems to be linked with a whole spectrum of conditions associated with an impairment of carbohydrate tolerance. This is why I feel this whole group of conditions is cross-related and tends to "run in families." The related conditions are obesity, diabetes, low blood sugar, alcoholism, schizophrenia, manic-depressive states, suicidal tendencies, high blood pressure, early heart disease, migraine headaches, allergies, peptic ulcer, gallbladder disease, and high birth weights.

In addition try to recall whether any of your blood relatives had symptoms such as the following: cravings for sweets or starches, excessive hunger or thirst, night eating, alcohol intolerance, overreliance on medications, insomnia, daytime sleepiness, undue laziness, bizarre and inconsistent behavior, emotional instability, inability to concentrate, fainting spells, blackouts, dizziness, or fits of rage or hostility, just to mention a few.

Don't be alarmed if I've just described some of your closest relatives. These symptoms aren't *necessarily* due to a genetic inability to metabolize carbohydrates, but they *might be*. The more of these things that occur in your blood relatives, the greater the suspicion of your having the gene for carbohydrate intolerance, and the more compelling the urgency that a glucose tolerance test be done.

THE DIET HISTORY. I consider this to be the most important area of all in my workup of a new patient. If your doctor neglects to ask you about it, volunteer the information you think he may find significant. Tell him such things, if they are so, as "I go on candy binges," or "I can't live without my ten cups of coffee a day," or "I'm up after midnight eating whatever's not nailed down." He needs to know these important facts to find your correct diagnosis and recommend corrective treatment.

NEXT COMES A COMPLETE PHYSICAL EXAMINATION. When I do this, I look for certain findings of nutritional problems.

For instance, stretch marks in a young man, particularly if they are pink or red, suggest intolerance to carbohydrates. So does edema of the feet and legs in women, dowager's hump, facial hair, or midline pubic hair that extends upward toward the woman's navel.

White spots on the fingernails suggest a deficiency of the important trace metal zinc. Crowded upper incisor teeth and inability to pigment from sun exposure suggest the presence of kryptopyrrole, a condition requiring massive amounts of vitamin B_6 and some zinc. A whitening around the circumference of the iris of the eye suggests a defect in carbohydrate and lipid metabolism. A heavy back and upper torso with slim or muscular legs in women suggests prediabetes or diabetes and demands a glucose tolerance test.

LABORATORY TESTS. The single most important test is the glucose tolerance test, as I have discussed. Of great importance, too, is the lipid profile which determines cholesterol and triglycerides. Your blood count, of course, will be done, as well as general tests of health, such as liver and kidney function tests. Most doctors do this as a battery of tests called an SMA-12. I include tests of thyroid function, an electrocardiogram, and a chest X ray, as well. Other tests that may be done are of levels of potassium, magnesium, calcium, zinc, or copper in the blood, the analysis of hair (or blood) for trace mineral composition, and tests of vitamin levels. Other tests can be valuable too. For instance, insulin levels are very much to the point and at the crux of most of the theories of this book.

WHEN ALL THE RESULTS ARE IN. If your doctor finds no diseases or other abnormalities that are causing your symptoms, suggest to him that you would like to experiment with your diet by cutting out junk food and trying to find the vitamin and mineral intake level that gives you the best result. Would he then be willing to follow your progress? It's hard to imagine that he would refuse you such a reasonable request.

CONVINCING THE RELUCTANT PHYSICIAN. That's the doctor who thinks everybody has a nutritious diet, who won't want to give you a glucose tolerance test, who doesn't believe in vitamin supplements, or who thinks everybody needs a lot of carbohydrates.

Your first job must be to convince him to perform the glucose tolerance (GTT) on you (or authorize a lab to do it). He may say low blood sugar is hogwash, a fad, a myth, and that your fasting blood sugar was normal, therefore, there is no reason to do a GTT. Far be it from me to suggest that you consider changing doctors, but that's mighty strong language to direct against the most valuable test in medicine.

In case his resistance is not quite so strong, let's review the arguments you can use to convince him. You might start off with "It's my money and my veins, and I'm willing to undergo the nuisance, so how can it hurt me?" If he still balks, remind him of the relation that your symptoms have to eating, if you've noted any, or of any such dead giveaways as cravings for sweets, excessive thirst, excessive urination, attacks of light-headedness or shakiness that occur when hungry, or awakening at night to raid the refrigerator, or falling asleep in the daytime when you want to be awake. The supreme giveaway, of course, would be if you are able to report symptoms that are relieved temporarily by food or beverage, such as sweets, coffee, or alcohol. Tell him of any data about relatives with diabetes or some of the other manifestations of carbohydrate intolerance mentioned earlier. If you had any symptoms during your home glucose tolerance test, that should convince him by demonstrating the link between your sugar intake and your symptoms.

But if all else fails, try: "If it turns out that I am suffering from a carbohydrate disorder, wouldn't you be considered negligent if you refuse to perform the test?" At that point, I guess you could roll up your sleeve for the test to begin.

WHEN TO TELL HIM YOU WANT TO CHANGE YOUR DIET. Now let us assume you have had your checkup, including your 5- or 6-hour glucose tolerance test, and you are sitting in your doctor's office going over some of your findings together.

If the doctor has found a disease or a condition causing your fatigue or depression, then obviously you will follow his advice and treat it immediately. For example, if you had a chronic fever and an increased number of white blood cells along with your fatigue, you may have a chronic infection. Or the symptoms could have been caused by insufficiency of the liver or the kidneys. Or your doctor may have discovered you have an allergy, a glandular insufficiency, a sluggish thyroid, or even cancer. Any of these conditions, to mention just a few, might be responsible for your fatigue or depression.

But the chances are your doctor has told you that you are in good health, or that you are in good health except for a slight upset in your blood sugar curve. Or he may give you a diagnosis of nervous exhaustion or fatigue secondary to being depressed about your life situation.

If so, tell him you want to see what you can accomplish by changing your diet. When you suggest this, be sure to specify which diet you have in mind and outline the particulars of the diet so he knows exactly what you are talking about.

STARTING THE DIET. If your doctor has found nothing really adverse about your health, I know of no reason not to start the diet. The only reasons not to would be if you must restrict proteins, as in far-advanced kidney disease, or if you have a severe fatty food intolerance. If you have a *serious condition which is undiagnosed* or if you are pregnant, you should only go on Diet #4 until the nature of your condition is clarified. Otherwise it is quite safe to embark upon one of the other diets.

If none of these conditions exists, then ask your doctor if he would object to your trying the diet for one or two weeks just to see how you would feel on it. Usually he will be reasonable enough to let you try it, or he may have another idea that he may want to try first. If it's a new idea that sounds workable to you, why not oblige your doctor and try it to see if it does work? If it's an old idea that didn't work, remind him that you've already tried that and found it unsatisfactory.

If he is an open-minded physician, you should be able to convince him to let you try the diet if only because you and he know you can't tell if anything is any good unless you try it.

IF HE STILL SAYS NO. Should, however, his attitude be completely negative and should he say to you, on general grounds, "I don't like the diet, it's dangerous, and it can't possibly work," just remember my words. I love the diet; I know it's safe; and it very possibly might work. Now you have two conflicting medical opinions, one from a doctor who knows you, but not the diet, and the other from a doctor who knows the diet, but not you.

I propose that you try the diet and see who was right. Once you've seen how the diet and the nutritional supplements work, then you will no longer need to speculate on its possible effects, because you will have experienced them.

A BASIC PRINCIPLE OF THERAPY. How could your reluctant physician recommend your stopping something that works? He may be chagrined or personally affronted but what can be say, except: "It seems to be working; so keep it up. I'll continue to follow your progress to make sure it continues to work."

10

How to find your own best diet

Now you are ready to start on your diet. You've analyzed your symptoms, identified your health goals, visited your doctor, had your glucose tolerance test and medical evaluation, and are ready to undertake your Great Diet Experiment. The question now is, which diet should you go on?

You recall there are four basic diets.

Diet #1 The Superenergy Weight-Reducing Diet. For those who want to lose weight as well as gain energy.

Diet #2 The Superenergy Weight-Gaining Diet. For those who want to gain weight as well as more energy.

Diet #3 The Superenergy Weight-Maintenance Diet. For those who want to keep their weight the same but gain all the other benefits.

Diet #4 The Special Situation Diet. For those who are pregnant, undiagnosed, on special medication, or otherwise need more carbohydrates.

Lest the choice appear a little confusing, keep in mind that these diets are so similar that they might all be considered variations of the same diet. If you follow the guidelines, each of you will end up with the one diet which is best for you, no matter how you begin to approach it. They might really be better thought of as four basic approaches to finding Your Own Best Diet.

CHOOSING YOUR DIET. Since you have a pretty good idea of what your ideal weight would be, you will find it easy to determine which one of the four basic approaches you want to start with.

If you consider that you have a "weight problem," if you tend to gain weight no matter how little you eat, if you are more than ten pounds over the weight considered "ideal" for your body, or have in the past been considerably overweight, then Diet #1 would be the best approach for you.

On the other hand, if you have never attained a weight as high as you would like or are underweight now, then Diet #2 is the one you should try.

If you are pretty happy with your weight now and you have never had to be concerned about it, if you are now within ten pounds one way or the other of your ideal weight, but just not feeling as great as you think you might, then Diet #3 might be your best starting point.

If you are in a special medical situation, such as being pregnant, about to undergo surgery, or are postoperative, or on a medication that affects your diet, then you would be more prudent to start with Diet #4, switching over later to the definitive diet that is right for your weight.

Diet #1 is a ketogenic very low carbohydrate diet.

Diet #2 is more lenient as to carbohydrates, but heavily weighted as to proteins and fats. It is nonketogenic, averaging 70 to 120 grams of carbohydrates per day.

Diet #3 is a diet intermediate between numbers 1 and 2, designed not to change your body weight.

Diet #4 is nothing more than a set of rules involving the elimination of sweets and starches, sometimes alcohol and caffeine.

A SPECIAL NOTE IF YOU ARE THIN: If you are overweight, Diet #1 is ideal. You may see many of your friends go on Diet #1 and be struck with the high proportion of them who not only lose weight but exclaim over the improvement in their health, energy level, and emotional state. But if you are thin, don't be tempted to go on it with them, because, for you, this level is too strict, and you will not feel your best.

You may have read that there are sometimes symptoms associated with a ketogenic diet. And you may also have read that I rarely see them. The explanation is simple. I don't put a thin person on Diet #1. When a thin person goes on a diet so low in carbohydrate that he must use his sparse stores of fat as fuel, he runs the risk of developing symptoms such as fatigue, weakness, listlessness, nausea, or even vomiting. For the overweight dieter this virtually never occurs.

So, for those of you who are not overweight, Diets #2 or #3 will provide the same Superenergy advantages, but without the likelihood of causing such symptoms.

IF YOU HAVE GOUT. Those who have a tendency toward high uric acid levels may have a flare-up on Diet #1. A person with a clinical history of gout who has had attacks of joint pains *definitely* should avoid the strict level that is found in Diet #1, unless he is on an adequate dose of antigout medication and the diet is approved by his physician. Diets #2, 3, and 4, on the other hand, carry very little risk of a gouty flare-up.

IF YOU ARE PREGNANT. Statistical evidence indicates that it is not good to lose weight by any means during pregnancy, because it leads to a higher percentage of pregnancy complications. Therefore, I would recommend that the strict diet (#1) be undertaken only under the supervision of the obstetrician who will be managing the case, and that it be used only if necessary to *prevent* an undue weight gain, not to induce a weight loss during the pregnancy.

Diet #4 is a good choice of diet during pregnancy because it does not involve major dietary changes, yet is amply provided with the vitamins and minerals that are essential to the mother and the developing baby. Study after study has shown that there are fewer pregnancy complications when the mother is on a good diet. Diet #4 contains folic acid, pyridoxine, vitamin E, and all the vitamins so vital to pregnancy.

Diet #4 also is valuable during the postpartum period until

the nursing time is over, at which point the new mother can begin afresh with the idea of finding her ideal nonpregnant diet.

THE DIET MONITOR. In my office we have a Diet Monitor which is actually a ketone meter. It gives a numerical readout of the ketone concentration of the breath, which, in turn, is in equilibrium with ketone blood levels.

I have correlated patients' fatigue-energy scores with their ketone readings, and in most cases, the higher the ketone reading, the higher the energy score. This research provides the basis for my statement that Diet #1, the most ketone-producing diet of all, is the best fatigue-fighting diet of all.

But all four diet plans should make you feel better and note an upsurge in energy.

The major differences in the diets relate to the amount of carbohydrates allowed.

They all restrict sugar. They all restrict other refined carbohydrates, such as macaroni, white bread, white flour, or cornstarch.

They all have a specific plan for intelligent use of vitamin and mineral supplements.

WILL THE DIET REALLY WORK? If your fatigue happens to be caused by chronic anemia from a bleeding ulcer or a chronic low grade infection or some other disease, it would not be likely that the diet would change it. But if there is a nutritional basis for your fatigue, the diet should work.

SO, I WANT YOU TO TEST YOURSELF AND SEE WHAT HAPPENS. You may test yourself and find no benefit at one diet level, and then will have to try a different diet level to find the one that works.

But I'm certain of this: the overwhelming majority of you, like the majority of my patients, *will* benefit.

REMEMBER, GOOD RESULTS DON'T COME IMMEDIATELY. Your body needs an adjustment period, so don't change to another level until you have given the new diet a chance. That means, unless you feel worse, give it a week or two. These diets, which seem so elementary, cause a radical change in the delivery of your metabolic fuels, and your body may not adjust to the changeover at once. You have been, if you are like most of us, living on simple carbohydrates as your primary fuel source, but now you will be switching to your fat stores if you are overweight, or to dietary protein and complex carbohydrates, if you are not. It can take several days, even weeks, before your body adjusts fully to the new primary source of energy fuel.

So at the risk of getting a little ahead of our story, let's make note now of what you may find at first.

THOSE FIRST DIFFICULT DAYS. The first three or four days on these diets are sometimes tough. Everything you are used to reaching for is on the no-no list. You can't find any interesting snack foods, and you may feel let down, restless, maybe even a little more tired.

Don't give up: many people feel this way when they start out. It will change overnight on the third or fourth day, perhaps as late as the fifth day. But most probably you will wake up one of these early days feeling very noticeably improved.

One typical dieter said on day three she thought she would throw up if she saw another hard-boiled egg. But on day four she had a complete sense of well-being, was able to meet every event of the day with enthusiasm and equanimity, had not the usual midday slump, and found herself walking around with a smile of contentment.

And most encouraging . . . often the people who don't tolerate the transition phase well are the very ones who can feel the best.

ONE EXAMPLE. Mrs. Otto Preminger is such a case. By the end of the third or fourth week she reported to me that she had never felt better in her life; that her fatigue, which was the reason she consulted me, was completely gone and her energy, boundless. But during the first two weeks of her diet, she had actually felt worse. Had it not been for my knowing there was a pot of gold at the end of the rainbow, she might well have abandoned the program and never experienced the benefits that she now enjoys.

IF YOUR DIFFICULTIES CONTINUE PAST A WEEK. If your new diet does not seem to do the job so that you feel worse instead of better, it may be that you are still deficient in vitamins and minerals and need to build up your reserves first.

If this were to happen, the rules of Diet #4 would serve best for this nutritional buildup. Then after several weeks, you might try one of the other diets again and find that you feel quite well.

YOU CAN SWITCH AROUND. The fact that you start with one particular diet does not mean you will necessarily stick with that one forever. As your needs change, you may find yourself switching to a different diet, or a different level. It is quite reasonable to try variations to see if you feel better on one than another.

You may start with Diet #1 because you are twenty pounds overweight. Then after a month or so, you might find you are down to your best weight so you would switch to Diet #3 to maintain that weight. If you start gaining again, you would go back to Diet #1, or perhaps try some level in between.

Or perhaps you start out on Diet #3, but find it is not solving your afternoon fatigue problem as much as you would like and you don't have the better-than-ever feeling yet. So you will try Diet #1 for a while and see if that does the trick.

DIFFERENT PEOPLE NEED DIFFERENT DIETS TO CORRECT THEIR SYMPTOMS. There is no one sure-fire diet that can work for everybody, and anyone who makes such a claim is over-simplifying.

The true test for any diet is its usage. Does it correct your symptoms? The answer may be complicated because there are so many things involved in dietary manipulation. A new diet might be correcting a hidden vitamin deficiency, or a mineral deficiency, or both. It might be correcting a manifestation of a food allergy. It might be correcting low blood sugar. But the fact that there are many factors does not mean that there is no way for you to find your own perfect diet. And when you find the right diet for you, you will know it was worth the effort.

INDIVIDUAL DIET EXPERIMENTATION IS IN DIRECT CON-TRAST TO THE WAY MOST DIETS ARE PRESCRIBED. The physician's magazine *Patient Care* described the average physician's technique for dispensing diet advice as this:

"You have only a few minutes to set up the diet and motivate the patient. So you hand him a favorite among 100 odd lists that have been sent to you free and unsolicited. You (1) scratch out a few foods you think will worsen the patient's clinical problem; (2) add a helpful item here and there; and (3) give him a little pep talk that boils down to 'here take this and try it awhile.' And the patient comes back in a few weeks, frustrated, off the diet, and ready for a pill. You realize the problem is not with the diet itself, but for some reason the patient didn't follow it."

That's not the kind of diet I want to give you.

I WANT YOU TO HAVE A DIET THAT IS JUST RIGHT FOR YOU. I want you to have a diet that satisfies you, that fits your particular life and tastes, that keeps you at the weight you want to be, that gives you the nutrition your body needs, that keeps you full of energy and feeling your best. I want it to be personalized to provide you the best possible response, plus the most enjoyable eating. Your enjoyment is important, because it is to be a lifetime diet, not so much a diet as a new way of eating.

Now it's time to begin the diet of your choice, an experiment both for yourself and for the world. For you, this diet experience might end up being only an unsuccessful experiment, or it can end being your new lifetime diet.

THE GIANT NATIONWIDE STUDY WE WANT YOU TO BE PART OF. No matter what the results, I am asking you to be a part of a unique nationwide study.

I don't really know how the results will come out; they might even prove an embarrassment to me. But, because I know the outcome of this regimen among my own patients, I am eager to have the results of this study made public.

Therefore, I will be asking you, each and every one of you, to record your experiences with your diet so that for the first time in history people will know the effect that a book about diet really has upon its readership. The U.S. Senate appointed a select committee to study just this question; now we will be able to give them the answer.

The results of your individual dieting experiences will be

tabulated and computerized. To do this, I will ask you to fill out the questionnaire and mail it when your initial phase of dieting is completed. One portion of it is to be filled out before you begin the diet, the other after you have been on the diet one week. If you turn to the questionnaire in the back you will notice that for everyone there are four areas to be studied: energy, mood, weight, and medical experiences. In addition, there is room to evaluate three other symptoms that you hope the diet will improve.

Now is the time for you to consider what you would like your new eating regimen to accomplish. Are you troubled by headaches, dizziness, arthritis, abdominal pains, heartburn, fluid retention, palpitations, chest pains, shortness of breath, night sweats, leg cramps, hot flushes, nausea, diarrhea, seizures, irritability, insomnia, mental confusion, or whatever? If you have symptoms to list, now is the time to select up to three, those that bother you most, score them as we discussed previously, and record the scores. Please do it now because what you do will influence millions of people.

Now let's start Day One of whatever diet you have chosen.

11

Diet #1. The superenergy weight-reducing diet

If you are overweight and fatigued, you can try many diets, but I'll wager this: You will find none the equal of Diet #1. The low-carbohydrate diet is far superior to the low-calorie diet in the management of obesity, and especially in the management of fatigue in the overweight person.

The low-carbohydrate diet has the advantages of ease of following, palatability, enjoyability, rate of weight loss, efficiency and safety. It is more adaptable to modifying a dieter's eating behavior, to eating in restaurants and gatherings, and to fashioning a lifetime regimen of good eating habits. It provides additional therapeutic benefits in conditions such as high blood pressure, edema, ulcer, heartburn, heart failure, angina, migraine, allergy, depression, triglyceride elevations, and all blood sugar disturbances.

But especially is it superior in that it abolishes forever the concern, the fear, the discomfort, of the symptoms of hunger.

THE MOST CONSISTENT AND PREDICTABLE EFFECT IS UPON HUNGER. Hunger is the bane of the low-calorie dieter's life. It more than any other factor is responsible for the pathetic 98 percent relapse rate that has been found to follow low-calorie reducing. But on this diet, hunger *cannot* take place.

Virtually every patient, having been on the diet, reports

97

back to me, "Doctor, I'm not hungry anymore." If you're trying to lose weight, what could be of greater value than that?

This no-hunger aspect of the diet is the major reason people can stay on the diet for life.

THIS DIET IS DIFFERENT. For example, many of you are night eaters who eat all through the evening, even after a full dinner, sometimes even awakening after bedtime to raid the refrigerator. You may look with shame upon your "compulsive" behavior and may even have sought psychiatric help for what appeared to be an emotional problem. But, night eating doesn't need to be eradicated with hours of psychoanalysis; it needs only three words of counseling: "Stop eating carbohydrates."

You would be surprised to know how many symptoms you have that are really symptoms of hunger. Weak spells, crankiness, inability to concentrate, yawning, headaches, lightheadedness can all be due to hunger. Watch. When the hunger goes away, these symptoms will go away.

Those critics who proclaim that "the Atkins diet is just another low-calorie diet" have missed the point entirely. Yes, people do eat less; and the intake of calories, and of fats, is lower; that has been shown scientifically. But the great effect of this diet is on the *behavior* of the dieter. This turning to food when things go wrong, or when they go right, is governed in large part by the fact that the individual is really hungry. Take away the hunger, and the behavior toward food becomes normal.

I am impressed with the success of a series of psychological techniques given the name "Behavior Modification." But, what could modify the behavior of the big eater more surely than to wipe out the very hunger signals that lead to the food-oriented behavior?

MOST OF THE PATIENTS I SEE HAVE ALREADY BEEN DEFEATED BY THE HUNGER OF THE LOW-CALORIE DIET. Many of the persons now eating themselves into self-destruction used to be very diligent about dieting, but gave up when the hunger became unbearable.

My most difficult task in treating these people is to convince them to try again, that defeat is not inevitable. They cannot comprehend that one diet can be so different in its effect. They cannot believe that they will no longer have to deal with the hunger that frustrated all their previous attempts and made them fail. But, once on this diet they see it provides something no ordinary diet does—*weight loss without hunger.*

I HOPE THAT BY NOW YOU CAN'T WAIT TO START DIET #1. It's really very simple to comprehend. The diet will seem extremely generous to most people, particularly to seasoned dieters. But never forget that in one way it is extremely strict— in the rigorous way it cuts down carbohydrates. And it is carbohydrate, not fat, that the fat person, with his already overactive insulin response, cannot handle properly. Proteins and fats *can* be fattening, but *only* when carbohydrates are present. To reach this remarkable stage carbohydrates must be excluded nearly completely.

There are many foods that contain no carbohydrates, and they can be eaten in as great quantity as you wish because they do not add to the carbohydrate count. Fortunately, these are the main courses, such as steak, chicken, roasts, and eggs.

But if an item contains a large amount of carbohydrate, it is not permitted. Thus the diet boils down to two lists, foods that are allowed and foods that are not: yes or no, black or white. Learn what you *can* have; everything else you can't have.

There is also a third grouping, and those are foods that contain some, but not zero carbohydrates. These foods are allowed in limited quantities, different quantities for different levels of the diet.

These various levels give you the flexibility you need to lose weight at different rates, to find the level at which you feel your absolute best, and, especially, to take into account the way in which your metabolism responds.

YOU COUNT CARBOHYDRATES INSTEAD OF CALORIES. The starting level—the one called biologic-zero—has only about ten grams of carbohydrates for you to eat each day. You then work it up gradually to the level of carbohydrate that seems to be ideal for you.

You will know it's ideal because you will be aware of an

elevation of mood, a calmness, a lack of hunger, an increase in energy, as well as a steady comfortable loss of girth. When you go past this point, eating carbohydrates beyond your own personal Critical Carbohydrate Level, you'll know, because the appetite will return, and so probably will your old fatigue and other symptoms.

THE MOST IMPORTANT LESSON TO LEARN ABOUT OVER-WEIGHT. The key concept is that the response to any given diet varies widely among different individuals. I see this every day in my practice; people working with low-calorie diets see it just as much. Those of you who have belonged to diet clubs must have noted how some of the members drop thirty pounds in a few months, whereas others have lost only four pounds, and some may even have gained! Many of the poor responders insist that they have followed the diet. My patients on a ketogenic diet have different rates of response also. I can be sure they are following because my office staff measures their ketone excretion in their urine with Ketostix, and in their breath with our ketone analyzer. It would be nearly impossible to cheat on this diet without this equipment detecting it. So if a patient tells me, "It's my metabolism," I am inclined to believe him.

ONE LAST WORD OF ADVICE BEFORE STARTING THE DIET. Some medications can interfere with the success of this regimen, and if you are taking them you may have to consider discontinuing them or finding a substitute. Many drugs seem to act as insulin stimulators.

The first that comes to mind is estrogen, the hormone used to combat menopause and contained in birth control pills. Estrogen exaggerates insulin problems, not only diabetes, a fact which is well documented, but also hypoglycemia and obesity. So, if you are a little bit sugar-intolerant, estrogens make you more intolerant. If you are having trouble losing weight and if you are taking estrogen birth control pills, ask your doctor about switching to another contraceptive technique. If you are taking estrogen for menopause, you may be delighted to find that on our high vitamin regimen, especially with high intake of vitamin E, many women are able to give up or reduce the dosage of their estrogen pills and have none of their menopausal symptoms.

Since edema is a very common physical finding with car-bohydrate intolerance, many of you may be taking diuretics. Others will be on them because of high blood pressure. Keep in mind that the diet, particularly during the first few weeks, is itself a potent diuretic. The combination of the diuretic pill and the diet usually causes *too much* water loss and may deplete you of potassium, sodium, and calcium, with resulting symp-toms of exhaustion, leg cramps, or muscular weakness. That is why I usually recommend that my patients discontinue diuret-ics about a week before starting the diet.

YOU SHOULD NOT DISCONTINUE THESE MEDICINES WITH-OUT CONSULTING YOUR PHYSICIAN. Your doctor knows your case, and knows whether or not you need one of these medica-tions. Do not go off the medication without asking your doctor to follow your progress carefully.

YOU MUST ALSO STOP TAKING DIET PILLS. My pet peeve has always been appetite suppressants—diet pills.

The worst problem about them is not so much their immedi-ate effect, but the later effect upon your metabolism. When the body tries to readjust to normality, there will be an increase in hunger and a series of biological readjustments that can lead to weight gain despite dieting! The magnitude of this effect can be so great that virtually the only people who can't lose weight on Diet #1 are from the group exposed to prolonged diet pill usage. That's why I insist that my patients discontinue diet pills for at least two weeks, preferably much longer, before starting the diet.

Now if you are on appetite suppressants and if it so much as runs through your mind that you *can't* stop them, then you had better consider that you are probably *addicted* to them. If this is the case, it becomes imperative that you stop them at all costs.

You have seen your doctor, you have had your glucose toler-ance test, and you have given up diet pills if you are on them. Now it is time to go on the diet. Here are the basic rules.

THE TEN COMMANDMENTS OF THE SUPERENERGY WEIGHT-REDUCING DIET.

1. Your diet for the first week will be made up entirely of the

Permitted Foods and nothing else. If you can't find a food on your permitted list, that means its carbohydrate (or alcohol) content is too high, and it is therefore not allowed at all.

2. You may eat as much of Permitted Foods as you want because quantities will be limited by your hunger signals. Even though you eat as much as you need of these foods, this should be less than previously, because of a decrease in your appetite.

3. Start off with six small feedings a day, eating a snack every three or four hours. If this proves unnecessary, you may then eat fewer times. All feedings should contain some protein.

4. Eat breakfast every day. This should be postponed only if you find no inclination to eat in the morning.

5. Take the recommended megadoses of vitamins and minerals as discussed in Chapter 18. This is an essential part of the Superenergy Diet.

6. Avoid all sugar and flour. Read all labels; anything containing a form of sugar or refined starchy carbohydrates is out.

7. Caffeine, as in coffee and cola, should be restricted. Three cups a day is a reasonable limit. If you usually consume more, you should try to eliminate it completely during the first few weeks.

8. Alcohol will act like a carbohydrate in preventing fat mobilizing and must be restricted. None is permitted during the first week. Maximum later is to be individualized. People who consume large quantities or who have a "drinking problem" must avoid alcohol completely.

9. Exercise as much as possible, developing a daily program of calisthenics, sports, cycling, walking, or jogging. However, avoid strenuous exercise during the first four days of dieting, since these are the days of fuel changeover.

10. See your doctor before you start, again after a few weeks, and again after a few months.

WHEN WE SAY NO SUGAR, WE MEAN ABSOLUTELY NO SUGAR. Sugar is not the high energy food its manufacturers would like us to believe it is. It is energy-depleting in the long run. And it is more fattening, calorie for calorie, than fat is.

You must not only avoid table sugar, but sugar in all its hidden forms. Avoid foods that contain sucrose, dextrose, lactose, glucose, fructose, sorbitol, mannitol, dextrins, corn or maple syrup, brown sugar, raw sugar, invert sugar, or even honey. Do not have anything with "natural sweeteners" or "nutritive sweeteners."

A special word of caution: When sugar is in a medication, such as cough syrup, laxative mixtures, lozenges, or chewable vitamins, the law does not require that it be listed, but you can taste its sweetness. If you must take such a medication, remember that there is a sugar-free alternative for just about everything. Ask your pharmacist's help in finding it.

BUT LIVE IT UP ON PROTEIN. If you wish, you may start the day with bacon and eggs; have a cheeseburger (no bun, of course) and a green salad for lunch; snack on assorted cheeses; have a shrimp cocktail (no red sauce), plus steak or chops or any meat, a green salad, and our diet cheesecake or sugarless gelatin for dessert.

With all of this, you will have taken in less than 10 grams of carbohydrate.

ON THIS DIET YOU CAN HAVE SOME FATS. Some rather unscrupulous people have criticized this diet, saying it's a high fat diet. Well-publicized diet studies have shown it to be actually a somewhat reduced fat diet. It *allows* fats, but it does not *force* them. Naturally, you don't gorge yourself on fats. In fact, you don't gorge yourself on anything because you're not as hungry as you used to be.

But you do eat *some* fat. Animals . . . including people . . . *need* some fats. They are *essential* nutrients. Without them, many of the body's essential chemicals cannot be made. I have seen women on diets so low in fat that they couldn't manufacture enough female hormones to have a regular menstrual cycle!

Fats and oils are also necessary to keep your skin and your vital mucous membranes smooth and lubricated. Fats in your diet help stabilize your blood sugar level. Fat is the fuel least convertible into glucose, and least stimulating to your insulin response. And fats allow you variety in your diet and keep you from feeling deprived. You can use mayonnaise on your cold tuna or turkey and butter sauce on your seafood or your vegetables, and thereby avoid the main unpalatability factor of low-calorie diets.

ON THIS DIET YOU CAN HAVE SALADS AND SALAD DRESS-INGS: Roquefort, oil and vinegar, mayonnaise, Green Goddess, Caesar, creamy garlic dressings. Leave out the croutons and use crumbled fried pork rinds or chopped eggs or real crumbled bacon. Dark green leafy vegetables like raw spinach are the most nutritious ingredients.

ON THIS DIET YOU CAN HAVE SNACK FOODS. You can have not just celery and carrot sticks, but cheeses of every kind, olives, hard-boiled or deviled eggs, many luncheon meats, or seafood appetizers, and all the protein leftovers from yesterday's dinner.

ON THIS DIET YOU CAN HAVE DESSERTS. The first week you can have carbohydrate-free gelatin desserts. In the following weeks, you can have our special sugar-free cheesecake, maca-roons, diet pudding, mocha pie, chocolate mousse, as long as you prepare them with artificial sweetener instead of sugar. And you can have heavy cream fashioned into real whipped cream.

ON THIS DIET YOU CAN HAVE A BIG BREAKFAST. In fact, I recommend it to give you a reserve of energy for the day. People with weight problems often eat no breakfast and little lunch, then eat huge dinners at night. Reversing this pattern should be a dieter's major objective. But, no cereals or pastries for breakfast. Instead have ham and eggs, an omelet, smoked fish, or even a steak.

FIRST-WEEK PERMITTED FOODS. Here are the things you can eat the very first week of the diet.

Meat—Steaks, corned beef, lamb chops, pork chops, tongue, ham, hamburgers, fresh sausage. In short, any kind of meat in any quantity (except organ meat or meat with carbohydrate fillers such as prepared sausage, hot dogs, corned beef hash, meatballs, packaged cold cuts).

Fowl—Duck, turkey, chicken, anything with wings. (No stuffing.)

Fish—Salmon, tuna, any kind of fresh or saltwater fish: any kind of lobster, shrimp, or crab, prepared without flour or breading. Oysters, clams, mussels, scallops, and pickled fish can be added only later in limited quantities.

Eggs—Boiled, fried, scrambled, poached, or omelet.

Cheese—Four ounces a day of any true cheese. May be hard, semisoft, or soft. No cream cheese, cottage cheese, or cheese spreads until later.

Condiments—Salt, pepper, mustard, horseradish, vinegar, vanilla and other extracts; artificial sweeteners; any dry powdered spice that contains no sugar.

Drinks—Water, mineral water, Vichy, club soda, Perrier water, sparkling water, sugar-free diet soda, sugarless lemonade or limeade. Herbal teas, tea and coffee, per specific instructions.

Desserts—Gelatin with artificial sweeteners.

Soups—Chicken broth, beef bouillon.

Fats—Butter, margarine, oils, shortening, lard, mayonnaise, in judicious quantities. Four teaspoons of cream a day (cream has less carbohydrate than milk, so it is preferable to milk). Some of the fat should be in the form of polyunsaturated vegetable oils (the essential fatty acids).

Fruit—None, except for the juice of one fresh lemon or lime per day.

Vegetables—To be added only after first week.

Salads—Two small salads a day of any of the following: Any leafy greens, celery, chicory, Chinese cabbage, chives, cucumber, endive, escarole, fennel, lettuce, parsley, peppers, radishes, scallions, fresh spinach, watercress. Begin with a limit of only two cupfuls per day, loosely packed.

Garnishes—Bacon, fried pork rinds, grated cheese, herbs, hard-boiled egg, sour or dill pickles (no more than one small one), olives (no more than six).

Appetizers and snacks—Aspics artificially sweetened, cheeses, chicken, deviled or hard-boiled eggs, meatballs (without filler), pâté, salmon, sardines, sausages, shrimp, steak tartare.

DIET #1 NO-NO FOODS. Do not eat any of the following the first week *or any week.*

Bananas	Honey
Beans (except green or wax)	Ice cream
Bread	Jam or jelly
Cake	Macaroni
Candy	Pancakes
Cashews	Peas
Catsup	Potatoes
Cereal	Raisins
Chewing gum	Rice
Cookies	Spaghetti
Corn	Sugar
Cornstarch	Sweet pickles
Crackers	Sweet relish
Dates	Sweetened yogurt
Figs	Syrups
Flour	Yams
Fruit (dried)	

Caution: This list is by no means complete.

THE FIRST WEEK. This first level is a biologically zero carbohydrate diet. This means that, even though there are a few grams of carbohydrate in it—about 10 to 15 grams—your body responds as if there were no carbohydrates. This level should be followed for at least a week.

For best results, keep a written record. Look up the foods you are eating in any carbohydrate counter book (or in the table in the back of this one) to make sure the carbohydrates do not total more than 10 grams in any one day. List your energy and mood scores every day, as well as any other symptoms you are concerned with. Record your weight and Ketostix findings. At the end of the week please record your results in the back of the book for the nationwide survey.

And at the end of this first week, it's time to take inventory for yourself. Ask yourself, "Have I lost weight? Do I have more energy? Has my mood improved? What about my other symptoms? In short, how well is the diet working?" Because if all is going well, it's time to progress with your diet to another level.

THE SECOND WEEK. The second diet level has about five more grams of carbohydrate per day than the first level. In other words, you may go to a 15-to-20-gram intake, utilizing the second level grouping of foods.

These foods can be eaten in any combination as long as your total carbohydrates for the day do not total more than 15 to 20 grams. You may choose from formerly excluded vegetables, cottage cheese, nuts and seeds, the organ meats, the excluded seafood items, frankfurters, sausage, or you may have more salad greens.

You can also supplement the basic diet by using the recipes we have compiled in *Dr. Atkins' Diet Cookbook.*

THE THIRD WEEK. Each week now you will begin to add carbohydrate very gradually. So the third week you can add 5 grams of carbohydrate more . . . ½ cup of avocado or a dozen olives or a small glass of tomato juice . . . making a total now of 20 to 25 grams per day. Then every week for several weeks add 5 grams more, until you reach the level best for you.

By gradually adding the carbohydrate in those stages, you can continue to keep your body burning fat.

You can confirm that this is so by observing that you are losing weight, and that you're not as hungry as you used to be, and that you feel an unusual sense of well-being.

CONTINUE TO INVENTORY YOUR PROGRESS UNTIL YOU FIND YOUR IDEAL LEVEL. At the end of each week, take the same progress inventory as you did at the end of the first week, because you must raise or lower the level of the diet according to your response. If you continue to feel well and lose weight, you can add 5 grams of carbohydrate more. If you don't feel as well or if you stop losing, you should drop down to Level One for a few days, then resume the level of the previous week. This is your Critical Carbohydrate Level for losing weight and having the maximum Superenergy response. For most overweight people, this usually ranges between 20 and 50 grams of carbohydrates per day.

MANY PEOPLE LIKE TO USE THE KETOSTIX TO HELP FIND THEIR CRITICAL CARBOHYDRATE LEVEL. They know the diet is working if they're not hungry and are full of energy. It is not working if they are hungry or tired. But they like to use the Ketostix to provide biochemical confirmation that stored fat is a significant source of metabolic fuel. Ketostix are inexpensive test sticks you can buy in any drugstore without prescription.

To use them, just hold the strip where the urine will wet it; or collect a sample of urine in a paper cup and put the tip of the test stick in it. The stick will turn purple if your body is properly burning off its fat to produce ketones, and a very slight surplus is excreted.

Usually the deeper the purple shown on the Ketostix, the less the hunger and the better you feel. The paler the color, the more the possibility of hunger. However, you will soon find which shade of purple correlates best with your own best energy levels, and this, for you, is the ideal level.

As long as the test stick shows some degree of purple or lavender, you are probably dieting correctly. But any day in which the sticks go from a deep purple to a light shade or to beige, you should ask yourself whether you may have had more carbohydrates than you thought you did.

Sometimes people will stop showing the purple reaction, yet will continue to lose weight and feel well. This occurs when there is only a moderate increase of ketones in the blood, but not enough to spill over into the urine. This can be perfectly all right, provided that there has been no increase in appetite or drop in energy compared to the early weeks, and that the weight loss is continuing.

The other consideration some of you will have to remember is that maintaining the purple color reaction in no way *guarantees* the weight loss. Chapter 20 will tell you more about this type of problem.

YOUR LIFETIME MAINTENANCE LEVEL. Once you have attained your Critical Carbohydrate Level for losing weight, do not go above it until you have reached your ideal weight. Then you can add a few more grams of carbohydrates from the foods allowed, up to the point where you do not regain any weight and you still feel Superenergy and no return of the old symptoms which the new diet may have relieved. This is now your Lifetime Maintenance Level, and you should not go above it. It will soon become clear to you what the best level of the diet is for you. Most of us tend to follow the highest level we can get away with, simply because it allows for the most enjoyable and most nearly normal eating. But there is very little reason, on medical grounds, not to recommend the strictest level. There are not many people with overweight problems who feel better, or do better medically, at a 40-gram carbohydrate level, for example, than they do at 10 grams.

YOUR DOCTOR AGAIN. You remember how avidly I insisted that a doctor had to be brought into the picture. Well, here is where he comes in again. You know how you feel; be it better or worse, you don't need a doctor to tell you that. But you cannot know how such items as your cholesterol, triglycerides, uric acid levels, or your blood pressure are doing without your doctor checking. I have conducted thousands of such checks and have learned that this low-carbohydrate and high vitamin-mineral regimen generally brings about improvements in these areas. But exceptions do occur upon occasion, and you would want to be aware of them so you could correct the problem. Should an abnormal reading occur, it usually responds to a combination of increased intake of certain vitamins and minerals, a low fat variation of the diet, or, on occasion, medications.

These problems occur less often when dieters maintain the vitamin and mineral regimen outlined in chapter 18.

HOW FAST ARE YOU GOING TO LOSE? Remember the diet is not meant to be speedy. It's meant to be effective and forever! It's designed to be so livable that you will stay on the diet forever and always keep your weight where you want it, and continue to feel your best. There are tremendous variations in how virtuously people stick to the diet; and there are striking differences in individual metabolism and response. But after one week the average overweight man takes off seven pounds, and the woman five. After two weeks, ten pounds for the man, seven for the woman. After three months there might be a thirty-three pound loss for the man, and twenty-two for the woman. These are averages based on a sampling of significantly over-weight patients who didn't cheat once.

But even when there was some cheating, those who got back on the diet and showed perseverance found their results were quite rewarding. When I tabulated the results of eighty-three consecutive patients with more than fifty pounds to lose who stayed under my observation for six months or more, even with some cheating, seventy-four of them lost more than twenty pounds, and twenty-six lost forty pounds or more. The rest lost at least eight pounds.

The important thing about a diet is not how fast it is, but how easy it is to follow. The main problem with diets is that they're not being maintained. The truth is that of the millions of Americans who go on diets every year, few actually keep the weight off. The usual quote is that out of any given 100 se-riously obese patients on any weight control program, only two can be expected not to regain the weight within a year after losing it.

This diet is quite different. Perhaps the greatest reason for its success is the fact that it creates such a sense of well-being and Superenergy that people don't *want* to go off it.

12

Why Diet #1 works so well

To follow Diet #1 properly you must consult with your physician. But suppose your doctor's knowledge of the low-carbohydrate diet is rather sketchy and he tries to dissuade you from following it.

In order to know for yourself, to discuss the diet in depth with your doctor, and to make all the right medical decisions, I want you to be well acquainted with the scientific basis of the diet.

TO UNDERSTAND THE PRINCIPLE, ASK THIS QUESTION. "What is the purpose of fat on our bodies?" Answer: It is our primary reserve fuel. When you understand that, you will soon see how Diet #1 works. For most of us, over 90 percent of the energy which is stored in our bodies is stored in the form of fat. When we restrict carbohydrates, we get the body to use that reserve stored fat for its fuel. We tap into this fuel source and thereby get rid of the excess fat in the very way nature meant for it to be used.

The reason the single best diet for the treatment of obesity and fatigue is a low-carbohydrate, high-nutrient diet is that it takes fullest advantage of this biologic truth: *The less that the most ready fuels (alcohol and carbohydrate) are available to the body, the more fully will the body use the storage fuel—body fat.*

Early in our existence, the ability to store fat as the reserve fuel supply had a strong survival value to get through times when food was scarce. It should come as no surprise to anyone who understands the wisdom of nature that our bodies thus have the metabolic capacity to break down this stored fat and use it for energy.

This breakdown of stored fat into the fuel we use is an everyday process of metabolism. All of us utilize this fuel to some extent every day, much more when we are losing weight, and most, when we are not eating carbohydrates.

HERE IS WHAT HAPPENS. In an ordinary diet, about half of the energy comes directly from the starch or sugar we eat. The other half comes from the breakdown of the protein and fat we eat.

At first when we have not eaten, most energy comes from the storage form of carbohydrate, called glycogen, but these supplies are used up in two days.

The major storage form of fuel is body fat, called triglyceride. When the two-day glycogen stores are gone, and no ready carbohydrate fuel is taken in, the triglyceride moves out of storage and takes over as the primary fuel source. It does this mainly by breaking up into two metabolic fuels—free fatty acids and ketone bodies.

The free fatty acids primarily provide the fuel for muscular work, whereas the ketone bodies are used best by the brain cells. When fat breaks down so that these two types of fuels are detectable, the person is said to be in a state of ketosis.

Ketosis is simply the state in which our fats have broken down into the chemical form where they, rather than glucose, can be used for energy. It would be more accurate, but more unwieldy, to call it "free fatty acidosis and ketosis."

The greater the amount of excess fat that's being burned up, the greater the amount of free fatty acids and ketones that will be present. In general, the more ketosis you achieve, the more weight you are losing.

That's why the diet that is designed to produce ketosis will prove to be the most efficient weight-shedding program you have ever been on.

IF I AM OVERWEIGHT AND PLAGUED WITH FATIGUE, DOES THAT MAKE DIETING DOUBLY DIFFICULT? No, it doesn't, because fortunately the very diet that is best for weight loss is also best for conquering fatigue.

Patients on various levels of carbohydrate intake almost always achieve the best results from the lowest carbohydrate intake.

Part of the reason is that when the stored fat becomes the primary fuel source, it releases its energy fuels over a longer span of time, in contrast to carbohydrate-based energy, which is quicker, but more short-lived. So the high energy level is more sustained.

THE REASON FOR THE SUSTAINED ENERGY. Metabolic processes take place at varying rates, and these rates are governed by hormones and other chemicals circulating in the blood. In this case, when carbohydrates have been cut out of the diet long enough to allow for all the glycogen stores to be used up, a group of substances called lipid mobilizers comes into play. One of these is Fat Mobilizing Substance. When these mobilizers are pouring into the bloodstream, your body can readily utilize the ketone and fatty acid fuels, and at this point the fatigue disappears.

YOU CAN TEST THIS RELATIONSHIP BETWEEN ENERGY AND KETONES YOURSELF. You may use the Ketostix.

If you are metabolically normal and follow Diet #1 correctly, you will note, after a few days, that the Ketostix are giving the positive purple reaction. If this is the point at which you notice an improvement in your energy level and your mood, a decrease in your appetite, and a lessening of some of your symptoms, then you have proven that you are one of the many people who feels better when a large portion of your fuel requirement is coming from your fat stores, in other words, when you are in ketosis.

In some cases, the improvement is immediate; in other cases, the improvement follows the turning-purple test by a few days. But either way, if the presence of ketones has heralded a noticeable improvement in your well-being, you have just learned a valuable personal lesson in nutrition: *I feel better when I'm burning my ketones.* Knowing that, you are able to structure the diet that works best for you.

THE DEHUNGRIFYING EFFECT. Ask about the effects of Diet #1, and the most commonly heard response will be "I'm not hungry on this diet." The absence of hunger can convert a compulsive eater into a disciplined dieter, a night-eater into a sound sleeper, a diet Yo-Yo into a never-regainer. Dr. Yudkin was able to demonstrate this hunger-suppressing effect with a diet not nearly as effective as this one. Dieters invited to eat all the protein and fat they want cut their caloric intake by 40 percent below their usual level. After you've been on this diet just a few days, you will be struck with a startling loss of appetite. Compulsive eating patterns will cease, as if by magic, and cravings that you felt were a part of you will vanish.

How does this loss of appetite come about? The explanation is incomplete but it is based on one of nature's protective devices. When we are subjected to starvation, and the lipid mobilizers and ketone bodies are present, there is a dramatic loss of appetite. Although this has been demonstrated many times in test animals, and in humans, it is not clear which, the ketones or the fat mobilizers, are responsible for the loss of appetite.

Dr. George Blackburn, after hundreds of observations, concluded hunger is inversely related to ketone levels and as little as 20 grams of carbohydrate twice daily altered the ketone levels *and* the hunger. It was actually shown that as little as 7½ grams of carbohydrate changed the ketone levels considerably. If only noncarbohydrate foods are added, the fat mobilizers and ketones still abound, but when carbohydrates are added, these substances are lost, and hunger returns.

THE OTHER REASON IS INSULIN. Overweight people, as well as hypoglycemics and early diabetics, put out too much insulin. As Drs. Neil Grey and David Kipnis have shown, restricting carbohydrates causes a marked lowering of insulin levels in overweight subjects. And Dr. George Cahill showed that when insulin secretion is reduced, then our stored fats break down and are mobilized to serve as fuel.

OTHER HORMONES ARE INVOLVED, TOO. Ethan Allen Sims

showed that when carbohydrate intake is low, the levels of cortisol are lowered. And Dr. John Yudkin showed that a high sugar intake raised these cortisol levels dramatically.

Elevated cortisol produces a form of obesity involving the torso, chest and back, causing a round face, but slim arms and legs. Women may have facial hair growth, men, reddened stretch marks.

The important metabolic consequence of too much cortisol is diabetes. Cutting sugar, and other carbohydrates, out of your diet will go a long way toward improving this imbalance.

OTHER ADVANTAGES OF THE KETOGENIC DIET. This ketogenic diet is a remarkable therapeutic tool in other ways. For example, it will also get rid of excess water and is beneficial for those who tend toward fluid retention. Because this ketogenic diet acts like a diuretic, it is remarkable in the control of mild and moderate degrees of high blood pressure, as well as congestive heart failure, or any condition causing edema.

THE DIET ALSO BENEFITS HYPOGLYCEMIA. You may wonder how the removal of the traditional "energy" foods can give you *more* energy than you had before. If you've been reading carefully, you'll know it's because this diet corrects hypoglycemia—not just the *disease* that some people have, but the *tendency* that all of us are prone to.

How does this work? In the first place, when your stored fat is used for fuel, its slow release of energy dampens the fluctuations of blood sugar that take place on an insulin-provoking sugar and starch diet.

Second, recent scientific studies have shown that ketone bodies in the bloodstream will prevent the adrenalin response to falling blood sugar levels. Drs. J. P. Flatt and George Blackburn of Harvard devised an ingenious experiment. They gave test animals a large dose of insulin and measured both the drop in the sugar levels and the amount of adrenalin put out. Then they repeated the same challenge while the animals were receiving an infusion of ketone bodies. They found that, although the blood sugar levels still fell, this time the adrenalin release was significantly less than before.

Many of the symptoms of hypoglycemia really come from this adrenalin release—the nervous sweaty attacks, palpitations, headaches, waking in the middle of the night. These symptoms vanish on the diet.

IS THERE METABOLIC WASTAGE? After I told in my first book of the patients I had observed who shed eighty-five pounds while consuming three thousand calories daily for four months, I found that many scientists were unable to accept what I had seen. Yet there are millions of people who would lose weight on a low-carbohydrate diet containing the same number of calories now causing overweight.

For this to happen, the low-carbohydrate diet must produce a metabolic advantage and the calorie theory must have a loophole. There are many bits of evidence that it does, and none to say that it does not. The definitive study is yet to be done.

In 1965, Dr. Fred Benoit of Eugene, Oregon, and his associates, studied seven obese subjects very thoroughly, comparing a 1,000-calorie ketogenic diet including only 10 grams of carbohydrate with a total fast. *At the end of ten days those on the ketogenic diet actually lost more body fat than those who had eaten nothing at all.* Since then he has confirmed the results in ten more subjects. The subjects on the ketogenic diet did not suffer fatigue or nausea, but had an unusual feeling of well-being. "The striking thing was the euphoria," Dr. Benoit later commented to me.

This important document should have laid the calorie hoax to rest because it proved that an overweight person could lose as much or more fat eating 1,000 calories of noncarbohydrate food as he would by fasting.

AND SO THEY WERE ATTACKED. The-calorie-is-a-calorie theory has always been the major scientific distortion propagated by the food industry, since it justifies the inclusion of all sorts of fattening junk foods into the regimen of a weight watcher. And so, one of the nutritionists long friendly to the sugar industry wrote that he found fault with the Benoit data. Why? Because if the Benoit data were correct, then the calorie theory must be wrong, and the calorie theory *can't* be wrong.

THE OVERFEEDING EXPERIMENTS. More evidence against the calories-are-the-only-things-that-count theory was offered by Dr. Ethan Allen Sims, who tried to create experimental obesity in prisoner volunteers. He found he had to give calories in quantities far beyond that calculated from a calorie balance sheet. And Dr. George Bray, in his overfeeding experiments, found that only 50–60 percent of the ingested calories could be accounted for. How were the other calories lost? How can the calorie theory stand up to that kind of scientific data?

IN SUMMARY: The diet works because it specifically mobilizes fat, stimulates the release of ketones and fat mobilizers, thereby suppressing hunger; causes a disproportionately greater loss of fat; helps eliminate excess water; stabilizes blood sugar; lowers insulin levels and cortisol levels; and delivers a metabolic advantage.

DIET #1 IS BEST FOR LOSING WEIGHT AND IS BEST FOR ENERGY. It is the best basic diet for obesity and the most suitable as the basic diet to combat fatigue. It is the best diet for attacking high insulin levels that overweight and tired people have.

It is the best diet for combating hunger. And if you're tired and overweight, getting rid of hunger can be the key to your mastery of both. Think about how often you are tired when you're hungry. The two symptoms appear together more than not.

Diet #1 is the best way to conquer both.

13

Diet #2. The superenergy weight-gaining diet

So many times at social gatherings I meet attractive slim people who, upon hearing my name, say, "Dr. Atkins, I don't need your diet, I'm skinny." Or "I don't have to diet, I never gain weight." In one way, I feel more concern for this segment of the population than the ones who usually get the sympathy—the overweight—for the simple reason that the misconception that slim people don't have to diet leads them to more improper nutritional practices than any other group.

COMMON MISTAKES OF THE SKINNIES. Noting that their overweight acquaintances get fat from eating sweets, thin people often make the big mistake of filling themselves up with empty calories, which in fact are antinutrients. Slim people may use sugar in huge quantities, unaware that this is what prevents proper nutrition from filling out their slim frames.

The underweight person must stress proteins and fats and those carbohydrates which have not been refined. And he must be fully aware of what vitamin and mineral supplements can really accomplish.

So often thin people try to gain weight by drinking malteds and eating a lot of desserts and exceedingly rich junk foods. They wonder why they don't gain weight, without realizing what all those sugars and starches might be doing to them *inside*. It rarely occurs to them that their diet might be the cause of fatigue or other unexplained symptoms.

DIET #2 WILL HELP SOLVE THESE PROBLEMS. Diet #2 is for those of you who are tired, or depressed, or have other diet-related symptoms, and who also happen to be underweight. It was not designed for the primary purpose of helping you gain weight, but for giving you energy.

Chances are that it will help you gain weight, but a few of you still will not put on a single pound. Believe it or not, it is much more difficult to get a truly slim person to gain weight than to get an obese person to reduce. I can recall many patients who visited my office for whom lasting weight gain eluded all our efforts. Fortunately, this group is in the minority, and most of you can expect to gain some body weight coincidental with the improvement in your general health and symptoms.

So, if you're tired, lethargic, tense, or irritable, and happen to be underweight, what are you going to do?

THE KETOGENIC DIET IS NOT FOR YOU. Unfortunately, the diet I consider to be the single most effective Superenergy diet, Diet #1, is not best for you. Thin people don't seem to tolerate it; they don't have enough fat to mobilize to provide a ready reserve fuel supply. Take away enough carbohydrates and the underweight person will be forced to burn up his vital tissue proteins, one thing that no dieter should do.

Slim people must have a diet that is *not* ketogenic.

But you can still utilize two of the most important lessons about nutrition—the benefits of swearing off sugar and other refined carbohydrates, and the beneficial effects of taking vitamins and minerals in meaningful and realistic quantities.

These nutrients take on an even greater meaning for you, the slim person, than for others, since you cannot rely on the mechanism of ketogenesis to protect you against the adrenalin response or to stabilize your fuel supply. Since you will not be relying on fat mobilization, you must do it by avoiding the insult of too much sugar or starch in a short time, and by a steady supply of fuel you can use directly.

YOUR BASIC ACTION PLAN. Let's suppose you are my patient, and we have just completed the review of your symptoms, physical findings, and laboratory results. Suppose we learn that you are fatigued, obviously underweight, but free of any known disease except for a possible suspicion of low blood sugar. How would I change your diet?

The basic principles of your diet are:

1. Your new diet must be higher in calories than your present one, otherwise you would not be likely to put on the desired weight.
2. All your calories must consist of foods which contain other important nutrients, and very little should be of the empty calorie, antinutrient variety, such as sugar, refined flour, or alcohol.
3. Feedings should be frequent and preferably balanced as to protein, fat, and unrefined carbohydrates.
4. The ideal level of carbohydrate for you must be determined through trial and error.

THE TWO REAL CAUSES FOR BEING THIN. People who are underweight and find it difficult to gain, and who are otherwise healthy, usually have problems representing some combination of two factors.

One is that they are more inefficient in their use of food as fuel for metabolism. A higher percentage of their food energy is wasted, dissipated as heat, much as inefficient machinery gives off "friction" instead of work energy.

The other is that the appestat, the hypothetical hunger signal which regulates our body weight, is set so low that the presence of appetite or hunger is not made known as readily. These people often literally forget to eat.

RULES TO START GAINING BOTH ENERGY AND WEIGHT. With these special considerations in mind, these are the golden rules for the first week of your Superenergy Diet #2.

1. Determine your vitamin and mineral regimen per chapter 18 and start following it for at least four days before you begin the other diet changes. This serves two main purposes: to begin to correct any *glaring* deficiencies *before* you begin the metabolic changeover, and to help you know whether any benefits or side effects can be attributed to the vitamins rather than to the diet.

2. Determine your present total daily carbohydrate allowance by figuring your intake of carbohydrates, using a carbohydrate counter. If you are now eating less than 100 grams, increase your carbohydrate intake to that level. This is where most people begin.

3. Schedule five or six convenient times spaced throughout the day for eating or snacking. Three might represent your usual mealtimes, and two or three would be snack times between them and at bedtime. That way you will be eating something every three or four hours while awake.

4. Divide the number of grams per day by the number of feedings. This will give you the approximate number of carbohydrate grams you should eat at each feeding. You will probably have somewhat more in your larger meals, somewhat fewer in your snacks.

5. Carbohydrates should primarily be unrefined starches, such as whole grains, lentils, vegetables, and particularly nuts and seeds. Fruits are less desirable at first than vegetables for they contain a simple sugar rather than a complex carbohydrate. Fruit juice can be used in small quantities. Honey should generally be avoided. Milk, containing the simple sugar lactose, should also be limited at first. These will be added later.

6. No sugar. This often produces the outlandish sight of a skinny person ordering diet soda, but it will make a huge difference in your energy level. This also means no corn syrup, dextrose, or glucose.

7. No white flour, cornstarch, white rice, or other refined carbohydrate. Eat brown rice and whole grain bread items instead.

8. No caffeine for this beginning week. This includes coffee and cola beverages and a few others such as Dr Pepper. Check the labels on drink containers.

9. No alcohol. For most people this rule applies only to the beginning stage of the diet.

10. Select the permissible carbohydrates according to the above rules and decide which ones you will be eating, in what amounts, and at which times. Then fill in the remainder of your diet with foods that are primarily protein and fat. These are: eggs, meats, fish, fowl, and cheese.

11. Eat as much as you can comfortably enjoy, without

overstuffing yourself. Concentrate on the *frequency* of your feedings rather than the quantity.

FOLLOW THE DIET FOR AT LEAST ONE WEEK. If, in that time you have cheated to the extent of eating sweets, an entire dessert or candy bar, or have given in to your old habits of cola beverages, or coffee, or alcohol, keep trying until you get it absolutely perfect for one week.

THEN IT'S TIME TO TAKE INVENTORY. Refer to your fatigue and symptom scorecard and make an entry on the important diet questionnaire in the back of the book. This will help you decide whether or not you are beginning to notice some benefits and to what degree.

If the improvement is dramatic, then you are ready to begin making your diet more livable. These are the questions you will want to answer:

1. Are all the feedings still necessary? Or do you still feel as well if some of the snacks are eliminated?

2. Are you gaining or losing weight? There is usually a two-to-three-pound loss the first week if the total carbohydrate intake has been drastically reduced. There should be some re-gain the second week. If not, the total carbohydrate count should be *increased*. If the weight remains the same or goes up, the carbohydrate count need not be increased.

3. Which foods would you like to add? There is now room for more of the *simple* carbohydrates, such as milk, un-sweetened yogurt, and fruit. Foods sweetened with a *little* honey might be added now, and perhaps a glass of wine or an ounce of hard liquor, unless you happen to have a drinking problem.

If there has been no improvement in your energy, you must determine whether you need *more* or *less* carbohydrate. And this will take some trial and error. One of the best ways to help make the decision is to buy a package of Ketostix at the drug-store. Use them to test your urine as I explained on page 108. If the Ketostix give a positive or slightly positive reaction, then your carbohydrate level should be *increased*, for ketosis would signify you are *losing* weight, something you can ill afford.

Increase your carbohydrate intake 20 grams per day, adding each week until you arrive at the level which provides your optimal well-being.

ADDING MORE NEW FOODS. You have been able to add milk, fruit, yogurt, and a little honey in addition to the nuts, vegetables, and whole grains making up your carbohydrates. And now that you have established your new eating pattern, it would be perfectly acceptable for you to experiment to see if you can tolerate some caffeine, or some alcohol, if that is what you are missing most. Add one of them at a time, gradually, and see if you have a decrease in energy, or if your fatigue or other problems return. If your energy level stays high, you may add them to your diet, otherwise it will be best to drop them.

Sugar, when it appears as a *minor* ingredient, as in Russian dressing or coleslaw, probably could be reintroduced at this point also.

To gain or maintain the weight you want and still maintain reduced carbohydrate intake, it may be necessary for you also to increase your intake of fat. A small percentage of people will, on such a diet, develop a significant increase in cholesterol level, which carries enough risk for you to be aware of it. Your responsibility to yourself is clearly not completed until you have gotten your *second* set of blood tests to see how you responded biochemically to the diet. As we will discuss further in chapter 22, despite the intensive propaganda campaign being waged, you should know that a slight elevation of your cholesterol level is not the worst complication in the world. There is a host of disabling symptoms that you may have that have more need for correction than high cholesterol. Chances are it will not go up, but if it does, you and your doctor have a clinical decision to make. Do the benefits outweigh the disadvantages? This depends on how much better you feel. If you feel very little improvement, you would be better off to limit your saturated fat intake and increase your vegetable starch intake. But if you feel great improvement and are one of those whose cholesterol level goes up, you will have to consult with your doctor to make a decision.

A GOOD FOOD AND THE BAD FOODS. Foods that are really great for you are nuts and seeds. They are packed with nutrition, have the perfect balance, and are marvelous for the stabilization of blood-sugar problems.

The especially bad foods for you are refined carbohydrates. You should definitely not have cakes, cookies, candy bars, sugary soft drinks, macaroni or spaghetti, or any pastas. When you buy carbohydrates, make sure they are not refined. Learn to cook and eat potatoes with the skins on. When you buy rice or bread, buy the whole grain varieties.

DIET #2 EAT-ALL-YOU-WANT FOODS. These are the foods to be taken without limit, since they have only small amounts of carbohydrate:

Meats—all cuts, all kinds. This includes organ meats.

Eggs—any style.

Fowl—any kind and any style.

Protein concentrates—such as protein wafers, liquid predigested protein, and soy protein vegetarian burgers.

Nuts and seeds—these are so important, they are included here, although they really belong in list number two.

Fats and oils—vegetable oils, butter, margarine, mayonnaise, shortening. (The percentage which should be unsaturated depends on personal responses; *some* unsaturated fats should be included.) Heavy cream and sour cream are allowed in any quantity.

Condiments—salt, pepper, paprika, oregano, onion salt, garlic salt, any dry spice. Soy sauce, Worcestershire sauce, any seasoning in which sugar is not a major ingredient. Artificial sweeteners, but not sorbitol or mannitol. Vanilla, chocolate, other extracts. Mustard, vinegar, horseradish, cinnamon, nutmeg, cloves, capers, and many others.

Desserts—sugarless gelatin, flavored and unflavored. Any artificially sweetened or sugarless dessert. Whipped cream can be used if made without sugar.

Olives—black or green.

Pickles—dill or sour.

Beverages—water, tea, vichy, club soda, lemon or lime juice, Sanka, decaffeinated coffee, all as much as you want; regular caffeinated coffee is to be avoided. Clear broth, consommé, madrilene. All sugarless diet soda (except colas or other sodas with caffeine).

Salad—all salad vegetables, such as leafy greens, celery, cucumbers, avocado, radishes, peppers, tomatoes, onions are allowed in any quantity. Salad dressings which do not contain sugar or sorbitol are permitted (Italian, oil, vinegar, spices, cheese dressing are all okay).

DIET #2 COUNTABLE FOODS. These are the foods which must be counted to measure their carbohydrate gram count, but they are permissible, in fact, necessary. Look up their gram counts in the carbohydrate gram table.

Vegetables—all are allowed except those which have been partitioned and a nutritional part discarded. So you would not eat white (polished) rice, polished oats, skinless potatoes, cornstarch, etc.

Vegetable juice—permitted.

Fruit juice—limit to less than a glass per day.

Grains—only whole grains are permitted. Ordinary bread, crackers, cake mixes, etc., are made of white flour, which is prohibited.

Fruit—apples, pears, oranges, grapes, and cherries, being sweeter, are allowed in small quantities. Melons, berries, bananas, avocado are all preferable.

Milk—no more than two cups for an adult, three for a child. Yogurt and buttermilk would be included in this count. Be aware of the possibility you may have a lactase deficiency, especially if diarrhea follows milk-drinking. If you do, milk should be avoided.

Snacks—popcorn, fried pork rinds, whole grain wafers, sugarless cookies, corn chips, nuts, seeds.

Alcohol—wine in cooking. Otherwise, your limit would be two drinks per day.

DIET #2 NO-NO FOODS. Do not eat sugar. This includes sugary desserts, jams and preserves, sugared soft drinks, candy, cookies, corn syrup, dextrose, honey, catsup, sweet relish.

Do not eat white flour, or any food from which fiber or bran has been removed.

Alcohol and caffeine—to be determined by your own ex-

perimentation. Your limit, if trial shows these are not trouble-makers for you, should be two drinks per day and two cups of coffee.

KEEP YOUR CARBOHYDRATES UP, JUST MAKE SURE THEY ARE THE RIGHT KIND. When you start on this diet, look up every carbohydrate you eat in the carbohydrate counter tables.

You have to do two things: First, find a low enough level to give you the high energy benefits of the low-carbohydrate diet. But second, have enough carbohydrate so you do not lose weight. We have found that thin people lose very easily, even eating a lot of food, if the diet is low in carbohydrate. I, as one of the people who tend to gain, envy the ease with which the thin person loses weight just with the slightest reduction in carbohydrate.

During the first week you may lose a few pounds, but don't worry about this loss, you will gain it back after this first week when you begin to add the larger amounts of carbohydrates.

It may be at this point that you start to gain weight, and this then would be the ideal level for you.

You will be looking for the lowest level of carbohydrates at which you can gain some weight. Additional weight gain should not be accomplished by further increases in carbohydrates, but rather by further increases in protein and fat.

Once you have reached your ideal weight, you will stay on this level of diet. This is why I want you to count your carbohydrates, so that when you find your right level, you will know just what the right amount of carbohydrate is for you.

Should you begin to overshoot the mark and gain past what you consider to be your ideal, you have two options. You can either cut your total caloric quantities by reducing your fat intake, or you could go down to a lower level of carbohydrate and again stabilize your weight. Figure out which way makes you feel better.

IF YOU STILL HAVE NOT GAINED WEIGHT OR ENERGY. This diet should make a real difference to you in gaining weight and energy. But if the diet at its highest level of carbohydrates and fats still has not done the job for you, there are several things you should check into and do.

Make sure you are not skimping on breakfast. You must get some real food energy at this time because it reduces the likelihood of a physical and mental letdown in midmorning. Coffee or fruit juice alone for breakfast is not enough. If you can't eat a substantial breakfast first thing, then try to eat somewhat later.

Your vitamins and minerals program should be expanded as chapter 18 shows.

Force yourself to take something to eat on schedule even if you don't feel particularly hungry. You may be the kind who gets too busy and forgets to eat.

IF YOU SMOKE CIGARETTES, STOP IMMEDIATELY AND COMPLETELY. The most effective measure in conjunction with our diet for the smoker to put on weight and to increase energy would be to stop. The more you smoke, the greater the chances are that this is playing an important role in your failure to gain weight and in your being tired. For the first few days after you stop smoking, you may feel worse, but as your body readjusts and frees itself from the effects of the cigarettes, you may expect to feel the improvement.

Make sure that your carbohydrates are being spaced throughout the day. On Diet #1 overweight people tap the storehouse of energy in their fat depots. *Your* diet will supply energy from the greater amounts of carbohydrates allowed, and from the high amount of the protein- and fat-containing foods you will be eating.

HAVE LOTS OF THE RIGHT FOODS ALWAYS ON HAND. Make a list of all the foods or combinations of food that have the good nutritional value that you want and that you also really enjoy . . . cheese and crackers, nuts, sunflower seeds, olives, avocado, deviled eggs. Protein wafers won't do much for putting on weight, but they are an excellent means of getting protein conveniently every three hours to fight fatigue or any other hypoglycemia symptoms. They are sort of an easy-carry portable energy machine. Go to the store and buy everything on the list you can find. Then when it's time for a snack, you'll have something right there at your fingertips.

If your energy still is flagging, consider the use of fructose. The fructose diet is described in the next chapter.

SOMETHING ELSE TO CONSIDER. There may be other reasons why you can't gain weight.

There are many nondiet causes of underweight, and if you simply cannot gain weight even after trying all the things discussed in this chapter, you should work with your doctor to see if you might have some other condition.

A WARNING YOU SHOULD NEVER IGNORE. You should never ignore unexplained weight loss. It can be an ominous symptom of a serious, even life-threatening disease and demands immediate medical investigation, particularly if your weight should suddenly begin to drop. See your physician.

If the weight loss is associated with thirst or increased urinary frequency, it could mean diabetes. Unexplained weight loss can also be caused by something as serious as cancer, especially if associated with fatigue. So if you have fatigue in association with unexplained weight loss I would suggest that you call your physician and make an appointment immediately!

14

Diet #3. The superenergy weight-maintenance diet

It is not easy to devise an antifatigue diet without changing a person's body weight, but this Superenergy Diet #3 is designed with this goal in mind. It is for anyone who wants to keep his weight within a ten-pound range or for anyone who for medical reasons should not gain or lose weight.

Diet #3 embodies all the principles of nutrition that have helped others achieve Superenergy, except for one thing. It is not ketogenic because ketone body production is associated with weight loss. This diet is designed to find the common point where your carbohydrates are cut down, but short of the point where ketosis (fat breakdown) takes place. For most people, this comes to around 60 carbohydrate grams per day.

If there's a tendency to gain on this level, then you drop the gram count, perhaps to the 50-gram level. If you still gain, you'll try 40 grams.

If there's a tendency to lose on it, you increase the gram level to 80 or 90.

WHAT IS ALLOWED ON DIET #3. All meats are allowed, including seafood, fowl, even those meats which contain some carbohydrate, such as liver, sausage, or bologna.

Eggs are allowed, any style.

Cheese is allowed, any kind.

All salads are allowed, as much as you want.

129

All those vegetables allowed on Diet #1 are permitted, up to several cupfuls per day. Refer to the list of vegetables on Diet #1.

Fats and condiments—as in Diet #1.

In the case of bread, you may use two or three slices of gluten bread per day, or one slice of stone-ground wheat bread, or two slices of whole rye flatbread. (Do not exceed 15 carbohydrate grams per day in this category.)

Olives, nuts, and seeds are allowed, as much as you like, with the exception of chestnuts, water chestnuts, and cashews, which are high in carbohydrates.

Fruits and fruit juices should not be allowed during the first two weeks of the diet; further observations will dictate whether or not they can later be added gradually.

DIET #3 NO-NO FOODS. You should not eat any of the following:

Refined bread	Cookies	Macaroni
Cake	Crackers	Pancakes
Candy	Refined flour	Sugar
Cashews	Ice Cream	Syrup
Catsup	Jam or jelly	

THE SIX RULES OF DIET #3

1. Develop a vitamin and mineral regimen as outlined in chapter 18.

2. Eat as much as you want of meats, seafood, eggs, cheeses, and salads.

3. Start with six small feedings a day, eating some protein every three or four hours, including breakfast-time.

4. As long as you are at the weight you desire, eat as much as you want of the listed vegetables. If you begin to lose weight, then you may begin to add some fruit, primarily melons, berries, and citrus. If you begin to gain weight, switch to Diet #1.

5. Avoid sugar, refined flour, and white rice. Eat only whole grain products.

6. Check your individual reaction to coffee and alcohol and limit them to an amount that does not produce rebound fatigue.

DIET #3 IS GETTING RESULTS ALREADY. It has already proved to be of extreme value in psychiatry, according to Dr. Richard A. Kunin of San Francisco. After reading my first book, Dr. Kunin decided to try a group of seventy-three patients on a diet that placed them at the transition point between ketosis and non-ketosis. He found that 82 percent of them reported improvement in their symptoms by using that diet *or* Diet #1. In contrast, 81 percent of them reported worsening when they resumed their usual high carbohydrate intake.

WHEN SUPERENERGY IS NOT YET YOURS. If the comprehensive vitamin-mineral program and the low carbohydrate but not ketogenic diet does not solve your personal energy crisis, two quite different possibilities exist. Your carbohydrate intake may be too high—or it may be too low.

Just as the overweight person almost invariably finds he has more energy when he is in ketosis and his fat stores are providing a large share of the fuel, so too do many normal weight subjects. Diet #1 should be tried in such cases. By eating generously, weight loss can usually be halted after a few pounds.

IF THAT MANEUVER DOESN'T WORK. You may be someone who *needs* carbohydrate fuel. If you are, there are two dietary modifications of Diet #3 that I have used with consistently good results. One variant involves a special form of sugar called fructose. The other involves whole grains and lentils.

Either variation makes a good starting point. You might even choose between them according to whether you miss sweets or starches more. The final choice should be the one which gives you the most energy.

THE FRUCTOSE DIET. Fructose is a simple sugar, as is glucose. Table sugar—sucrose—is a molecule of glucose combined with a molecule of fructose. Starch is a complex of glucose molecules.

To be metabolized, fructose, unlike glucose, does not require or call forth insulin. Thus it provides a readily available carbohydrate source for energy, but one which does not evoke the insulin overresponse that characterizes the person with low blood sugar and is the most common cause of fatigue.

DR. PALM'S DIET. No one has described the advantages of fructose better than Dr. J. Daniel Palm, author of *Diet Away Your Stress, Tension and Anxiety.* Dr. Palm feels the key to using fructose successfully is to exclude almost all other carbohydrate except fructose. In that manner, he has been able to give as much as 100 grams of fructose daily with good results. I have been using it in much smaller quantities than that.

I found Dr. Palm's laboratory proof—that subjects on his fructose diet put out significantly less adrenalin by-products, presumably because of much fewer hypoglycemic stimuli— very convincing.

FRUCTOSE CAN BE TAKEN IN SEVERAL WAYS. You can take two fructose tablets (2 grams each) every two hours, making about sixteen tablets distributed throughout the day.

Or you can make lemonade with it, using about six teaspoons to a quart, and drink it throughout the day.

Or you can use fructose as you would ordinary sugar. To get the full antihypoglycemia effect, you may need a teaspoon or two of fructose each hour, which effectively curtails insulin release. Or you may need to use it only certain times of the day. Test it for yourself, watching for that point at which you might feel an energy letdown. If you feel fatigue, tension, or uneasiness, then you know it's time to take fructose again. Sometimes you will feel relief in minutes.

Used correctly, fructose should give you a steady assured source of energy without any of the letdown of ordinary sugar.

Six teaspoons of fructose makes 30 grams. The remainder of your diet might provide 30 more grams of carbohydrate making a total of 60 per day. If an undesirable loss of weight takes place, you might increase your fructose intake.

If you start to gain weight then you should decrease the carbohydrates by either decreasing the amount of fructose or the amount of carbohydrates in your other food.

Dr. Palm calls fructose "nature's tranquilizer" and reports that it eliminates hunger in dieters and eliminates the demand for alcohol in alcoholics and the craving for sugar of hypoglycemic persons. He feels it helps the overweight person reduce, but I have not found this.

He also found using the combination low-carbohydrate-plus-fructose diet reduced or eliminated migraine headaches in longtime sufferers and generally made hyperactive children more manageable.

YOU CAN USE FRUCTOSE IN ANY RECIPE CALLING FOR SUGAR. Just remember that fructose is two-thirds again sweeter than sugar. So if five teaspoons of sugar are called for, you need only three teaspoons of fructose.

It also makes a super substitute for artificial sweetener in the recipes in *Dr. Atkins' Diet Cookbook.* Remember it still counts for five grams of carbohydrate per teaspoon.

CAUTION: WATCH YOUR TRIGLYCERIDES. Many investigators, despite Dr. Palm's studies, have found that fructose can raise the level of triglyceride in the blood. If you stay on fructose, make sure to test your triglyceride level.

For best effects fructose should be given with the mineral magnesium in the amounts outlined in chapter 18.

Do not make the mistake of assuming that fructose is the same as the sugar in fruit or juice. Fruit sugar is actually half glucose and has the effect of stimulating, rather than pacifying, your insulin response.

Perhaps the greatest frustration is that fructose, widely used in Europe, is very difficult to get in America. Those in the know attribute this fact to the widespread influence of the sugar industry. Fructose with its natural sweetness and its ability to bypass the insulin hypoglycemia cycle, is, like cyclamate, too dangerous a competitor to sugar.

THE DIET #3 ALTERNATE METHOD: OLD-FASHIONED GRAINS. This alternate method uses oats, groats, barley, millet, maize, and all the old-fashioned nonrefined whole grains, instead of fructose. Plus nuts, lentils, and brown and wild rice.

The six basic rules are the same. The no-no foods are the same. You simply get your carbohydrates from these whole grain cereals instead of from fructose. Try both avenues, and see which one makes you more satisfied and more energetic.

NOTE: Be careful of some of the commercial whole grain

cereals that have a lot of raisins and honey. They may work very well for you, but they can be disadvantageous to the person who has hypoglycemia because honey and highly concentrated dried fruits can be more than the metabolic machinery can handle. Check your own reaction to any cereal product. And of course make sure there is no sugar in it.

Read labels carefully on cereals and breads. The term "whole wheat bread" does not always mean the bread is made entirely of whole wheat flour, but may be whole wheat flour added to a blanched white flour.

Check with the health food stores to find new products coming out using whole grains.

Consider lentils as part of your carbohydrate intake also. Lima beans, baked beans, kidney beans, peanuts, and soybeans are excellent.

HOW TO FIND OUT IF YOU'RE BETTER ON FRUCTOSE OR ON GRAINS. It's really quite simple: Just try both. Try two weeks on fructose, then two weeks on grain, and see if there is any advantage to one over the other. Which fits in better with your lifestyle? On which program do you feel better? In my practice, I usually start my carbohydrate-dependent patients on the fructose and gradually wean them over to the whole grains, week by week.

FIGURING OUT YOUR CARBOHYDRATE LEVEL ON THESE VARIATIONS. What do you miss most? If you would like to add sugar or flour, don't expect to get it. But it would be reasonable to expect most anything else, including a glass of wine.

Remember, your first step is to find out where your weight keeps level, and the second step involves finding what level gives you the most energy. You can do this by adjusting the amounts of fructose or whole grains, or by adding or subtracting the carbohydrates you are getting in other foods.

If you find you do better on fewer carbohydrates, but lose weight, you will end up eating more fats. In this case, your doctor must check your blood lipid levels.

REMEMBER: In an experiment don't try to change more than one variable at a time because, if you do and you feel better, you won't know what did it, or if you feel worse you won't know what is responsible. If you try two or three measures simultaneously, you won't know which one did the trick.

Some people find it helpful to keep a notebook to help notice relationships.

NOW THAT YOU'RE READY. Before you start this diet to see if it makes you feel better, be sure to fill in the questionnaire in the back of the book indicating which variant you used.

15

Diet #4. The special situation diet

This is a short-term diet for persons in a special situation. Perhaps you are pregnant; perhaps you are about to go into surgery; perhaps you have been sick and your doctor has not yet made a diagnosis.

In all of these situations you want to increase the quality of your diet to give yourself every nutritional advantage possible to aid your situation, but you do not want to make drastic changes in your physiology and metabolism.

Diet #4 will give you many advantages in the waiting time you have before trying the more ambitious Diets #1, 2, and 3.

It is also a marking-time diet to keep in mind when you're traveling, when you're in any situation where you're unable to follow your regular diet completely. It can be used to mark time until you can get back to your usual diet.

THE RULES TO DIET #4.
1. Avoid sugar.
2. Avoid starch, all refined flour.
3. Avoid alcohol and caffeine.
4. Take your vitamins and minerals as outlined in chapter 18.

IF YOU ARE GOING TO THE HOSPITAL. The first thing to do is tell your doctor what kind of diet you are on and get his advice.

He may want you to continue it. But usually it is simplest to switch to Diet #4 about ten days before going to the hospital and continue it right through your hospital stay and your convalescence.

You will have to watch particularly for sugar in the hospital since few hospital dietitians seem to have accepted the responsibility for keeping sugar out of the patients' diets. Simply send the desserts back to the kitchen; or if you have a choice of menu, as many hospitals allow these days, try to choose the things that you know are on your diet and don't accept the ones that are bad for you.

It is not hospital policy to allow any pills, even vitamins, to be taken by hospital patients on their own. You must ask your doctor's permission to take vitamins. He should be reasonably cooperative because all doctors recognize the need in times of special stress. However, many physicians in hospitals still do not give vitamin and mineral supplements to their patients despite the fact that study after study has shown that they do speed healing and recovery. Zinc, for example, has been shown to increase healing tremendously and to help prevent post-surgical blood clots. And vitamins A, C, and E have also been found to be useful in surgical recovery.

Thousands of hospital days could be saved if physicians would only use vitamin and mineral supplements to help patients heal faster and get out of the hospital and back to work sooner.

16

Why vitamins and minerals are important

Most physicians have been brainwashed into thinking vitamins are generally useless. I was no exception.

Now I'm very enthusiastic about the many possibilities of nutrition breakthroughs in medicine, but it took me a long time.

I don't know why medical school teaches a doctor to be militantly antivitamin, but it does. It puzzles me how we have harbored such an antipathy toward the only form of therapy we can turn to which is virtually devoid of any side effects or toxicity potential.

WHEN I WAS AN INTERN. I recall well, as an intern and resident at prestigious teaching hospitals, the scorn I felt for the outside practitioner we called an LMD (local medical doctor), who gave B_{12} shots or treated a patient with "vitamins," the latter word uttered with complete disdain.

But I also recall well the inspiration provided me by one of my professors. His favorite saying: "A good doctor learns from his studies; a great doctor learns from his patients."

I never forgot that, and I always made it a point to learn from my patients. I listened when they told me that a vitamin that I "knew" to be useless seemed to clear up a certain complaint, or that an idea they had gathered from a magazine or newspaper seemed to work for them.

WHEN MY PRACTICE GREW. Once I was established in my practice I continued to listen to my patients and to test new ideas with small clinical trials, slowly sifting out which of the many claims made about vitamins had some merit and which did not.

There were disappointments, but overall I saw that nutrition medicine could work at preventing disease as well as treating it and could help the well person feel better as well as the sick person get well. Nutrition medicine was the one major thrust that we weren't using in everyday medical practice.

DRUGS VERSUS VITAMINS. Vitamins do not compete with drugs within your body. But they do compete in the marketplace—and for this reason an economic war is being waged, and your bodies are the battlefield.

When a vitamin is used to treat anemia, or leg cramps, or menopause, or mental illness, it is being used as a therapeutic agent, even though it still retains its identity as a food supplement. As a therapeutic agent, it becomes competitive with drugs and pharmaceuticals, and there begins the problem.

Our federal government has an agency, the Food and Drug Administration, designed to *police* the drug industry, but which in reality serves to *protect* the industry. It is seeking authority to regulate and control all nutrition supplements.

Their latest proposal is that if any vitamin preparation contains more than one and one-half times their recommended daily allowance *then you cannot buy it yourself as an over-the-counter product.* You either have to buy a huge number of the smaller dosage capsules, paying more, of course, and being forced to take two, or ten, or fifty, or a hundred small capsules just because you can't buy one big one. Or you have the choice of finding a physician who believes in vitamins and minerals and getting him to write a prescription for the larger size capsules. That means, of course, in addition to the cost of the vitamins you would have to pay for the office call and the prescription.

There has been a major furor over the FDA's proposal. Bills were proposed in both houses of Congress to prevent the FDA from taking this action. A groundswell of public opinion deluged Congress with mail criticizing the FDA's proposals. Several people, including Dr. Linus Pauling, are even bringing lawsuits against the FDA.

The conflict remains unresolved because of the question: Are vitamins a drug or a food?

Should the FDA have jurisdiction over vitamins or shall these nontoxic nutrients be left in the hands of the public?

Several problems arise when the FDA can control vitamins. For one thing, vitamins are in the public domain; no manufacturer can hope to recapture the considerable costs necessary to prove to the FDA that the regimen is effective when he only has a fragmentary share of the market and no patent protection as he would with a new drug.

And the FDA, for reasons obviously beyond those involved in merely protecting the interests of the consumer, has always sided against the nutrient industry.

THE FDA SHOULD NOT BE ALLOWED TO REGULATE VITAMINS. If you know anything about nutrition, you know that a nutritional support system can work only if *all* the nutrients are present. Vitamins work as a team and a single missing nutrient can keep vitamin therapy from working. So if the FDA limited even one vitamin, it could render therapy nearly useless.

This is what *has* happened in the case of folic acid. As long as there is no easy way to administer this essential vitamin in the dosage necessary to provide a proper response, vitamin therapy cannot work at its most effective level.

WHAT YOU READ. In newspapers and magazines you have been exposed to a bewildering barrage of claims about the benefits of vitamin therapy and counterclaims that we don't need any surplus vitamins at all. The counterclaimers seem to be more numerous, so most people, hearing the frequent statements that vitamins aren't necessary, don't even try them.

One of the questions I ask new patients is whether they take vitamins and, if so, which ones. The majority either take no vitamins regularly or follow regimens which are woefully inadequate in several major nutrients. When these dietary histories are cross-indexed with existing medical problems it shows that *those who need vitamins most are the ones least likely to be taking them.*

WHAT ABOUT STUDIES SHOWING NEGATIVE RESULTS WITH VITAMINS? What about studies showing that certain vitamins don't work? To a person with a nutritional background, these studies seem incredibly naive. Usually they involve administering a vitamin just as a drug is given—merely giving it alone. No other nutrients except the one in question are given, and no attention is paid to the patient's diet. But vitamins can work only as part of a nutritional team. They cannot work alone. Nor can vitamins work against the obstacle of an improper diet. For example, vitamin therapy cannot work when an underlying hypoglycemia is not controlled. This could be the hidden factor in whatever studies with vitamins have shown negative results. The studies did not disprove the value of vitamins, but only proved that in addition to the vitamin supplements, the diet also needed to be modified to make it possible for those vitamins to be effective.

If I had designed one of those amateurish studies, I would have been ashamed. But the doctors who deserve the greatest shame are the "experts" who accept these studies as valid, give credence to them, and quote their results.

An example is the scathing attack by the American Psychiatric Association upon niacinamide therapy for schizophrenia after a series of studies showed that this remarkable vitamin, *when used alone without a dietary change,* had very little effect on most mental disease patients. The Association ignored the studies in which the vitamin was used successfully in conjunction with dietary improvements.

There are some patients who will improve their energy level upon changing to a low carbohydrate eating pattern before any vitamins are administered. There are some who will respond favorably to the vitamins before the diet is begun. But the vast majority will show this favorable response only when *both* are begun and done correctly.

Vitamins, even when they are desperately needed, when used without the proper diet, rarely produce much tangible benefit.

WHY ARE VITAMINS DOWNGRADED BY THE ESTABLISHMENT? In my view, the main reason is the opposition of the food industry, which would be embarrassed, and the drug industry, which would suffer from the competition. There are historical reasons that may explain the medical thinking.

Vitamins were first discovered, in a way similar to bacteria, as a result of the "one cause—one cure" theory. Scurvy, beriberi, pellagra were caused by deficiencies of certain vitamins. Thus developed the corollary concept: if the absence of a vitamin does not cause a disease, then that vitamin is not required.

The concept has led to some remarkable incongruities in establishing dosage levels of many vitamins. If you only ask how much vitamin C prevents scurvy in humans, the answer is 30–60 mg. Yet those animals who make their own vitamin C, manufacture it in the equivalent of what would be 2,000 to 15,000 mg. for humans. Dr. Man-Li S. Yew at the University of Texas tested one species that, like humans, cannot manufacture its own vitamin C. He found out that the human equivalent of 3,500 mg. had to be given to get maximum wound healing, growth, and resistance to stress.

Thinking restricted to the prevention of illness caused by a deficient vitamin leads to far too low RDAs (recommended daily allowances). Going beyond these levels often leads to a world of therapeutic benefit.

Further confusion arises from failure to recognize that a vitamin can have more than one use, and that a biologic function can be served by more than one vitamin.

For example, the discovery that deficiencies of vitamins B_{12} and folic acid caused pernicious (megaloblastic) anemia set back progress in thinking about these vitamins for a generation. It allowed some fairly influential scientists to overlook the fact that these vitamins have some very important functions in the body beyond that of preventing anemia.

AND THIS THINKING PERVADES THE FDA. The extent of this fixation on cause and effect is so great that in April, 1971, the FDA took the 5 mg. dosage form of folic acid—even with a doctor's prescription—off the market. They did this not because they had found it to be dangerous in any way, but merely because larger doses were ineffective in correcting megaloblastic anemia. The FDA took the stance that folic acid is a drug, rather than a vitamin, and therefore, subject to the regulations that demand efficacy be proven.

Think of the significance of this decision. The FDA has the power to declare a vitamin to be a drug and then demand that it be effective in treating a disease! Decisions like this favor the drug industry in their economic competition with the nontoxic nutrient industry.

HOW DOES THIS AFFECT YOU? It can keep you from obtaining a vitamin program that works effectively. Folic acid deficiency was one of the most frequently found shortages in the government surveys of both the United States and Canada. Not only do I find it effective in 5 to 15 mg. doses, but Drs. H. L. Newbold and Kurt Oster, who have done the most clinical work with folate in general medicine, psychiatry, and preventive cardiology, have concluded that 40–80 mg. per day is a more appropriate dose.

In Canada, where the 5 mg. dosage is quite appropriately sold over the counter, a daily dose of 20 mg. can be purchased for about nine cents. In the United States where only the 1 mg. dose is purchasable, and only with a doctor's prescription, the daily cost of taking twenty pills runs between fifty cents and a dollar. If the FDA's proposal to limit the dosage forms of other vitamins is put into effect, then the cost of vitamin therapy will escalate beyond the average person's ability to pay.

THE FDA IS TELLING YOU WHAT YOU CAN AND CANNOT BUY. The new rulings that the FDA is trying to put through— that you cannot buy vitamins and minerals in large doses—is tantamount to ruling that you must get a doctor's prescription to eat a slice of liver or a sweet potato, because both of these contain two to five times as much vitamin A as the FDA's maximum. To stop a cold by taking the amount of vitamin C that is recommended by most researchers you would have to take 100 tablets a day!

WHAT THE FDA THINKS OF YOUR INTELLIGENCE. The FDA's publicly stated position is: "Lay persons are incapable of determining by themselves whether they have or are likely to develop vitamin or mineral deficiencies."

By what right does the FDA use your tax money and mine

to keep us from using vitamins and minerals? These are nutrients that have nurtured man for 200,000 generations.

We may have to fight for our right to take vitamins. In California the fight has already started. Federal raiders there seized a quantity of vitamin E and multivitamin tablets from one pharmaceutical company. There was no charge that the products were contaminated or dangerous in any way. The charge was they were misleadingly labeled because they were called "dietary supplement." This, says the FDA, is false and misleading.

As *Rodale's Health Bulletin* (June 24, 1972) says, "The FDA has a right to their opinion, but they do not have the right to tell us we cannot go out and buy vitamins when we want them. It is an outrageous intrusion into our freedom of choice."

THE RDAS ARE NOT ENOUGH. The official recommended dietary allowances, commonly known as the RDAs, are designed only for the average person who is completely healthy and eating a completely satisfactory diet. In fact, even Dr. Alfred E. Harper has conceded that the recommended dietary allowances "do not cover the needs of those who are ill, nor do they take into account losses of nutrients that occur during the processing and preparing of food." And he says, the requirements differ with age and body size, with differences in genetic makeup, with growth rate, pregnancy, lactation, and with sex, with activity and with environmental conditions. And Dr. Harper is the chairman of the very committee that makes up the recommended dietary allowances!

WE WANT OPTIMUM HEALTH, NOT MINIMUM. The amounts of the RDAs are only the amounts needed to prevent you from getting such diseases as rickets or scurvy. They are not aimed at the preservation of optimal health; they are not aimed at the subtle deficiencies you might have.

The "facts" upon which the recommended daily allowances are based are quite shaky. Many nutritionists disagree violently with the recommended amounts and think they should be much higher.

Even an AMA nutritionist once described how the Food and Nutrition Board puts together the recommended daily dietary allowances. "It evaluates the data, published and unpublished, does some guessing and comes up with some figures."

Well, I'm happy to have so-called experts give me facts and even their opinions. But I do not want them to do my thinking for me. And I certainly do not want them to legislate that I cannot think differently.

MOST PEOPLE NEED TO GET MORE THAN THE RDA. Some need much more.

A typical case. Ann Clark, a brilliant young lady, consulted me because she had read my first book and felt I could help her with her overweight and hypoglycemia. I placed her on Diet #1 and a fairly potent vitamin regimen including at least 200 mg. of every known B complex constituent. She lost the weight, and her fatigue disappeared. But certain lifelong symptoms remained, even after years of the regimen. She frequently perceived herself as being outside her own body, looking down upon herself and other people in a room.

An avid reader of nutrition books, Ann suspected that these represented the dysperceptions of schizophrenia, even though her psychiatrist had not told her so and had merely said: "That's a very common symptom." From her reading, she began to add vitamin B_3 in the dosage of 6 grams (6,000 mg.) compared to her usual dose of 200 mg. and to the RDA of 20 mg.

Within four days her depersonalization disappeared, and with it she noticed a new clarity of vision, of sound, and of memory. When she does not take these doses, the symptoms return.

Ann's is not an isolated case. There are currently hundreds of nutrition-oriented psychiatrists who use vitamins to produce similar results with predictable regularity.

THE RESULTS ARE HARD TO CHALLENGE. But explaining them is a little more difficult. Some have posed the concept of *vitamin dependency*, which means that such people are not just deficient in the intake of these vitamins but, because of a missing enzyme or an error in their metabolism, require much larger amounts of certain vitamins. Several such defects have been identified, and more will be identified in the future.

HOW TO DETERMINE WHETHER YOU NEED EXTRA VITAMINS OR MINERALS. There are different kinds of tests for vitamins: blood tests, urine tests, some done with samples of hair. They are valuable, but are experimental and fairly expensive. A person might spend a great deal to check out very few vitamins. This might not be too much, since the presence of one nutritional deficiency more than likely heralds the presence of some other deficiency. One should never make the mistake of stopping at correcting the first deficiency he finds. If you've got iron-deficiency anemia, yes, correct it, but don't stop there thinking you have the entire answer.

If you can afford the testing, get it done, but it is not necessary. A therapeutic trial is better—giving the vitamin and looking for the response.

WHAT ABOUT FINDING VITAMINS IN NATURAL FOODS? I want you to eat good nutritious foods and hope that you will prepare them in the way that will preserve the most nutrients, that is, buy fresh, eat soon, don't peel, cook only until tender.

However, just eating well-selected foods would only give you the optimum amounts of vitamin and minerals you need for super health if taken for a rather lengthy period, and then only if there were no metabolic block.

Our food supply has changed since nineteenth-century man did without vitamin supplements. Now we eat 1,100 calories a day in the form of stripped-down sugar and flour, which our bodies must metabolize by using the vitamins and minerals we get from the rest of our diet. This type of "antinutrient" was a much smaller factor a century ago.

THE ONE THING THAT IS PROBABLY IGNORED MOST. Those who say that we get enough vitamins and minerals in our everyday diet don't take into account that so many things in our modern-day life destroy the vitamins and minerals that we should be getting: the processing and storing of foods; the vitamin-stripping refining of flour and sugar; TV dinners that mean you cook food twice, increasing vitamin loss; additives that prevent the absorption of nutrients so your body can't even use them when they are there. Increased intake of polyunsaturated fats can produce vitamin E deficiency. Cigarette smoking destroys vitamin C. Many medicines cause vitamin deficiencies. Antibiotics change normal intestinal bacteria which ordinarily synthesize certain vitamins. Diuretics can wash out potassium, sodium, and other minerals. Environmental pollutants increase need for vitamins C and E. And our soil is depleted of certain key trace minerals. All this translates into deficiencies in our diet that weren't there in "the good old days."

ANOTHER UNBELIEVABLY IGNORED FACT. Our metabolic responses vary greatly, and so do our needs for vitamins and minerals. The activity of certain enzymes has been found to differ by as much as fifty times from one person to another.

The needs for vitamins differ just as greatly. What is a satisfactory amount for one person may not be nearly enough to supply the body needs of another.

BUT THE MOST CONVINCING PROOF OF WIDESPREAD VITA-MIN DEFICIENCIES IS THE REMARKABLE SUCCESS OF VITAMIN THERAPY. I am quite content to rest my case on that point. And that's where you come in—you will provide the proof—or disproof. After you have tried the vitamin regimen, along with the diet suggestions, will you please fill out and return the questionnaire in this book? If I'm right about the widespread prevalence of vitamin and mineral deficiencies, then the majority of you will report the ways in which you have improved physically, and mentally. If I'm wrong, your answers will show that too.

Actually, the efficacy of vitamins has already been shown in many areas. Excellent results have been gained in schizophrenic patients. Treatment includes large doses of vitamins B_3, B_6, and C and sometimes vitamin E, plus an antihypoglycemic diet with avoidance of sugar, reduction of starch, and elimination of caffeine. Sometimes thyroid medications are used. Some people also seem to respond well to folic acid plus vitamin B_{12}, while others do worse on folic acid and better on zinc and manganese. Sometimes response is rapid and dramatic with improvement in three or four days; at other times it may take a year.

Dr. David Hawkins, one of the early pioneers in the field who has now treated more than five thousand patients, says the new treatment has been so effective at the mental health center where he practices, that the rehospitalization rate has been cut in half. One local social agency found a huge number of their most difficult clients . . . including alcoholics, unwed mothers, student dropouts . . . were helped by the orthomolecular treatment. The agency was able to double its case load with the same budget and eliminate its waiting list for the first time in fifty years.

Dr. H. L. Newbold in his excellent book *Meganutrients* estimates that between 50 and 75 percent of schizophrenic patients can benefit from an ideal complete orthomolecular regimen, based on the correction of vitamin dependencies.

THE SAME REGIMEN IS ALSO PROVING HELPFUL IN ALCOHOLICS AND DRUG USERS. Case after case has been reported of people who have been able to give up their habit after going on a low-carbohydrate high-vitamin diet.

GREAT RESULTS ARE ALSO BEING FOUND WITH CHILDREN. Those with behavior disorders or who are having difficulty with school are helped tremendously by a new diet plus vitamins.

Dr. Bernard Rimland of the Institute for Child Behavior Research in San Diego, who previously never believed in vitamins, began using vitamins on children after he kept hearing reports from parents and physicians who had tried them.

He decided to do a test of his own with three hundred child patients at his institute. Each parent was required to obtain the cooperation of a local physician to check the child's progress, and astoundingly there was so much physician resistance to the vitamin treatment that many families had to drop out because after going from doctor to doctor they could not find anyone open-minded enough to test whether the vitamins had any effect. Each child daily took vitamin B_3, B_6, pantothenic acid, vitamin C, and sometimes dilantin. There was definite improvement in 45 percent of the children.

THE NEW FRONTIER OF MEDICINE. I have been meeting with many of the leaders of the orthomolecular movement. All agree that these principles of megavitamin therapy have much wider application than in the treatment of nervous and mental diseases. A virtually untapped area of exploration lies in applying these nutritional principles to everyday problems of medical care. You will find that nutrition can help you combat symptoms of fatigue, sleeplessness, recurrent headaches, joint pains, moodiness.

I have tried to approach these everyday problems in medical care using vitamins as therapeutic agents. It has been gratifying to deal with treatments that have almost no potential of producing side effects. I have been able to see such symptoms as insomnia, hot flushes, hay fever, leg cramps, arthritis, skin rashes, hair loss, edema, depression, forgetfulness, emotional outbursts, anxiety, headache, and plain old tiredness clear up by using vitamins in these doses.

The nutrition regimen you are about to begin will start you on the way to learning how meganutrition may apply to you.

17

What you should know about vitamins and minerals

As we study specific vitamins and minerals, we find example after example of ways in which dosages above those recommended by the FDA play a role in nutrition medicine. (Nutrition medicine is the diagnosis, treatment, and prevention of disease with nutrition techniques: vitamins, minerals, and a change in diet.)

We'll discuss the vitamins and minerals in the following sequence: first the water-soluble vitamins, C and the Bs; then the fat-soluble vitamins, E, A, D, and K; and then the minerals and other nutrients.

VITAMIN C

The need for extra vitamin C in man is quite logical. Most animals have the enzymes to synthesize their own vitamin C. Man and apes do not. The animals that do manufacture vitamin C seem to produce it in quantities at the tissue saturation level. This led Dr. Irving Stone and Dr. Linus Pauling to speculate that the proper dose for man would be in the 2,000 mg. or more range, and led to their recommendations of vitamin C in high doses to treat colds.

The experiences of other doctors in treating colds support the recommendation. Dr. Edme Regnier reported "symptoms were tremendously reduced." Dr. H. Curtis Wood, Jr., reported "excellent results" in hundreds of cases.

Since then, four major controlled, "double-blind" tests in Glasgow, Toronto, Dublin, and a Navajo boarding school have been published. All confirm that moderately large doses of vitamin C reduced the incidence and/or the severity of the common cold.

WILL VITAMIN C HELP IN OTHER ILLNESSES? There is evidence that it will. The latest report from Japan shows that in doses of 3 to 6 grams daily it is effective in preventing viral hepatitis. In test tubes it has been shown to inactivate viruses of poliomyelitis, herpes simplex, and rabies.

Dr. Fred Klenner, of Reidsville, North Carolina, has accumulated a vast clinical experience with vitamin C, given in 10 to 60 gram doses, often intravenously in the successful treatment of a wide variety of viral and bacterial infectious diseases.

Vitamin C has long been recognized as essential to the formation of the connective tissue called collagen. In this role, it protects the gums from bleeding, the blood vessels from easy bruising, and it improves the healing of wounds.

As a detoxifying agent it has been found useful to treat several kinds of poisoning. It also helps remove accumulations of toxic heavy metals, copper, lead, and mercury, and has even prolonged life in terminal cancer patients.

VITAMINS AND SMOKING. Vitamin C also seems to neutralize some of the effects of cigarette smoking. One estimate is that one cigarette uses up 25 mg. of vitamin C. A heavy smoker who does not take supplements of vitamin C will be deficient in that vitamin. A one-pack-a-day smoker must take 1 to 3 grams of ascorbic acid to maintain blood levels of that vitamin.

SCHIZOPHRENIA. Vitamin C is an integral part of the antischizophrenia program of orthomolecular psychiatry. When a very large dose of vitamin C is given to schizophrenic patients, they do not excrete the extra vitamin C as completely as do normal people. Their tissues take it up to correct the deficiency state, as much as 3 to 40 grams being necessary to cause spillage in the urine. With vitamin C there is usually a significant improvement in the impaired perception that characterizes schizophrenia.

CHOLESTEROL. Like so many other nutrients, vitamin C is developing quite a track record in reducing serum cholesterol and triglycerides. At the Institute of Human Research in Czechoslovakia, Dr. Emil Ginter gave vitamin C daily to middle-aged men and women and found that in those with high serum cholesterol readings the cholesterol dropped; triglyceride values decreased to almost one-half their previous level.

Many studies have confirmed the beneficial effect of vitamin C in atherosclerosis. Its effectiveness may be due to the fact that it is essential for the conversion of cholesterol into bile, which can be excreted. Or it may be effective because it increases the concentration of substances called chondroitin-4-sulfates, as Dr. Anthony Verangieri of Rutgers University has demonstrated. These same substances have been used experimentally to treat coronary atherosclerosis and were reported to produce an 80 percent decrease in the death rate.

OTHER EFFECTS OF VITAMIN C. In a study of 500 patients who had low back pain, Dr. James Greenwood, Jr., of Baylor University, found a significant number were able to avoid surgery after taking approximately 1 gram of vitamin C per day. Their pain recurred when the vitamin C doses were stopped.

The need for vitamin C is increased during and following serious illnesses, injury, intestinal bleeding, burns, or surgery; and in severe burns or extensive surface injuries vitamin C levels may fall rapidly to zero. Wound problems occurred eight times more often in patients with vitamin C deficiencies than in those with adequate vitamin levels. Giving vitamin C shortens convalescence time.

Dr. Richard Passwater, author of *Supernutrition*, postulates that vitamin C can protect us against carcinogens (cancer-inducing chemicals). He has been able experimentally to reduce the incidence of carcinogen-induced cancers in mice by 90 percent if he simultaneously administers vitamins C and E, plus the trace mineral selenium. And Tulane urologist Dr. Jorgen E. Schlegel has been using vitamin C effectively to prevent recurrences of bladder cancer. Vitamin C can also prevent the formation of nitrosamine, the cancer-causing chemical our body produces after we eat foods preserved in nitrites, such as bacon.

WHAT CAN VITAMIN C CONTRIBUTE TO SUPERENERGY? Not much work has been published on this subject. Dr. H. L. Newbold has observed that "people with low blood sugar generally feel much better on liberal amounts of ascorbic acid." Dr. Carl Pfeiffer has demonstrated that vitamin C has an antianxiety effect, measurable on the electroencephalogram. And Drs. Kubala and Katz were able to demonstrate a significant increase in "mental alertness" and in the IQ measurement of children given enough vitamin C to raise their blood levels.

In my own experience, vitamin C has served as a fatigue fighter, fatigue tending to reappear whenever a patient has neglected to take his usual dose. I also find it useful sometimes in the treatment of allergic conditions such as asthma and hay fever.

THE B COMPLEX

B₃ (NIACIN)—THE VITAMIN THAT BEGAN THE MEGAVITAMIN MOVEMENT. Orthomolecular medicine, the medical treatment of the future, began quietly. Drs. Abram Hoffer and Humphry Osmond in Saskatchewan, Canada, could not shake from their minds the similarity between the psychosis of pellagra, the niacin-deficiency disease, and schizophrenia. In 1952, they treated their first schizophrenic patient with vitamin B₃ and, fortunately for the world today, their results were dramatically successful. I say fortunately because probably less than half of all schizophrenics might respond to such a simple therapy. The two pioneers persisted, learned the efficacy of this vitamin, then of other vitamins given in conjunction, first in schizophrenia, then in other psychiatric problems. They enlisted the interest of a few other psychiatrists, then a few more, who in turn performed other studies, all expanding upon the role of vitamin therapy in a variety of conditions. In 1968, Linus Pauling coined the term "orthomolecular psychiatry" and later, he and Dr. David Hawkins coedited a book with that name, a landmark for the new science.

Orthomolecular psychiatry should by now be a part of the mainstream of psychiatric therapy. But it had the misfortune to be developed during the heyday of the "drugs-for-psychiatry" movement.

Niacin was the cornerstone of this movement based on megavitamin therapy. It was administered in doses of 3 to 20 grams, which is 150 to 1,000 times greater than the 20 mg. RDA.

ARE THERE OTHER CONDITIONS WHERE THIS DOSAGE CAN BE OF VALUE? The mega-dosage has been used clinically in the treatment of children with hyperactivity and learning disabilities, behavior disorders of aging, alcoholism, drug addiction, and other psychiatric illnesses. It has been widely used to lower cholesterol levels, as well.

B_3 has also been used to help smokers reduce their dependency on nicotine, to allow reduced dosages of tranquilizers, and even to help some arthritic conditions.

That large doses of this vitamin would prove necessary was foretold in the 1930s, when anti-pellagra pioneer Dr. Tom Spies found dosages up to 600 mg. were often necessary to treat pellagra effectively. Although we recognize full-blown pellagra as a rare condition, more subtle varieties of it are quite common. Dr. Hoffer described adults with emotionality, depression, and a lack of humor as "minipellagrins." And Dr. R. Glen Green of Saskatchewan gives a brilliant clinical description of "subclinical pellagra" which he found to be quite common and quite responsive to niacin therapy. It is characterized by mild and occasional disturbances of sensory perception such as seeing words moving on a page, or subtle changes in the perception of taste, smell, sound, or body movement.

There are a few precautions. Large doses of niacin can produce an uncomfortable warm itchy "flush" an hour after taking it. Niacinamide avoids this, but occasionally worsens a depression. Peptic ulcer, hyperacidity, and diabetes can be aggravated. An occasional patient may experience headache or nausea. In all these cases, the dosage should be reduced.

HOW DOES NIACIN WORK? It is part of the two most important hydrogen transporting coenzymes (NAD and NADP) in the body. Since more than fifty enzymes have NAD or NADP coenzymes in them, the number of chemical reactions dependent on niacin is almost limitless. It also counteracts the low histamine levels found in a variety of conditions such as sexual dysfunction, hyperactivity, and insomnia.

This fatigue-fighting vitamin also raises the blood sugar levels in the hypoglycemic person. In addition, dietary sugar consumes niacinamide, thus increasing its requirements.

VITAMIN B_6. Pyridoxine—B_6—has long been known by the megavitamin therapists to be one of the most effective agents in their arsenal. And for me, it has been one of the most important additions in the fight for Superenergy.

There are reasons for this. First, the pyridoxal structure governs dozens of chemical reactions, especially those involved in the metabolism of protein. Second, deficiencies are widespread because B_6 is removed from flour in the milling process, but is *not* included in the mandatory enrichment program. To make matters worse, there are many best-selling vitamin preparations almost fraudulently labeled "high potency" which are very low in B_6 content, some containing less than one milligram. In addition, B_6 is easily destroyed by cooking, food processing, and refining. Its level is lowered by the Pill and by the estrogens used to treat menopause. It is wrong to stay on those medications without significant B_6 supplements.

Pyridoxine has been used to treat nausea, including that which follows surgery, edema, toxemia in pregnancy, and premenstrual edema, and it is perhaps the most useful vitamin-diuretic; I have confirmed its ability to combat water retention many times, circumventing the need for diuretic medicines.

Pyridoxine plays an important role in fat and cholesterol metabolism. It can correct a common type of nutritional anemia. It is used to prevent kidney stones. Dr. Platon J. Collipp and his associates showed it can improve asthmatic children significantly.

It can even have dramatic effects on some kinds of childhood epilepsy. One investigator found infants with abnormal brain waves improved within minutes when vitamin B_6 was injected.

Scientific papers have also been written describing its use in Parkinsonism, peripheral neuritis, acne, psoriasis, hair loss, ulcers, and a variety of psychiatric problems.

Dr. Carl Pfeiffer uses it extensively to treat the high histamine levels, low zinc and high copper levels, and the high level of kryptopyrrole which are often seen in schizophrenics.

All these abnormalities return to normal when 600 to 1600 mg. of B_6 are given. These same chemical abnormalities occur in many psychiatrically "normal" patients; when they are corrected, many of these individuals' symptoms clear up. One of these symptoms is inability to lose weight while dieting carefully. I have found that many such people will lose weight when these doses of B_6 are given along with zinc.

DO YOU REMEMBER YOUR DREAMS? Everybody dreams, but not everybody can remember the details. Dr. Pfeiffer discovered that this ability, when lost, will come back when the proper amount of B_6 is given. If you can't remember your dreams, increase your intake of this vitamin to the point where you can.

Many of my patients report that they did remember their dreams regularly but "stopped dreaming" after childbirth or since going on the Pill.

Drs. John Ellis and Roger Williams have shown the value of B_6 in the treatment of rheumatoid arthritis.

Ellis's sign helps test for B_6 deficiency. Bend your fingers so the tips touch where your fingers join your hand. If they don't touch, you may well have a B_6 deficiency.

I consider B_6 to be one of the most essential vitamins for Superenergy. When I evaluate a B complex formulation, or a multivitamin pill, the first thing I look for is its B_6 content. I find little use for those that contain less than 25 mg.

VITAMIN B_1—THIAMINE. This was the first B vitamin discovered, being isolated in 1911 from the rice polishings that prevent beriberi. It is essential to the functioning of the central nervous system. When it is deficient, there can be numbness in the arms and legs, or a tingling or burning sensation. Powers of concentration, memory, mood, and perception may be affected. Fatigue and depression can be caused.

Like other B vitamins, thiamine is lost in the milling of wheat or the polishing of rice. And thiamine requirements are much higher among people who consume sugar or significant amounts of alcohol. The government's RDAs fail to take this into account.

Five hundred to 2,000 mg. daily will provide the key to fatigue problems in some patients.

Deficiencies of thiamine are somewhat less prevalent than others of the B complex, probably because thiamine is included in the enrichment program and stressed in multiple vitamin preparations, but it has been used to treat hundreds of conditions and must be included in any program involving the B complex.

VITAMIN B_2—RIBOFLAVIN. Cracking and inflammation at the edges of the lips, a reddened inflamed tongue, and bloodshot, burning, tearing and light-sensitive eyes are signs of B_2 deficiency.

Riboflavin levels were found to be low in the plasma of many rheumatoid arthritis patients. Another study links B_2 deficiency to mental depression, and recent work suggests it may play a role in the prevention and cure of cataracts.

B_2 is replaced in enrichment programs and has not been widely used in megavitamin regimens.

It should, of course, be included in quantities proportionate to the B_1 and the rest of the B complex.

ONE OF THE "BIGGIES" FOR SEEKERS OF SUPERENERGY —PANTOTHENIC ACID. This B vitamin has a key role in energy metabolism because it is part of coenzyme A which helps form the most pivotal of all metabolic compounds—acetyl coenzyme A. Acetyl Co A, as it is called, is the common end point of the metabolism of protein, fat, and carbohydrate, and it can break down to form energy or can be used to manufacture cholesterol, the steroid or sex hormones, or antibodies.

Pantothenic acid was discovered by nutritionist Roger Williams. It is used in megavitamin therapy and has been safe at any dose tried up to this point.

Pantothenic acid is a biochemical precursor of the adrenal hormones and is found in great quantities within the adrenal gland tissues, so nutrition pioneers have tried it in those conditions where adrenal hormone therapies might be used—arthritis, allergies, asthma, stress reactions and hypoglycemia. Dr. Elaine Ralli and her associates, for example, found that patients given high doses seemed better able to withstand emotional stress. I have confirmed all of these applications in numerous patients; it is safer than cortisone or other steroids and should be tried first, reserving the stronger therapy for those cases where pantothenic acid (and the other vitamins that must accompany it) does not do the trick. Dosages must be in the 500–1500 mg. range. Note that when given in the form of calcium pantothenate, it can induce drowsiness. This quality can make it valuable as a "sleep" vitamin.

INOSITOL. This is a B vitamin which I personally have found to be invaluable. No one has yet proved any clearcut deficiency state and so the FDA carries it under the heading "Need in human nutrition has not been established."

But inositol is one of those nutrients that is lost when whole wheat, which was its major source, is refined into flour, some 87 percent of it being lost in the process; and it is not restored through enrichment.

Inositol is a constituent of an important class of body chemicals called phospholipids, which are important in atherosclerosis prevention and in brain metabolism. Both cholesterol and total lipid levels have been reduced by giving 3 grams of inositol daily to older patients.

Inositol's effect on the brain is similar to that of a moderate-to-mild tranquilizer-sedative. Dr. Pfeiffer finds 2000 mg. per day to be an effective treatment for high blood pressure. I have found 2000 mg. of inositol taken at bedtime to be a remarkable sleeping medication in many patients; and 650 mg. makes an effective daytime sedative. And how much safer it is than sleeping pills!

CHOLINE. This B vitamin is a provider of the methyl group which is needed for an endless variety of biochemical reactions, but it is not essential because other nutrients—methionine, betaine, vitamin B_{15}, folic acid, and B_{12}—can serve the same function. However, all these nutrients are often in short supply and methyl groups must be provided through some means.

Dr. Lester M. Morrison and W. F. Gonzales reported the effectiveness of choline in reducing the death rate in a matched study of 230 patients. For some reason, this promising lead never has been followed up.

BIOTIN. Like the rest of the B complex, biotin serves as a coenzyme for a large number of enzymes. Eating too many raw egg whites will destroy biotin. But biotin is readily made by intestinal bacteria, and so little is needed that deficiencies are unlikely.

PABA. Para-aminobenzoic acid plays several roles in the body, and for a very high number of my patients is a key to Superenergy. In fact, whenever a patient does not achieve Superenergy from the standard vitamin-mineral regimen and the diet, the addition most likely to wipe out fatigue is PABA, given in doses of at least 1000 mg.

In a Soviet study 450 mg. of PABA was shown to lower cholesterol in one-half of the patients tested.

PABA is known to act as an effective sun protectant. It has been used with benefit in a variety of skin conditions. I have found it to be dramatically effective in some of my patients with bone and joint disorders.

Since a 1941 study by Dr. Benjamin Sieve, several studies report that PABA is effective against graying of the hair, but the majority opinion is that PABA is not effective in combating gray hair. So, why don't we keep a registry to settle the question once and for all? Will every reader whose gray hair turns dark at the roots after taking PABA (the dose would have to be over 1000 mg. per day) please include that information on the diet questionnaire you return to us?

FOLIC ACID—A KEY TO VITAMIN THERAPY. How often have you heard people say: "I've taken a lot of vitamins, but I don't feel any better"? The overwhelming majority of those people for whom vitamin therapy does not seem to work either do not follow a careful enough *diet* along with their vitamins, or their vitamin regimen does not contain enough folic acid.

Folic acid deficiencies are widespread. The Ten-State Survey showed low levels of folate in the red blood cells, a rather far advanced deficiency finding, in over half the population of Michigan. A Canada survey found it to be the single most prevalent deficiency among the nutrients tested.

The reasons for folate deficiencies are clear. Folic acid is easily destroyed by cooking or canning; 50 to 95 percent may be destroyed by these processes. Alcohol intake interferes with its use also. Alcoholics, in fact, are almost all severely deficient in folic acid. They cannot absorb it or vitamin B_1 or B_6 from food even a week after they stop drinking.

The Pill, as well as estrogen and pregnancy, causes a major loss of folic acid. Vitamin C increases urinary excretion of folic acid and therefore the body's demands increase. Further, many people do not absorb it properly.

The FDA has placed an exceedingly low restriction on the folic acid content of multivitamin pills—just one-tenth of a milligram—and reduced the largest dose available with a doctor's prescription to just one milligram. Contrast this with the Canadian regulations which quite properly allow for the over-the-counter sale of a 5 mg. preparation.

Nature put folic acid in the B complex, but the FDA took it out.

Folic deficiency is a well-known cause of megaloblastic anemia, but the earlier stages are much more prevalent than the late anemic stage. According to folic acid expert, Dr. Victor Herbert, the symptoms may include irritability, forgetfulness, weakness, tiredness, diarrhea, headache, palpitations, and shortness of breath. To this list Dr. Carl Pfeiffer adds: agitation, moodiness, depression, delusions, hallucinations, and paranoia. I will personally confirm its great value in correcting these symptoms, and add one more—the decreased sex drive seen in heavy drinkers. One alcoholic relabeled it "frolic acid."

It should be given with caution in patients with seizure disorders, and always with vitamin B_{12}. Not all patients feel better on high doses of folic acid. Some will feel worse. I'm sure this correlates with Dr. Pfeiffer's work showing that many patients have low levels of histamine, which is raised to normal with folic acid. However, a small number of patients have histamine levels which are too high, and they get worse on folic acid.

VITAMIN B_{12}. May the Lord forgive me for all the times in my early career when I thought that doctors who gave their patients B_{12} shots were quacks. I have since learned how often that type of therapy works as a fatigue fighter.

Much of what was said about folic acid can be said about B_{12}. It, too, is corrective of an anemia, pernicious anemia. But all too often the thinking of the medical profession goes something like this. "B_{12} is used in the treatment of pernicious anemia, so using it for any other condition is quackery." Scientifically, nothing could be further from the truth.

B_{12}, the cobalt-containing vitamin, is part of a coenzyme involved in the metabolism of proteins, fats, and carbohydrates. It is involved in the formation of the sheaths of nerve fibers and its deficiency produces a well-recognized form of neuritis. Poor growth, a sore tongue, and most of the symptoms of folate deficiency are seen in B_{12} deficiency.

B_{12} is sometimes difficult to absorb when taken by mouth. Therefore, it is customarily given by injection.

Actually, it is not easy to become *deficient* in B_{12} because it is stored rather well in the body. However, it is not readily available in vegetable foods, being found mainly in animal protein foods, and vegetarians often get a B_{12} deficiency. B_{12} is lost in women on The Pill, people taking large amounts of vitamin C or the drug dilantin, or those who consume alcohol in large quantities.

PANGAMIC ACID—VITAMIN B_{15}. This vitamin is recognized in many nations, but not in the United States, even though it was discovered by an American, Dr. Ernst T. Krebs, Jr.

Pangamic acid, an important methyl donor, is used widely in Russia. During a 1964 Moscow symposium, thirty-four papers were read, all indicating a consistently reproducible benefit in heart disease. B_{15} tends to lower the cholesterol level and provides oxygenation to the heart muscle. It is valuable in combating alcoholism and alcohol intoxication. It reduces sugar levels in mild diabetes. And all without side effects.

Of interest to Superenergy seekers are the Soviet studies done on rowers. Lactic acid increase was less than half of its ordinary value when B_{15} was used, and the rowers reported less fatigue.

The distressing fact is that even though this international meeting was held in 1964, no one in the United States has picked up this valuable lead and evaluated it. The fact that the best of Soviet cardiologists participated in these studies involving more than one thousand patients has apparently not created a dent in American medicine.

I have used this remarkable vitamin, and there is no doubt

in my mind that it works extremely well and should be allowed to take its place with the other members of the B complex.

VITAMIN B_{17}—ALSO CALLED AMYGDALIN OR LAETRILE. This vitamin too was developed by Dr. Krebs, being extractable from seeds of many fruits, especially the apricot kernel. It seems to be a good treatment for sickle cell anemia.

Laetrile is the center of a furor over the fact that it has been used in over twenty thousand cancer victims as a palliative. It is quite legal in at least twenty-three medically sophisticated nations. Among many researchers, Dr. Hans Nieper of Hannover, West Germany, and Ernesto Contreras of Tijuana, Mexico, have reported many successes with a combination of nontoxic cancer chemotherapy based in part upon this vitamin's effect on the dividing cancer cell.

The closed-mindedness directed against this vitamin, which seems to prolong life, or at least relieve suffering, in otherwise hopeless cancer patients, will surely go down as one of the blackest pages in our medical history. It can only be a matter of time before research done in other countries demonstrates its efficacy to the point where the public will clamor for the proper clinical testing of laetrile.

The pertinence of this discussion in this context is not to tell you that B_{17} fights cancer or that it's good for your fatigue, but to show you the extent to which some medical leaders will go to suppress medical advances. The incredible story of the suppression of laetrile is chronicled in the books *B-17* by Michael Culbert and *World Without Cancer* by E. Glen Griffin.

THE FAT-SOLUBLE VITAMINS

The fat-soluble vitamins pose a problem that does not have to be faced with vitamins B and C, namely, they can accumulate in the body. In this group, overdosage can be a problem.

VITAMIN E—TOCOPHEROL. In no case are the battle lines against vitamins more clearly drawn than in the case of vitamin E. Doctors either think it's worthless or is the greatest.

I'm in the latter group . . . I think vitamin E can be of extreme value. It is one of the nutrients removed from wheat and not replaced; accordingly, the national intake is rather low, and deficiencies are quite possible.

Vitamin E seems to have a beneficial effect on wound healing and scar formations. Widely heralded as a treatment for heart disease, its use to diminish the cardiac pain called angina pectoris has provided "mixed reviews." But doctors have found benefit in peripheral artery disease, in easing pain of blood vessel spasms, and in preventing blood clots after surgery.

It has also been successful in treating hemolytic anemia, chronic cysts in women's breasts, leg cramps that occur at night, and various skin conditions.

Also heralded as a sex vitamin, it occasionally will improve male impotence. And I have confirmed in hundreds of patients that it effectively combats the distressing hot flushes of the menopause. When vitamin E is given early in the menopause, the menstrual cycle frequently returns and endometrial smears indicate a higher degree of estrogen activity.

I am convinced, too, of the usefulness of vitamin E in preventing some pregnancy complications, such as repeated miscarriages. It also combats the toxic effects of industrial pollutants, cigarette smoke, and polyunsaturated fatty acids.

There are many complex biochemical reasons that vitamin E might ultimately prove to help slow the aging process, one reason why I make sure to take at least 800 units daily.

FOR SUPERENERGY SEEKERS. Vitamin E has proved to be a useful part of our nutrition program. It seems to have a normalizing effect on blood sugar after a few months. It may promote a little weight gain. Therefore, I use larger doses in the need-to-gain Diet # 2 than in the weight-losing Diet #1.

Vitamin E should be used with caution if you have a tendency to high blood pressure or a history of rheumatic fever. But very little in the way of vitamin E toxicity has been reported even in large groups of subjects taking more than 2000 units daily. If one starts with 200 units and gradually builds to 600 to 1200 units, most toxicity problems are avoided.

VITAMIN A. The chances of your having a vitamin A deficiency are fairly great. Recently at the Western Hemisphere

Nutrition Congress, held in Miami Beach, Dr. John G. Bieri, National Institute of Health biochemist, said that vitamin A deficiency is probably the most common worldwide vitamin problem. Some surveys indicate that as much as 30 percent of the population has below average concentrations of vitamin A.

Vitamin A is essential to normal growth and to the health of the mucous membranes and skin. It is necessary to prevent night blindness. In this regard its dosage can be regulated with a do-it-yourself test. If you drive at night with oncoming traffic and can't distinguish the dividing line in your lane, it means you have night blindness and you need more vitamin A.

You should also suspect a vitamin A deficiency if you develop boils, acne, dryness, flakiness, skin rashes, itchy eyes, dry and brittle hair, loss of appetite, or increased susceptibility to infections.

In intriguing recent developments, vitamin A has been shown to have cancer-inhibiting effects in some animal tumors. It seems to protect body tissue against infection also; and at a recent American Chemical Society meeting, Dr. Eli Seifter of New York described it as a powerful agent against viruses, greatly enhancing the body's immune response. A team of surgeons in Phoenix, Arizona, found that the vitamin helped prevent stress ulcer bleeding in patients who were injured, burned or who had surgery.

Since vitamin A increases the lubrication of mucous membranes, it is of benefit to such diverse problems as irritation from contact lenses and dryness of vaginal membranes in intercourse.

Despite all the publicity about dangers of vitamin A, there are only a few recorded cases of persons who took too much vitamin A and suffered distress, and these were people who had taken huge doses of 100,000 and 600,000 units a day for months or years before they had reactions. Overdose is, of course, to be avoided, but don't avoid taking supplements because of false fears.

The general rule: any time it's necessary to go over 10,000 units a day it should be done only under a physician's care.

VITAMIN D. This vitamin can be considered a hormone. It regulates the metabolism of calcium and phosphorus. Too much is as bad as too little. Please avoid the pitfalls of too many amateur vitamin-takers—*don't* take three or more D-containing multivitamin pills daily without being aware of the risk.

VITAMIN K. This is a clotting factor which can be risky in large doses, therefore, it is rarely included in multiple vitamin preparations. It is plentiful in a diet consisting of dark green leafy vegetables, liver, and egg yolk.

MINERALS

Medicine is now just entering the era of the trace minerals. Really significant discoveries in nutrition are emerging from this exciting new area of research.

There are several groupings of minerals necessary to human nutrition. The soluble minerals, which are essential to life at the cellular level, include sodium, potassium, and chlorine. Then there are the minerals which are part of our bones: calcium, magnesium, and phosphorus. There are the other essential microminerals: iron, iodine, and sulfur. The rest are trace minerals—needed in only small amounts by the body, but vitally needed; they *must* be provided for the body to function because they cannot be synthesized.

SODIUM, POTASSIUM, CHLORINE. Since these are present in all foods, it is virtually impossible to have a deficiency of these elements under ordinary circumstances. But shortages can occur with prolonged vomiting or diarrhea, sunstroke, burns, dehydration, kidney disease, hormonal imbalances, diuretic therapy, or sometimes when salt restriction used in the management of high blood pressure or water retention is too effective, and the resulting weakness is called the low sodium syndrome.

Potassium losses may occur in very strict effective diets such as fasting, or a low-carbohydrate diet in someone with low potassium reserves, so dieting can be a risk if done in conjunction with diuretics or sodium and potassium restriction.

CALCIUM—THE BODY'S MOST ABUNDANT ELEMENT. We need approximately 1000 mg. of calcium per day. If our diet is deficient in it, the body will rob the calcium out of the bones, and osteoporosis (porous bones) will result.

According to the U.S. Department of Agriculture's survey, three out of every ten families showed calcium intakes below the recommended minimum.

Milk is the best source of calcium. But for those who must avoid milk because of lactose intolerance or because they must adhere to a low-carbohydrate diet, cheese, particularly the harder kinds, can provide the minimum requirement with just four ounces.

CALCIUM CAN BE GOOD TREATMENT FOR HYPOGLYCEMIA. Several of the hypoglycemia pioneers of twenty-five years ago used intravenous calcium infusions in the treatment of this condition. I am particularly aware of calcium deficiency when a patient complains of leg cramps, restlessness, irritability, or fatigue while climbing stairs.

Calcium levels tend to be depressed in a patient who has been on long-term diuretics. It will drop if someone who drinks a lot of milk suddenly curtails his intake, as when he goes on this diet. In these cases, adequate calcium supplementation must be provided.

Calcium, like cholesterol, is one of the substances found in the lining of the arteries in arteriosclerotic patches. This does not mean that calcium *causes* arteriosclerosis. Nonetheless, the removal of this calcium provides the basis of a very effective means of treatment, called chelation. Excessive calcium can cause tetany (spastic muscles) and kidney stones.

MAGNESIUM. Like calcium, magnesium is involved in the structure of bone and the transmission of nerve and muscle impulses. Magnesium, in addition, plays a key role in enzymatic reactions used to provide energy.

And magnesium *can* be deficient. Those who avoid nuts, seeds, and dark green vegetables and those who drink heavily run a good risk of being magnesium deficient. So, too, is magnesium deficiency a possible consequence of long-term diuretic usage, malabsorption, intravenous feedings, or kidney or liver disease. High sugar intake has been implicated as a cause of magnesium loss, and 85 percent of the magnesium content of wheat is removed by milling it to flour. Levels are lowered further if you use estrogen pills, or have high intakes of vitamin D or high fat intake.

Magnesium is essential for vitamins to be absorbed properly. Marginal deficiencies of magnesium can lead to atherosclerosis, depression, irritability, restlessness, convulsions, dizziness, muscle weakness, high blood pressure, sweating, painful cold hands and feet, and upsets in heart rhythm.

A proper amount of magnesium is tremendously important for a healthy heart, and death from heart attack is much less prevalent among people who live where there is hard water which has more magnesium. The death rate goes up if hard water is softened.

Dr. Roger Williams cites experiments showing that magnesium protects rats from atherosclerosis and brings about dramatic improvements in patients with angina. Excellent results are reported in South America, Europe, and Great Britain where magnesium is used in treating angina and even in treating patients during heart attack where it is injected immediately, followed by regular injections during the entire recovery period, to improve the rate of survival.

NOTE: It is important for the magnesium you take to be balanced with calcium, about one part magnesium to two parts calcium, a proportion found in the naturally occurring mineral called dolomite, an excellent supplement. Many mineral supplements have the proper 1 to 2 balance.

PHOSPHORUS. In the form of phosphate, phosphorus is essential in the chemical reactions involved with the liberation of energy fuel.

Phosphates should be in a balance with calcium, and this is regulated by the parathyroid hormone and by vitamin D. High protein food, except for cheeses, tend to be high in phosphorus, but low in calcium, so a calcium supplement is recommended in conjunction with most diets, including these.

SULFUR. This mineral exists as a sulfate or sulfhydryl molecule of the structure of the important sulfur-containing amino acids. Nutritional deficiencies of sulfur are not known to occur, but the sulfur-containing amino acids are quite essential to nutrition, and eggs provide one of the best sources.

IRON—THE MOST IMPORTANT OF THE MICROMINERALS. Iron is essential to the formation of hemoglobin, which carries the oxygen in the red blood cells. Iron has been well promoted as a dietary supplement, yet deficiencies are quite common.

Fatigue frequently is caused by iron deficiency anemia, either when dietary intake of iron is inadequate or when there is a chronic loss of blood such as from heavy menstrual periods or from a silently bleeding ulcer.

Common symptoms of iron deficiency are: weakness, depression, dizziness, and fatigue.

It is difficult to get enough iron in food. Even the Food and Nutrition Board notes that the RDAs "cannot be met by ordinary food products in respect to iron," and it says that there is iron deficiency in two-thirds of menstruating women and in most pregnant women. Millions of men have it too.

Even if you find you have iron-deficiency anemia, remember, it may not be the only answer. If you have iron-deficiency anemia, do treat it, but still go on with the rest of the diet too.

I do not recommend megadoses of iron because it can be deposited in tissues and cause side effects when taken in large amounts. I try to ensure that the iron content of supplements falls into the 12 to 18 mg. per day range. When treating a nutritional anemia, I make sure to provide vitamin C, zinc, B_6, and vitamin E as well as iron.

NOTE: It's best to take iron between meals rather than at meals, and it is best to take it in the form of ferrous sulfate and not in time-release capsules which cause late absorption too far down in the intestine. Don't take vitamin E and iron at the same time of day since they compete.

If you have thalassemia or sickle cell disease or a blood disease called hemochromatosis, iron should not be taken because it causes an iron overload.

Anyone who has an iron-deficiency anemia should work with a physician to find the underlying causes, since an ulcer, or even cancer of the lower intestine, can cause bleeding.

ZINC—MOST CRITICAL OF THE TRACE MINERALS. Zinc is a part of some two dozen enzymes including one which releases carbon dioxide from the blood, and one closely related to insulin.

Because so much zinc is removed in the milling, refining, and canning processes, probabilities of zinc deficiency are very real. And since zinc is an important constituent of egg yolk, those who have bought the "avoid eggs" propaganda are further subject to zinc deficits. Low zinc levels are often found in patients with leg ulcers, diabetes, alcoholic cirrhosis, schizophrenia, cystic fibrosis, and chronic infections.

Zinc is necessary for the uptake of vitamins B_{12} and A. It is a specific therapy for an impaired sense of taste. More than four thousand patients with this problem have been treated by Dr. R. I. Henkin and P. J. Schechter at the National Institutes of Health.

Zinc supplements do wonders at speeding up healing of wounds, skin ulcers, sores, burns, and surgical incisions. A U.S. Air Force study showed that men with standard treatment after a serious operation took sixty-two days for healing, but men taking a zinc capsule every day healed in forty-five days.

And latest animal research at the Human Nutrition Laboratory in North Dakota shows that if the mother has a zinc deficiency during pregnancy, the *offspring* are abnormally aggressive, are less tolerant of stress, have decreased learning ability, and smaller brains.

Zinc has begun to play a major role in nutritional psychiatry, particularly since the painstaking biochemical discoveries of Dr. Carl Pfeiffer, whose work exemplifies how knowledge of nutritional processes can lead to mastery of a seemingly hopeless illness.

Dr. Pfeiffer demonstrated that zinc is a biologic antagonist to copper and could normalize the high copper, low zinc levels seen in so many schizophrenic patients. (This, incidentally, is the same pattern repeatedly observed in women taking The Pill, and may help explain the psychiatric difficulties some of them get into.) Thirty percent of Dr. Pfeiffer's schizophrenic patients excrete a compound kryptopyrrole, which can be eliminated with large doses of zinc and B_6.

Zinc also can lower cadmium levels. Dr. Henry Schroeder's research indicates that high cadmium levels can be a major cause of high blood pressure. He recommends 30 mg. of zinc daily to lower cadmium. Because of the safety of zinc, I'm inclined to use somewhat larger doses.

Low zinc levels should be suspected if you have white spots on your fingernails.

MANGANESE. Like several other trace minerals, manganese is a factor in many coenzymes, in this case, involving the thyroid function and acetylcholine formation. It is almost completely removed from milled wheat. Deficiencies have been demonstrated in many kinds of animals, causing defects in brain function, fat and sugar metabolism, bone formation, growth, and reproduction.

It is obviously essential in man and must be provided for. It has been shown to work in conjunction with zinc in many of its reactions. It is absorbed rather poorly from the digestive tract.

COPPER—A GOOD-BAD MINERAL. Copper is essential to many enzyme reactions, but a problem occurs when levels get too high. Nutrition psychiatrists have found high copper levels in many schizophrenic patients. When these levels are lowered by increasing the intake of zinc and manganese, there can be a major clinical improvement.

Copper excess can produce everyday problems too, such as insomnia, depression, headaches, stretch marks, gray hair, and hair loss. And high serum copper levels are found in conditions such as viral and bacterial infections, rheumatoid arthritis, heart attacks, malignancies, cirrhosis, and leukemia. Even the copper from copper water pipes can cause a problem. In view of these findings, I now consider it wise to switch to vitamin and mineral preparations that contain zinc with very little or no copper.

IODINE. Iodine provides the thyroid gland with an essential building block for thyroid hormone. Iodine deficiency leads to a goiter; excess iodine is mostly excreted. This does not mean that large doses of kelp, the iodine-containing seaweed, can be taken with complete safety, since both under- and overactivity of the thyroid can result from excess iodine intake. But at least enough kelp or seafood or iodized salt should be included in your diet to provide one-tenth of a milligram of iodine per day.

COBALT. The prime function of cobalt is to be a part of vitamin B_{12}. In animals, there is a need for cobalt beyond that in B_{12}, but this has not been demonstrated in humans.

SELENIUM—AS IMPORTANT AS VITAMIN E. This is because many of their functions overlap. Selenium has effects as an antioxidant of fats, and scavenger of free radicals much the same way as vitamin E. It is important in the prevention of heart disease. High selenium soil areas seem to have a decreased incidence of cancer and of heart disease.

Not enough is known about selenium to state whether deficiencies are prevalent, or even possible. It is sparsely distributed in the vegetable kingdom, although adequately represented in meat.

CHROMIUM—THE ONE MOST IMPORTANT MINERAL TO PROVIDE FOR. Almost everyone on the American diet probably fails to get enough chromium. Although levels of minerals almost always increase with age, chromium does not. Dr. Henry Schroeder in his important book *The Trace Elements and Man* points out chromium was undetectable in the major artery of "almost every person dying of coronary artery disease . . . and was present in almost every aorta of persons dying accidentally." And he calculated that the 150 grams of sugar we consume daily leads to a net loss of 8.75 mg. of chromium per year, more than the body's total content! Until very recently, there was no way to take chromium in pill form so that it could be adequately absorbed.

Dr. Walter Mertz showed that chromium was necessary for the utilization of insulin; he called it the "glucose tolerance factor."

You can obtain chromium in the diet through brewers' yeast and some nuts.

OTHER MINERALS. Other minerals essential to man include molybdenum, vanadium, nickel, and tin. Others such as lead, mercury, cadmium, and beryllium may be toxic to man. Lithium and fluoride must be treated like pharmaceuticals, being capable of *either* clinical benefit *or* toxicity.

OTHER NUTRIENTS

There are many compounds found in the body that are considered nutrients, but are not vitamins or minerals. They can sometimes give therapeutic effects. Examples: the orotates, aspartates, deanol, betaine, and lecithin.

Individual amino acids, the building blocks of protein, can be of extreme value in medicine. For example, tryptophan, given in doses greater than 1,500 mg., makes a remarkable sleep-inducing sedative and antidepressant. Another, glutamine, has proved useful in reducing cravings for alcohol in heavy drinkers.

Then there are food sources which contain many nutrients, some of which may be as yet undiscovered. Therefore, their inclusion in the diet may provide benefits beyond taking all the *known* vitamins and minerals. The classic examples are brewers' yeast and liver extract. In this category I would also place ginseng, wheat germ, bran, kelp, and bee pollen.

18

Tailoring your own vitamin and mineral program

Now that you have a thumbnail knowledge of the philosophy behind vitamin and mineral therapy, how can you put it into practice so that it makes sense for you?

No two people's needs are alike; and neither are their responses to vitamins.

You will be evaluating two aspects of nutrition at the same time—diet and vitamin-minerals. In my practice, I start the diet and the vitamin-mineral supplements at the same time, but that's mainly for office convenience.

It is more scientific for you to start the vitamins first. That way if there is any benefit or problem you will know what is responsible.

However, most people are really eager to start the entire program at once while enthusiasm is high, so three or four days on the vitamins alone is plenty of time.

There are four phases of vitamin therapy:
1. Basic formula
2. Experimentation (building up)
3. Tapering down
4. Maintenance

YOUR BASIC FORMULA. The nucleus of the basic formula is a good multiple vitamin-mineral formula. There are several formulations that I find suitable. Most are obtainable from a health food store or a drugstore that carries some of the vitamins distributed by vitamin specialists rather than pharmaceutical houses. Many of the ethical drug companies' formulations are based on older formulas and tend to be pitifully low in B_6, zinc, and magnesium and too high in copper. Nor do they often contain significant amounts of the important nutrients PABA, choline, inositol, bioflavonoids, or biotin.

One typical multiple vitamin supplement I use has twenty-eight different vitamins and minerals, but I use it primarily for content of vitamins A (10,000 units) and D (400 units). (The remainder of the formula is of less importance as long as it will be supplemented by additions of B complex, C complex, E, folic acid, and trace minerals.) Take one of these each day to provide the base line.

THE B COMPLEX. My preference is for the B-50 formula which contains 50 mg. each of B_1, B_2, B_3, B_6, pantothenic acid, choline, inositol, and PABA plus 50 mcg. of biotin and B_{12}, and that tiny dash of folic acid that the law limits us to. Taken three times a day this guarantees 150 mg. each of eight B complex constituents. The best key to a B complex formula is B_6; it should contain 50 mg., or as a minimum 25 mg. of B_6. *Take three B complex capsules spaced through the day, preferably one at the end of each meal.*

FOLIC ACID. I cannot imagine that the proper dose of folic acid could be less than 3 mg. per day. Therefore, I recommend 1 mg. (with your doctor's prescription) three times a day for a starter program. Without a prescription one would have to take eight of the 0.4 mg. strength. Canadian purchasers can take 5 mg. once daily. Heavy drinkers and women on The Pill or estrogen should take 6 mg. or more.

VITAMIN C COMPLEX. When you take vitamin C tablets it is important that bioflavonoids, rutin, and hesperidin be included. There is a rather high incidence of canker sores, bruising, and bleeding gums—the very things vitamin C is supposed to prevent—if the preparation does not include the bioflavonoids. About 500 mg. of ascorbic acid and 100 mg. of bioflavonoids, taken three times a day, is suitable for the basic formula. Heavy smokers should use somewhat more. These doses of C can cause diarrhea in some persons. This may be because of the filler, and may often be circumvented by using another brand or ascorbic acid powder (4 grams in one teaspoon).

Many vitamin C preparations contain sugar or other carbohydrate as the filler, even though it will not be so labeled. This is particularly true of the chewable types. Eschew the chewable.

VITAMIN E. A conservative starting point might be to use 200 units of the d-alpha tocopherol form of vitamin E per day. This is probably safe even in the potentially risky situations of hypertension and rheumatic fever. Take with any meal, but not simultaneously with iron-containing preparations. The average dose may come to 800 units in men, 600 in women, more if menopause or vascular disease must be combated.

MINERALS. A good formula which is chelated (formed into a complex molecule) with amino acids should be used if possible. Your daily total should reach 30 mg. of elemental zinc, 15 mg. of iron, 400 mg. of magnesium, and 5 mg. of manganese. Chromium is currently a problem to find; when a product becomes available which provides an absorbable form of chromium, try to take 1 to 3 mg. per day.

Take minerals in divided doses immediately after meals.

If your diet is low in cheese or milk, calcium in the form of bone meal or dolomite should be added to the point where at least 800 mg. are taken per day.

BREWERS' YEAST. This important all-around nutrient source should be included, one teaspoon being a minimum dose.

MY IDEA OF A COMPREHENSIVE VITAMIN FORMULA. When Diet Revolution Centers, a nationwide group of diet counseling centers with which I'm affiliated, asked me to devise an all-purpose vitamin and mineral formula, I devised one that provides the following *total* daily quantities.

Vitamin A	10,000 I.U.
Vitamin D	400 I.U.

Vitamin B-1 (Thiamine)	100 mg.
Vitamin B-2 (Riboflavin)	75 mg.
Vitamin C	1,500 mg.
Niacin	50 mg.
Niacinamide	100 mg.
Calcium	600 mg.
Vitamin B-6 (Pyridoxine)	200 mg.
PABA	1,200 mg.
Calcium Pantothenate	150 mg.
Folic Acid	3.6 mg.
Vitamin B-12	750 mcg.
Vitamin E	200 I.U.
Magnesium	300 mg.
Manganese	6 mg.
Zinc	45 mg.
Choline	750 mg.
Inositol	450 mg.
Biotin	300 mcg.
Rutin	45 mg.
Bioflavonoids	300 mg.
Iron (as ferrous fumarate)	18 mg.
Iodine (as kelp)	225 mcg.

ONCE YOU HAVE ESTABLISHED YOUR BASIC FORMULA

Take the vitamin and mineral supplements for a few days just to make sure you're not getting any stomach distress from all the pills you've begun swallowing. Vitamins obviously were intended to be taken by mouth and are extremely nontoxic substances; therefore, if you have an unfavorable reaction, it could very well be to the binder or filler that comes with the vitamin. So many of my patients warn me: "I can't take vitamins," but usually a form that can be administered without difficulty can be located.

Now comes the big moment in which you turn your attention to diet. Pick the diet you will be following and do it so carefully that there can be no doubt as to your conformity. Find your best level and take inventory again. Reevaluate your energy and your mood scores. Do you feel better than ever, or is there room for improvement? Do some symptoms remain?

THE EXPERIMENTATION PHASE. If you're not yet at your best, it is appropriate to see what benefits you can derive from increasing dosages of certain vitamins and minerals.

There are several nutrients which you can take in what I call "step-out" doses. The idea is to try each new dose for a week and decide whether it has benefited you. In chapter 16, I pointed out that vitamins may have functions beyond those involved in being a part of an enzyme system. Oxidizers, anti-oxidants, methyl donors, hydrogen acceptors, free radical de-activators—all these are biochemical terms describing the other important nutritional roles that vitamins play.

IF YOU ARE WORKING WITH YOUR DOCTOR. Your doctor, if he is interested in your experiment, can help in this phase, because of the value that might result from vitamin B_{12} injections. Usually 500 to 1000 mcg. are given in one intramuscular shot. Those who feel B_{12} is a panacea and those who feel it is only of value in pernicious anemia are both quite wrong. When I give B_{12} I ask my patients to pay careful attention to how they feel over the next several days. After thousands of observations, I have noticed that they divide into three approximately equal groups: one group feels nothing different; one group thinks maybe the shot helped a little; and the other group reports that the shot had a dramatic effect, producing a striking feeling of well-being, but one that usually doesn't last.

If you're in that last group, you will then know you're a B_{12}-responder. If B_{12} works, you should plan to receive the injection at regular intervals. Learn when the "lift" begins to wear off and get a booster shot at that time. The interval between injections can be increased if you take some B_{12} by mouth (100–250 mcg. four times a day) or use the hydroxycobalamin injection instead of regular B_{12}.

THE EXPERIMENTS YOU CAN DO YOURSELF. PABA (para-aminobenzoic acid) can be the key to Superenergy for many people when taken in "step-out" doses of 1,500 to 2,000 mg. per day. The more convenient dosage form of 500 mg. sometimes requires your doctor's prescription. This dosage sometimes provides the bonus benefit of relieving symptoms of achy joints and muscles. I have never seen any complications develop from using these dose levels. In fact, the FDA has approved the potassium salt of PABA for usage in the dose of 12,000 mg. per day in the treatment of several rare conditions involving fibrosis of skin and muscle tissue.

If your fatigue is complicated by edema (water retention) or achy joints, or if you've been on The Pill, or if you can't remember most of your dreams, you are a good candidate to respond to pyridoxine (B_6) in dosages from 400 to 1,500 mg. divided throughout the day. Make sure you include 30 mg. of elemental zinc in this experiment. The only problem I have encountered with B_6 is occasional overstimulation and sleeplessness. This is actually a good sign, suggesting that your energy will respond to a lower dose.

OTHER EXPERIMENTS TO TRY. The "step-out" experiments can also be conducted with the other vitamins.

Try stepping out thiamine to doses of 500 to 1,500 mg.

Try stepping out pantothenic acid to doses of 500 to 1,000 mg.

Try stepping out folic acid to 10 to 30 mg. per day.

Try stepping out niacinamide to 500 to 2,000 mg. per day. For some people, niacin will work even when niacinamide does not. Watch for the flush.

Try stepping out biotin to 300 to 600 mcg. per day.

Give each vitamin a week or two of observation, and evaluate carefully, referring to your scores on your energy and symptom questionnaires. Once a specific vitamin has provided a definite benefit, keep it in your basic program as you go on to test the next vitamins. If the stepped-out dose does not give extra benefit, then drop it back to the level of your starting basic formula. Your end point should be where you can say to yourself, "I feel better than ever."

Some of these vitamins, such as folic acid, can make you feel either better *or* worse. If any one seems to make you feel worse, cut down on its intake until it is near the minimum daily requirement.

IF ALL ELSE FAILS. There are three nutrients that seem to help *everybody,* although not always dramatically.

The first is vitamin B_{15}, pangamic acid, which is available in this country as a combination of calcium gluconate and dimethyl glycine, 50 mg. The effective dose is 200–300 mg. daily.

The second is ginseng, which seems to have the same spectrum of activity as vitamin E, although its mode of action is unknown. Three to six capsules of a brand which has the Korean government stamp are effective.

The third is an increased amount of brewers' yeast. Two to six teaspoons per day may prove valuable.

At this point, if your symptoms remain, it is increasingly likely that nutrition therapy is not going to provide the help you need, but you have not reached the bottom of the nutrition barrel yet.

Vitamin E is important for energy. It is particularly valuable if your problems are menopausal or circulatory. But some caution is needed. It is one of the few weight-gaining vitamins I know and could slow down a weight-loss program, and it can elevate the blood pressure, or cause headaches. However, the gradual careful escalation of the dose to 800, then 1,200 and 1,600 units may get the desired results.

Further, there are some benefits which may result from increasing the intake of magnesium and calcium by taking dolomite, or from using lecithin (granules or liquid) in one or two tablespoon quantities per day.

WHEN THERE ARE SPECIFIC PROBLEMS. Nutritional remedies abound.

For insomnia or nervous tension, try the nutrition doctor's sleeping pill: inositol. Take 650 mg. to fight anxiety and 1,300–2,000 mg. to help induce sleep. Calcium and magnesium may also be helpful here.

For leg cramps, try magnesium, calcium, and vitamin E.

For the common cold, or the "grippe," increase your vitamin C intake to 4 to 6 grams per day, and take calcium pantothenate 400 to 600 mg. daily.

For minor burns and scalds, empty the contents of an oil-based vitamin E capsule and apply directly.

For mastitis, increase vitamin E to 1,200 units.

For canker sores, be sure bioflavonoids are included in your vitamin C preparation, and increase your folic acid.

AN UNEXPLAINED PHENOMENON. Often a person will feel great for a week or two and then begin to slip back to some of the old symptoms, without changing either the diet or the vitamin regimen. I can only speculate on why this might be. One theory is that the increased use of the vitamins corrects an imbalance and then proceeds to overcorrect it. Thus, the nutritional equilibrium becomes a dynamic one, subject to changing as time progresses.

The approach to this dilemma may involve searching for a missing nutritional link to be added, or it may involve cutting back on a nutrient being taken in high doses.

THE NEXT PHASE—TAPERING DOWN. None of us wants to spend the rest of his life taking unnecessarily large quantities of vitamins so the next phase is a very important one—decreasing doses where possible. This can be done after a while because needs diminish as the overall nutrition picture improves. The removal of the sugar, or the alcohol, or The Pill, or diet pills, or diuretics all serve to normalize a previously excessive need for some vitamins and minerals.

The tapering-down experiment is the same principle as stepping out, only in reverse. You cut back one at a time on those vitamins that are being consumed in especially high doses (or those that are particularly expensive). Reduce them 25 to 30 percent each week, one at a time. Continue to record your symptom score; if you notice any worsening, you may have confirmed that you do need the vitamin in question in the dosage you *were* taking. Repeat the maneuver somewhat later to be sure. Otherwise you will successively reduce your dose until you are down to what will be your maintenance formula.

FOR MAINTENANCE. It's hard to recommend much less than the basic multiple vitamin and trace mineral supplements plus some extra E, C, and folic acid. More often, if you are keeping close tabs on your symptoms you will find that many of the vitamins you have used do provide a noticeable effect, and you will decide to maintain their usage.

Make your judgment based on the results of your tapering-down experiments. You don't want to take more vitamins than you need to, but you want to keep those optimum dosages that truly keep you feeling your best.

There are theoretical considerations which make me conclude that 1,000 mg. of vitamin C is an irreducible minimum to provide proper resistance to infection and pollution. Similar studies involving vitamin E make it hard for me to suggest that vitamin E dosage should drop below 400 units. As a matter of fact, a Canadian study of vitamin E's effectiveness against angina showed an *increase* of this symptom when high doses were suddenly cut off. If this fact is borne out by further testing, it would suggest that vitamin E should be discontinued only with caution. Other nutrients that would have to remain as supplements even on maintenance include folic acid, pyridoxine, and zinc.

There is another consideration that's a little more subtle. Some vitamins seem to have a cholesterol-lowering effect. If you test at the peak of vitamin effect, your cholesterol level may be quite favorable. But if you retest after the vitamin dosage has been tapered down, the cholesterol level may have gone up. In that case, the vitamins are essential to normalize the cholesterol level, and the dosage should probably be reinstated at the higher level.

Also under stressful situations, higher dosages of vitamins C, A, pantothenate, and the rest of the B complex should be reestablished.

YOUR OWN NEEDS HAVE TO BE ESTABLISHED. If you have gathered from these three chapters that I have been recommending a form of self-experimentation, I cannot deny it. The one saving grace of vitamin and mineral therapy is that there is very little risk as long as certain precautions are taken. So far, self-testing is the most practical technique we have to offer; laboratory tests serve well but prove to be expensive guidelines.

AREN'T SOME OF THESE AMOUNTS TERRIBLY HIGH? They are much higher than the government recommended minimum daily allowances, but not nearly as high as some of the megavitamin doses being used by some nutritionists. Remember, these are not minimum needs, but Optimum Recommended Doses, that is, the amounts not for minimal health, but optimal health, the amount to make you feel the best you can.

I have arrived at these values after several years' experience with careful testing of my own patients. I am still testing new nutrients and doses as new reports appear, or after conferring with nutrition-oriented colleagues.

Naturally, when you take these or any pills, if at any time you have a reaction, stop taking them and determine which one, if any, seems to produce the reaction. It would be wrong to stop *all* vitamin therapy, when, in fact, the reaction was due to a single nutrient.

I WANT TO CAUTION YOU. The mere mention of vitamins and minerals on a label does not necessarily mean that the amount is significant enough to supply what you need. Check the supplements you buy against the recommended amounts to make sure you're getting what you should.

A microgram is not the same as a milligram. If I'm talking about taking 50 mg. and you see a formula with 50 mcg., that's one-thousandth of the amount that I'm recommending.

NO MATTER HOW WELL YOU EAT YOU CAN'T GET THESE DOSAGES IN FOOD. Since you won't be eating sugar or flour, the chances are that the rest of your diet will provide a considerable amount of vitamins. But are these enough? Many vitamins are lost in processing, freezing, cooking, and canning. And, since mineral content of a food is partly the function of the mineral content of the soil, different samples may give different quantities of these essential trace minerals. Enough nutrients are lost that it becomes uncertain as to what we're getting.

But the really important thing is that the large dosages, the ones that have been shown to be effective in clinical medicine, just don't occur naturally in food at those levels.

What we're trying to accomplish can't be done with food alone.

Your clinical deficiency may have taken ten, twenty, or even fifty years to develop, and now we're trying to correct it so rapidly that the improvement is immediately apparent. Accomplishing the same goals with nutritional food alone may take years. Wouldn't you prefer to know the answer within weeks?

19

Maintenance: your lifetime diet

After you have been on the diet for several weeks, you should evaluate it. Questions you should ask yourself: Am I less tired? Do I feel better? Is my mood, temperament, and energy better than before?

If you are on the right diet for you, the answers should be yes.

You should also ask: What is the diet doing to my weight? If a diet that relieves fatigue produces a final weight which is not ideal, then the diet needs to be modified.

THERE ARE TWO THINGS TO KEEP IN MIND. You are trying to achieve your best weight, as well as bettering the way you feel. There are two ways to do this. You can stay on the diet you began with and change carbohydrate levels within it. If it looks as though you're losing too much weight, you add more carbohydrates. If it looks as though you're losing too little, you reduce your carbohydrates even more.

Or you can switch to another of the four diet programs. For example, if you start to gain weight on Diet #3, you would switch to Diet #1 to see if it will cause your weight to drop.

When you switch a diet like this, ask yourself: "On which diet did I feel better?" If you feel better on the lower-carbohydrate diet, stay there. If you felt better on the original diet, then go back to it, or try a variation that is somewhere in between.

Through these experiments you can find the diet at which you feel best.

If you want to lose just a little weight and aren't sure whether to start out with Diet #1 or Diet #3, I suggest that you start with the stricter Diet #1.

The advantage of starting low in carbohydrates and then systematically building up is that you really can't miss the right level. At one point, you will pass through your ideal diet level.

YOU MIGHT WANT TO USE THE KETOSTIX. It isn't necessary to use them, but they can be a useful yardstick. Do you feel best when your sticks are deep purple, when they're lavender, or when they're negative (beige)? You can plan your diet to get that reaction; the fewer carbohydrates you eat, the more ketones you produce, the darker the sticks.

WHEN YOU FIND YOUR IDEAL LEVEL. Once you have found your best carbohydrate level and your best vitamin and mineral program, then stay with them.

When you find a diet that makes you feel as well as this one will, you will want to stay on it as you go through life. And you should. If a certain diet is best for your type of metabolism this year, it will probably be best for it next year, and ten years from now, as well.

Don't look upon a diet as an experiment that has a beginning and an end, but rather as a basis for a new nutrition lifestyle based on new values. With the new values, the long-term feeling of well-being must outrank for-the-moment eating pleasure, purpose must outrank convenience.

If you want to continue the feeling of well-being and the ideal weight you now have, you should make this your maintenance plan, your lifetime diet.

THE RULES THAT APPLY TO ALL FOUR DIETS

1. Continue your most effective vitamin and mineral regimen every day.

2. Stay away from sugar and refined flour completely.

3. Eat often . . . and when your energy seems to be flagging.

4. Use caffeine and alcohol in moderation, not exceeding the maximum.

5. Maintain the level of carbohydrate you have established as being the best for you.

THE MECHANICS OF MAINTENANCE. As long as you continue to feel well, you should stay at the most liberal level that keeps you feeling well, but you still have to be flexible, because your Critical Carbohydrate Level may vary at different times in life. So if you stop feeling as well as usual, you may have to temporarily drop your carbohydrate level again or step out your vitamin and mineral dosage.

Should you deviate greatly from your diet, go back to the basic diet for a few days and reestablish your ideal carbohydrate level. Then you can gradually put more carbohydrate back in your diet.

TEMPORARY DIFFICULTIES. Sometimes a dieter has trouble finding the level of feeling best. Or the dieter who wants to lose weight as well as feel better accomplishes the feel-good objective, but finds the scale will not move. Often the tape measure continues to show the loss of girth even when the scale doesn't, confirming that the diet is still working. But sometimes even this ceases to take place, and it is then time to reevaluate the basic structure of the diet. In the next chapter I'll tell you how I approach this discouraging problem in my own practice.

WHEN YOU HAVE REACHED YOUR GOAL. Let's assume your new diet has brought you your weight *and* Superenergy goals. You feel better than ever before and your weight is where you want it. The temptation is to say "I've done it" and begin again to seek out those scrumptious goodies you have put aside for all this time. If this is your reaction, restrain yourself. Remember what happened last time you terminated a diet.

Mac Palmer typifies dozens of other patients I have treated. Mac first came to me at age twenty-four weighing 293 pounds. His glucose tolerance and triglycerides were quite abnormal. Before coming to me, he had been treated by six different physicians, who prescribed diet pills or low-calorie diets or both. He never stuck to any of these programs very long and always regained more than he lost.

I put Mac on Diet #1. Within eleven weeks he had shed

fifty pounds and within eight and one-half months he had dropped an even 100 pounds. His blood picture was back to normal.

Mac was rejuvenated, his stamina high. He felt his weight problem was solved. But we never saw him again until more than four years had passed. When he came back, he was at 280 pounds, tired, depressed, and thirsty—all his symptoms (and lab findings) were back.

I asked how it could have happened. Mac is one of those who think a diet has a beginning and an end, and he began to partake of his favorite carbohydrates—and regained the weight just as fast as he had lost it. Because he and his parents were accustomed to changing doctors with every attempt to lose weight, he consulted another doctor who put him on a low-calorie diet. Mac couldn't overcome the hunger it produced so he quit and regained more, then went to another doctor and a third doctor a year later, weighing 270. Both touted him off his low carbohydrate diet.

None of these physicians bothered to find out how well Mac had felt losing a hundred pounds on the *only* diet he was *capable* of following or to learn that his blood levels of cholesterol, triglycerides, and sugar had all *improved* while he was on it.

Mac is back with me now, is once again cutting out his carbohydrates, losing rapidly and feeling better.

ADDING FOODS. You cannot abandon your new dietary principles. But you can add back some of the items you've been avoiding.

Now you may add in some of those vegetables too starchy to have been allowed before, or some whole grain items, or else expand in the nuts and seeds categories. Think of the less common, more nutritious foods such as groats, barley, millet, wild rice, buckwheat, maize, and lentils.

But what you're probably looking for is more fruit or juice, or a glass of milk, or some home-baked biscuits, or a glass of wine or a cocktail. Try them cautiously and gradually. If you don't regain your lost weight or relose your gained energy, these items can be a part of your regular lifetime diet.

BUT NOT SUGAR. But whatever you do, don't go back to sweets. If this diet has helped you feel better, it probably did so because it corrected a sugar intolerance, or quite possibly a sugar addiction. And if so, sugar, by triggering the pancreas to release a long-stored flood of insulin, may just begin that restless, exhausted, irritable, depressed reaction all over again. It's not much different from the risk an alcoholic takes when he goes for "that first drink." And in case you're still tempted, be aware that sugar is more fattening than other carbohydrates.

FRUITS AND JUICES. Fruit in our culture is generally considered an excellent food. Yet its major dietary constituent is a simple sugar, and the person who cannot handle sugar cannot handle very much fruit. And when concentrated into juice the difficulties are compounded. Although the average sugar-intolerant person can usually handle small amounts of fruit, he cannot expect to do very well if he takes it whenever he craves something sweet. You will have to test your own reaction.

THE CONCEPT OF PERMANENCE. All the while I'm treating a patient, I keep reminding him of two things: the improvement in his energy level and the changes on his glucose tolerance test, triglycerides, or other lab tests. I consider it most important that a person be well informed about his own metabolism. People who *know* they are hypoglycemic maintain a diet more carefully than those who *think* they are hypoglycemic. Knowledge helps provide extra motivation.

When you are tempted to go back to an undesirable favorite food, you must know clearly *why* you cannot have it. Otherwise, it's so easy to be talked into giving it up only temporarily. The hardest lesson that those of us with a disturbance in carbohydrate metabolism have to learn is that we will always have that problem, and that we will have to restrict carbohydrates for years.

THE GREATEST MOTIVATION OF ALL. You'll find this out for yourself. You will feel so good on the diet and so bad when you go off, that you will never want to go off it.

When you go off the diet, your fatigue returns. This provides a built-in punishment and reward.

If you go off the diet, you learn by sad experience that anywhere from immediately until seventy-two hours later you're dragging around again the way you did before you started on the diet.

It is important to understand this one-to-three-day delay can occur, otherwise you'll be blaming your Tuesday fatigue on your Monday dieting instead of on the Saturday or Sunday binge.

IF YOU'VE BLOWN IT. Don't fall into that common pitfall of saying "I've blown it; I might as well go all the way and eat everything." Remember that your weight gain (or energy loss) is proportionate to the *amount* of carbohydrate you've taken in, so simply go back immediately to where you started and build up your carbohydrates gradually again.

ONE TECHNIQUE. You will find it helps to keep your kitchen always stocked with the kind of foods you should have. Once you've found out what foods are on your diet, make sure they're always around in plenitude. Buy by the dozen or by the case when you find something on the list you really like and know you're going to use.

One of the biggest excuses that I've had to deal with in practice is when people go off their diet "because nothing else was around." *You* are responsible for what's around, so make sure it's plenty of what you should eat.

Plan ahead. Being a dieter is like being a pilot who must file a flight plan. Decide what foods you're going to have, and where you're going to be eating them. Write down your diet flight plan . . . and carry it out. Such advanced planning prevents finding yourself on a car trip, at a board meeting, or working late at the office with nothing to eat but Danish and coffee, atrocious food from a vending machine or simply running out of food at the end of the week when the stores are closed.

THINGS TO REMEMBER. Space your meals and snacks out over the day. If you have learned you need protein every three hours, have some as part of every snack, no matter how small the amount of protein.

Don't skip breakfast or start the day with coffee, a sweet

roll, and a cigarette. This will begin your hypoglycemic cycle all over again, with the caffeine, sugar, and nicotine triggering a flood of insulin into the system.

Spread your carbohydrates evenly through the day. If you are having 30 grams, don't have all thirty at one time, but rather ten on three different occasions.

ONE THING THAT ALMOST EVERYONE IS GOING TO DISCOVER. That is: with time the diet improves your body chemistry and general health so much that little indiscretions won't make you feel so bad. You will then be able to get away with a little more than you could before.

Your general nutritional level is so much better that it improves your ability to withstand dietary variations. Those who have vitamin or mineral deficiencies find that they are at first very susceptible to the slightest variations in the diet, unable to stabilize their blood sugar against changes. But after a few months of good nutrition the ability to withstand the insult of a load of sugar improves.

COFFEE, TEA, AND YOU. In some patients caffeine is as bad as sugar itself, causing a temporary lift, followed by a letdown far greater than the lift. But for some people coffee in small amounts can postpone fatigue.

My rule: Never drink more than four cups a day, and have a little snack with it.

Interestingly enough, the people who drink the most coffee—eight to ten cups a day—are the ones who usually need most to get off it completely. I did a tabulation of patients who drank more than six cups of coffee and found that 85 *percent of them* showed an abnormal glucose curve.

Each person has to evaluate coffee for himself. Heavy coffee drinkers had better switch to decaffeinated, but light to moderate coffee drinkers probably can continue. If you drink tea, make it moderately weak. If you have a three-cup-a-day habit and expand it to five or six cups, you may be getting yourself into trouble.

DO YOUR OWN CLINICAL TRIAL. Take three weeks of no coffee, tea, cola, or drinks like Dr Pepper that also contain caffeine. After three weeks with none of these drinks, see how you feel, then go back to drinking your regular amount and compare.

WATCH THE INSTANT TEAS. They may contain maltidextrin, a carbohydrate. Most luncheonettes serve such iced tea. This can introduce enough carbohydrate on a hot summer day to throw off your whole diet.

CAFFEINE CAN CAUSE ANXIETY SYMPTOMS. Dr. John F. Greden, Walter Reed Army Medical Center, Washington, D.C., warned psychiatrists at an American Psychiatric Association meeting that many patients with puzzling anxiety symptoms were simply drinking too much coffee, tea, and cola. He found too much caffeine can produce palpitations of the heart, upsets in heart rhythms, low blood pressure, circulatory failure, nausea, vomiting, diarrhea, stomach pain, nervousness, irritability, tremulousness, muscle twitching, sensory disturbances, and insomnia.

Only 50 to 200 mg. of caffeine are required to produce pharmacological actions. But three cups of coffee, two headache tablets, and a cola drink consumed in one day approximate 500 mg. of caffeine intake.

There is an average of 85 milligrams of caffeine per cup of brewed coffee, says the National Coffee Association, 60 milligrams per cup of instant coffee, and 3 milligrams per cup of decaffeinated coffee.

WATCH YOUR ALCOHOL. For hypoglycemics or for those who must lose weight, alcohol is undesirable.

In many ways alcohol works just like sugar—it provides empty calories and uses vitamins for metabolism and is therefore capable of producing a vitamin deficiency.

Excessive amounts of alcohol can make hypoglycemia worse. And there is an outstandingly high prevalency of hypoglycemia in alcoholics, perhaps 90 percent, according to Drs. Ronald Arky and Norbert Frienkel in Boston. Further, the hypoglycemic effects of alcohol are exaggerated by a low-carbohydrate eating pattern.

You will have to determine yourself how much alcohol you can handle and still feel well.

When you start your diet, you should have absolutely no alcohol. After you have reached your goal of feeling better than ever before, then alcohol can be reintroduced gradually. At each gradual, slow increment of alcohol, ask yourself if you have set yourself back or not.

Alcohol has calories, but no carbohydrates unless there are carbohydrate-containing additives. Alcohol's calories do inhibit the desired mobilization of fat; therefore, they may halt weight loss if that is your goal.

A REALLY BIG TIP—DON'T SMOKE. Smoking causes a fall in blood sugar by stimulating the adrenal gland. By joining the millions of people who have become nonsmokers, you may find considerably more energy.

DON'T FORGET TO EXERCISE. Would you believe that 45 percent of American adults today engage in *no* physical activities for exercise? So says the National Adult Physical Fitness survey.

This lack of exercise plus our overeating of carbohydrates makes for a dangerous situation.

Getting enough exercise is an integral part of feeling good. Sometimes we forget we have such sedentary jobs and so many laborsaving devices. To make sure you get enough exercise, you should specifically plan for it.

Tennis, handball, swimming, jogging, dancing, cycling, even walking will help.

Even if you don't need to lose weight, the exercise will firm up what's there. It firms up the flab, gets rid of the paunch and puts muscle where the flab was. It improves lung function, circulation, gives you a healthier heart, more energy, better color and skin tone, and even better looks.

IF YOU MISS THE TASTE OF SWEETNESS. At first you will. Partly because of habit, partly because sugar really does taste good, and probably because you're a little addicted to it, as we mentioned before. You become dependent because sugar causes an unbearable degree of hypoglycemia, and the symptoms are relieved by the ingestion of more sugar. The vicious cycle becomes an addiction.

ETERNAL VIGILANCE. As you maintain your diet, you must continue forever to look out for hidden sugars in innocent-looking foods.

Do you put ketchup on your hamburger? There is sugar in it. Do you spread relish on your hot dog? There's sugar in that. Would you like a can of soup? Sugar.

There is also sugar added to most canned vegetables, peanut butter, frozen items, even to dates, canned sweet potatoes, frankfurters, luncheon meats, pork sausage, tartar sauce, soy sauce, and cheese dips.

If it's any "convenience" food, be suspicious, since manufacturers put sugar in foods that the average housewife would never think to sweeten at home.

If the package says nonnutritive sweetener, it's okay, because that means it has saccharin or other artificial sweetener. But if the label lists "natural nutritive sweetener," that's a fancy way, or perhaps we should say deceptive way, to list sugar. Also, dextrin, sorbitol, and mannitol are sugars, so you should avoid products containing them.

If ingredients are listed, they are listed in order of amount. If sugar is listed first, it means there is more of that than of any other ingredient. Many manufacturers have developed the ploy of using two sugars such as sucrose and corn syrup so that sugars become the second and third ingredients.

The amazing thing is that after you have been away from sugar for a few weeks, you really won't miss it that much. You will probably find, as most of my patients do, that when you are at a party and succumb to a scrumptious-looking delicacy, it is so sickeningly sweet to you that after the second bite, you don't even want to finish it.

You will find more and more as your taste sensitivity returns, no longer overpowered by cloying sweetness, that you will begin to enjoy the subtle flavors of natural foods again. It's like giving up cigarettes . . . food suddenly starts tasting marvelous. You had forgotten how great it could taste.

ARTIFICIAL SWEETENERS WILL BE LIFESAVERS TO YOU . . . LITERALLY. There are many foods sweetened with sugar substitutes and if you find you still like the sweet taste, you must take the time to seek them out, from no-sugar soft drinks to no-sugar puddings.

The major artificial sweeteners are saccharin and cyclamate. In the United States cyclamate has been banned.

THE BANNING WAS ILL-CONSIDERED. It was based on the fact that a small percentage of rats fed high amounts of cyclamate—equivalent to our drinking a bathtub filled with diet drink each day—were alleged to have developed bladder cancer. Since later tests failed to confirm this, and the actual mixture fed to all rats was not kept to be analyzed for impurities, the findings are suspect. Most of the downfall of the artificial sweetener was due to pressure and publicity by the sugar industry.

I WOULD PREFER THAT ALL MY PATIENTS USE CYCLAMATES IF IT WERE POSSIBLE. In general I am against the unnecessary use of food additives, but I take cyclamate to be a major exception because it replaces sugar which has a far greater potential risk.

In Canada, saccharin and cyclamate are used together in a product called Sucaryl which many people bring back to use in the United States. The combination has a better taste than either sweetener alone and has the further advantage of reducing the intake of each. Cyclamate is also available in most European countries.

WHAT ABOUT SACCHARIN? Saccharin has been considered safe for human consumption for seventy-five years, but its safety has been questioned lately. In one study of 37,000 patients, however, absolutely no difference was found between rates of cancer in diabetics who use the sweeteners regularly and non-diabetics who don't.

DOES THIS DIET HAVE ENOUGH NUTRITION TO BE USED A LIFETIME? The low-carbohydrate diet has more nutritive value than the average "normal" diet. The average American consumes 371 grams of carbohydrate a day, of which 137 grams are in sugar and other sweeteners like corn syrup, 136 are in the form of flour, and 25 are in potatoes and rice. This leaves only about 73 grams for carbohydrates such as fresh fruits and vegetables which contain the greatest concentration of nutrients.

So the maintenance diet is not much different in nutritious carbohydrates, especially if we choose foods that are more nutritious than others, such as beans and sprouts and nuts and seeds.

And then of course the diet will include the large daily doses of vitamins and mineral capsules to provide nutrition far beyond that of the normal diet.

IN TIMES OF SPECIAL STRESS. If you've had a recent infection, or other physical or emotional stress, it is particularly important that you take the recommended dosages of vitamins and minerals and maintain your intake of protein.

Infection, injury, and emotional stress can all affect your nutritional status, causing a depletion of body protein, as well as of vitamins and minerals. So when you or someone in your family has a cold or other infection, or your body is under any special stress, make doubly sure that you stay on your diet, eating plenty of protein and taking every single vitamin and mineral you are supposed to.

Do the same during periods of emotional stress. It is natural to pay little attention to diet in moments of crisis, passing up meals, grabbing any junk on the run or living on cigarettes and coffee. So many of my patients' relapses begin in just this way. If it's not possible to stick to your diet, try at least to stay off sugar as much as possible, and be sure to take your vitamin and mineral supplements since you will need them more than ever.

20

If you are not getting results

I hope that you are now one of the new members of the "I-feel better-than-ever" Club and that you have felt the great transformation on this diet that most people feel. I hope you have more energy and a greater feeling of well-being, have more bounce and enthusiasm, have achieved your ideal weight, and have rid yourself of your most distressing symptoms.

But just in case you haven't yet reacted as most people do, let's consider some of the possible reasons.

DON'T GIVE UP. Every day many new things are being discovered in nutrition even though so much of it has not been well publicized. There's much more to nutrition than merely developing the proper balance between protein, fat, and carbohydrate. You need a sensible program of vitamins, for example, and your mineral intake must be in balance.

An unsolved case of fatigue can have many possible causes. You should not, if the first try doesn't work, give up and say nutrition can't provide the answer. Keep trying. Your conclusion about this project may influence you for the rest of your life.

THE FIRST THING TO CHECK FOR: HIDDEN SOURCES OF SUGAR. You may be taking in sugar that you're not aware of. The hidden sugar may be in your vitamin pills. Several vitamin C preparations have a gram of sugar in each tablet, even though there's nothing on the label to indicate it. Many vitamin preparations, especially chewable ones, have sugar as a filler, enough to throw the diet off. Capsules usually have no sugar. Go beyond the label; check with the pharmacist or nutrition center where you buy your vitamins.

The hidden sugar may be in cough syrup, lozenges, chewing gum, or mints, salad dressing, cole slaw, sweet pickle relish, or tartar sauce. The list goes on endlessly, seemingly innocent sources sufficient to throw the diet off.

If you are trying to lose weight, then watch too, for hexitols or sorbitol. These are metabolized as carbohydrates and should be counted as carbohydrate.

PERHAPS YOU'RE CHEATING ON THE DIET. Perhaps you think a few bits of something aren't going to matter. But they can matter. As little as 10 grams of carbohydrate can inhibit ketosis, or fat mobilization, or weight loss.

OR YOU MAY STILL BE KEEPING YOUR FOOD INTAKE TOO LOW. Often a person who has been on other diets sees this diet only as another restriction. This might lead to not eating enough proteins and essential fats to provide adequate nutrition, allowing hunger with its accompanying fatigue to remain. Eat up . . . the right things.

ARE YOU EATING SIX SMALL MEALS OR SNACKS A DAY? Be sure to stick to your frequent eating schedule. This will provide a constant source of energy without the insulin rebound.

It is doubly important for those who are trying to lose weight, because it has been shown in the laboratory that animals fed a few big meals, instead of frequent snacks, gained more and increased their production of blood lipids.

The same effects are found in humans. Dr. Paul Fabry, of the Institute for Clinical and Experimental Medicine in Prague, found in both children and adults, that far-apart meals, especially huge dinners, led to weight gain, raised cholesterol levels, decreased glucose tolerance, and even increased the rate of heart disease. So eating six small feedings a day instead of three substantial meals could break the energy and weight-loss barriers.

YOU MAY NOT HAVE FOUND YOUR PROPER LEVEL YET. If one level of the diet doesn't bring about your awaited feeling of well-being, then be sure to try the other levels. Review again the diet chapters to see if you worked through all the levels properly and whether you have added in the carbohydrates gradually.

The dilemma of remaining tired calls forth two choices. Either you may *increase* your carbohydrates, providing a ready source of immediate fuel. Or you may *decrease* them, which will allow you to get more fuel from free fatty acids and ketone bodies.

This clinical decision has confronted me thousands of times, and I have both stepped up and stepped down carbohydrate levels.

About four out of five patients do better when their carbohydrate level is lowered further, so I suggest you do this first. Try the first week schedule on Diet #1 to see if the lowest carbohydrate level produces the most energy. Then gradually work through the levels again, being careful not to go past your best level. If Diet #1 still does not work, increase to higher carbohydrate levels and see if that works.

ONCE YOU FIND YOUR BEST LEVEL. Then stay on the diet at that level. It is especially important that you don't go off the diet if you have hypoglycemia because hypoglycemia, should it persist, can become progressively more severe.

A third possibility is that you need to step out your vitamins as described in chapter 18. You may need more of some vitamin or mineral to reach the superenergy level. For example, doctors at Fitzsimmons Army Hospital discovered that there are patients who are hypoglycemic but who do worse on a low-carbohydrate diet because a specific enzyme, called fructose 1, 6 diphosphatase, is deficient. They discovered that it could be treated effectively with the vitamin folic acid in doses of 15 mg. daily. I found this to be most effective in many of my patients. This is just another example of how vitamin therapy, scientifically applied, can be used to combat fatigue.

CHECK YOUR MINERAL BALANCE. There may be an imbalance of the minerals you are taking, such as the ratio between zinc and copper, or some important trace minerals may be absent.

Several years ago one patient lost weight successfully, but no matter what she did, she complained of fatigue. After reading about research in copper, I took away her high-copper vitamins, gave her those with zinc, and her fatigue disappeared in a few weeks.

Many vitamin preparations contain too much copper and too little zinc. In addition, many homes have copper piping water systems which can cause elevated copper levels. Your doctor may find the answer when he draws your serum levels of zinc and copper.

YOU MAY BE LOSING TOO MUCH SALT. Salt deprivation or potassium deprivation are common in the early stages of the diet, especially if there has been a sudden weight loss. This can be corrected by eating salty foods and taking potassium supplements or eating parsley for potassium.

TRY TO EXERCISE MORE. Whether you're trying to gain weight or lose, exercise improves your circulation, wakes up sluggish hormones, and stabilizes your blood sugar. It can produce some important metabolic benefits.

Exercise is doubly good for the person trying to lose weight because it creates an extra demand for fuel, using up more stored fat by converting it into energy.

This may be why we are likely to have Ketostix more purple in the afternoon and evening after a full day of activity than in the morning, or why a vigorous workout in a health club can convert beige sticks to purple. This is direct evidence that exercise increases the burning of fat stores.

Exercise also has the obvious advantage of putting individual muscle groups into action. We know that if we only walk, let's say, and don't do anything involving our arms, our legs may get strong and firm, but our arms may get flabby. So the best exercise should involve all the muscles of the body: swimming, tennis, dancing, calisthenics, yoga, etc.

FOOD ALLERGY—A NEW CONCEPT. If you're having trouble with the diet, an allergy to specific foods may be the cause of your low blood sugar symptoms.

These allergies frequently cause fatigue, headache, and personality changes, just as does hypoglycemia. They can even cause an abnormal glucose-tolerance test. The most common allergy-causers in food are wheat, corn, milk, and chocolate.

It is very difficult to make the distinction between food allergy and hypoglycemia for the simple reason that a typical food allergy response involves hypoglycemia. Dr. William Philpott has shown that when the offending allergen is administered to patients with these allergies, a typical low blood sugar curve will result. In addition, many of the common allergens are carbohydrates, and these are automatically removed on a low-carbohydrate diet. If you are not doing well on the diet, you might raise the question whether an allergy to a food you are still eating is causing the problem. If trial and error testing fails to locate the food allergy, you might seek out a physician experienced in this new specialty, and be tested. For example, if your symptoms vanish whenever you fast, chances are you have food allergies, and the no-food diet has circumvented them.

FOOD ADDITIVES MAY BE YOUR PROBLEM. About a billion pounds of chemicals are added to our food every year, more than two thousand chemicals for flavoring alone. You may well be allergic to some of these additives.

One woman had a headache every day for two years until an allergist discovered she was allergic to the yellow dye in her vitamin pills and in a canned drink she liked. Other allergists have been able to correct learning disabilities in children by having them avoid the coloring and flavoring agents they are allergic to.

YOU MAY BE DRINKING TOO MUCH COFFEE OR TEA. Remember that coffee, cola, and tea stimulate the release of insulin, with the usual temporary lift in energy, followed by fatigue and hunger.

Most people can have two or three cups of coffee or tea a day, but if you react to fewer, you may have to give them up completely. Go without these beverages for a week and see whether there is a difference.

IT MAY BE BECAUSE YOU ARE SMOKING. There are many cases where cigarette smoking has prevented the correction of hypoglycemia. In fact some cases absolutely will not respond to diet treatment unless smoking is stopped. This may happen because smoking uses up vitamin C stores, or because smoking stimulates the adrenal gland.

HOW MUCH ARE YOU DRINKING? Don't forget that alcohol stimulates insulin production and some beverages contain carbohydrates. Most people on the diet are able to drink some alcohol, but you may be one of those who cannot: see what happens when you stop drinking.

IT MAY BE SOME MEDICINES YOU ARE TAKING. Many drugs, even aspirin, can cause hypoglycemia. Watch out for hormones, amphetamines, diuretics, some antihistamines, antiinflammatory drugs, analgesics, anticoagulants, antidiabetics, antibiotics, tranquilizers, clofibrate, acetaminophen, and propanolol.

Also make sure your medicines don't have caffeine or sugar in them.

LAST MONTH'S DIET PILLS MAY BE SLOWING YOU DOWN. Sometimes it isn't just what medication you *are* taking, but what you *were* taking that blocks the diet's progress. You may have stopped taking diet pills several weeks before you started the diet, but in many persons a rebound effect lingers on and keeps the diet from working.

Be thankful you're off the pills. You have no choice but to stay on the diet and hope that the aftereffects of the pills will pass.

SEX HORMONES. The sex hormones not only slow down weight loss, but stimulate the production of insulin. Estrogen, the female hormone, can do this when taken in birth control pills or as estrogen replacement for menopause. Testosterone, the male hormone, has the same effect.

Sex hormones have many important benefits, but you and your physician should also be aware that there are profound interrelationships between them and carbohydrate metabolism.

Estrogen seems to accentuate both low blood sugar and diabetes. So if you have either of these conditions, you should work carefully with your doctor to see, first, whether you actually need estrogen and, if so, what is the lowest dose that will provide the benefits you want. Some vitamins allow many women to discontinue or lower their estrogen doses, especially vitamin E, folic acid, and B_{12} as well as the nutrient source ginseng.

If you are taking birth control pills, you also have an increased need for vitamins B_6, B_{12}, C, and folic acid. Some contraceptive pill manufacturers, recognizing these deficiencies, now add vitamins directly to their pills.

If you are on The Pill, determine whether you have any of the following symptoms: irritability, headaches, excessive hunger or thirst, sugar cravings, depression, weight gain, decreased ability to concentrate, forgetfulness. These don't seem related, but experience has shown they often are.

If The Pill is being used only as a contraceptive, I strongly urge that a tired or overweight patient switch to another technique for contraception. Don't change any pills, however, without checking with your doctor.

ARE YOU TAKING TRANQUILIZERS OR ANTIDEPRESSANTS? Taking psychotropic drugs, those superpotent modern-day tranquilizers, may be causing your trouble. Most drugs of this type seem to increase insulin output and lead to weight gain and hypoglycemia. Lithium, as useful as it is, can produce a startling weight gain.

When these diets and vitamins are used with psychiatric patients, the dosage of drugs can usually be reduced, and sometimes even discontinued completely, because the nutritional regimen can often effect a dramatic improvement in depression, anxiety, and adjustment problems.

So if you are taking any medications like these, talk it over with the doctor who is giving them to you. Tell him you want to try the diet with lower dosages of the pills for a week or two, to see whether you can improve your situation.

IF THE DIET WORKS WELL, THEN SUDDENLY STOPS WORKING. Often the symptoms go away, only to come back. Sometimes, stress may be the cause. I often find that some stressful situation or anxiety-provoking crisis has come along to upset the balance. Not only does hypoglycemia cause stress, but stress in turn aggravates hypoglycemia. The stress can be emotional or it can be caused by a physical illness such as a respiratory infection or intestinal flu or surgery.

If this happens to you, going back to your lowest level of carbohydrates may provide the best metabolic regulation of your blood sugar during the stressful period.

ANOTHER POSSIBILITY. Despite the fact that an overwhelming number of cases of fatigue, depression, and other symptoms are correctable by diet, there are other possibilities to be considered. For example, the patient may have an emotional problem requiring psychiatric help.

IT'S ALSO POSSIBLE TO HAVE BOTH HYPOGLYCEMIA AND AN EMOTIONAL PROBLEM. Then they both should be treated. Even though many believe that heart disease may have an emotional basis, no one would tell the heart patient to forget his heart condition because "it's all in his head."

So, if you or your doctor believe you have an underlying emotional problem, you should be treated for it. Just make sure your hypoglycemia gets treated as well.

THERE COULD BE OTHER CAUSES TOO. This is one of the reasons I want you to have a physical examination before going on the diet . . . to check on other possible causes for your problems.

If you truly have followed the diet to the letter, have not cheated, and have checked into all of the potential trouble areas this chapter points out, and you still have fatigue or depression or other symptoms, I would strongly suggest that you see your doctor again.

You may have the type of hypoglycemia that has an organic cause, as is the case with a pancreatic tumor, or you may have anemia or other hidden disease. It is not natural to feel tired, and if the diet regimen doesn't correct it, then there might be some underlying problem that needs to be investigated and treated.

THE OTHER SIDE OF THE COIN. Suppose you have solved your energy or mood problems and have wiped out a whole roster of symptoms with your new diet program, but have not achieved the weight you want.

If your desire is to gain weight, but you have not succeeded, your task is not an easy one. Read again all the suggestions in the chapter on Diet #2, and especially try adding fructose as we describe in Diet #3.

Or perhaps you're feeling great, but you don't seem to be losing weight. Or you have lost some weight, but you are stuck short of your goal.

THE NORMAL RESPONSE TO DIET #1 IS TO LOSE WEIGHT. Any person with halfway normal responses will lose weight on the first level of Diet #1 (the 10 gram carbohydrate level) and will produce ketone bodies (the Ketostix turn purple).

This response is so certain and so predictable that I consider it to be an excellent test to check out the normality of a person's metabolism. In other words, if you don't lose weight on the diet, your metabolism *cannot* be normal. The only exceptions are people who have taken diet pills or injections in significant quantities, people on certain medications that have been mentioned, people who tend to retain fluid, and people who were on an equally strict or stricter diet when they began this one.

If there is no ketone production on a biologic-zero carbohydrate intake, this implies a block in metabolism. Something must be missing if you do not break down your fat stores into ketone bodies when no ready fuel is available.

HERE'S HOW I APPROACH THIS PROBLEM. If you are stuck, the first thing to look for is the carbohydrate content of your diet. Is your carbohydrate level as low as you think it is? The largest number of "failures" are those who think one little item can't possibly make any difference.

If you know you are accurate, then you must tighten the diet and go down to the next level of Diet #1 with 5 grams less than you are getting now.

KEEP TRACK WITH KETOSTIX. If they stay purple, you can be fairly certain you are at a low enough carbohydrate level.

If your Ketostix are not purple, try cutting out salad, cream, and everything except meat, seafood, eggs, cheese, and water to see if the ketones *can* appear. If the sticks do turn purple, you probably follow the diet correctly, and the fault lies elsewhere.

But here again, there is so much individual variation that even the Ketostix are not always a true yardstick. It is not rare to see patients whose Ketostix turn purple and yet who do not lose weight. And we also see people who never show purple sticks, and yet who lose weight consistently. Even though the sticks fail to provide the reassurance that they're losing, the scale and the tape measure do.

CHECK FOR HIDDEN CARBOHYDRATE SNEAKING INTO YOUR DIET. Just to give an example, those convenient little pink packets of artificial sweetener usually contain a gram of carbohydrate each, and that can add up if you use more than just a few. Sweeteners in liquid or tablet form do not have this extra carbohydrate. Even that single gram can be of enough significance to affect the result.

TOO MUCH SALT MAY BE CAUSING RETENTION OF WATER. Although the sharp drop in carbohydrates causes a ready loss of salt and water, the body does adapt partially to this during the second or third weeks. At this point salt in the diet can cause some water retention.

Protein foods tend to be high in sodium (salt), as can be some diet sodas, and even some drinking water. Cutting down your intake of sodium often helps.

YOU MAY HAVE TO EXERCISE MORE TO BURN OFF MORE WEIGHT. Although exercising isn't as fast as dieting, it's still effective, and the two together can work wonders. The effect of regular exercise is cumulative. A half hour of exercise every day for a year, can help you shed a lot of excess weight.

YOU MAY STILL BE REACTING FROM FORMER DIET PILLS. The prolonged use of diet pills seems to affect the appetite mechanism to the point where one cannot rely on his appetite to tell him when he has had enough. Diet pill victims may have to go a little bit hungry until the pill effect can be neutralized.

WHAT ABOUT QUANTITIES? If weight loss stops short of your ideal weight, even though you are producing ketones, you must conclude that the quantities within the diet are too great. The diet usually works best with just enough calories to stave off hunger. Too many people misinterpret the instructions regarding the diet as "Eat unrestrictedly." When they do this they will still lose weight in the beginning, which will reinforce their assurance that no heed whatever need be paid to quantities. In most cases, this practice will lead to a stalemate partway to the desired goal.

YOU MAY HAVE TO COUNT CALORIES IN ADDITION TO CARBOHYDRATES. I have never said that calories don't count, because I know of course that they do. I say that *carbohydrates* count *more*. If your case is especially difficult, you may have to count both.

For most people, restricting carbohydrates is all that is necessary. However, there is no question that a 1,500-calorie, 10-gram diet will take more weight off, and more quickly, than a 2,000-calorie 10-gram diet. So if you are having trouble losing, you should cut down on quantities, but not to the point where you have to put up with discomfort or hunger. All too often, this effort just doesn't pay. As a traditional overeater you may have built up a mistaken impression of how much food it takes to satisfy you. Try eating less on this diet and you'll probably find you are just as comfortable as when you ate more on a higher carbohydrate diet.

If you wish to decrease your intake of fat as well as keep carbohydrates low, you can easily modify the ketogenic diet so that it is even more restricted in fat. In *Dr. Atkins' Diet Cookbook* you will find an assortment of "Low Fat Recipes" that do precisely this.

THE REAL PROBLEM COMES WHEN YOU ARE DIETING TO THE POINT OF HUNGER AND STILL NOT LOSING WEIGHT. Anyone who treats a large number of overweight patients sees this phenomenon, called Metabolic Resistance to Weight Loss. But no one has ever identified the mechanisms responsible for this condition.

The most common patient of this type I have seen is one who has been exposed to prolonged diet pills, such as amphetamines. My own theory is that these medications create an aftereffect preventing the body from losing weight. I have collected hundreds of cases of this phenomenon. So, pills of this type have no place whatever in the management of chronic obesity.

In working out an effective diet for these difficult cases of metabolic resistance, remember this axiom: *"When calories must be restricted, in order to avoid hunger, it is imperative that carbohydrates be virtually eliminated."*

This means that a low-calorie diet should not contain a lot of vegetables and fruit, to keep the stomach filled with bulk, as in a Weight Watchers diet. These roughage items contain carbohydrate and prevent ketosis, thereby taking away the dieter's main protection against hunger.

THERE ARE DIETS TO CONQUER METABOLIC RESISTANCE. Perhaps the most effective diet is the regimen developed by Dr. George Blackburn of MIT and Boston City Hospital, "The Protein-Sparing Modified Fast."

A fast is the most effective way to lose weight, but on a prolonged fast one loses a lot of protein, essential body tissue.

Dr. Blackburn found that by adding perhaps 400 to 600 calories of lean protein foods, he could keep patients in nitrogen balance, meaning that there was no net loss of protein.

His diet consists of nothing more than beverages and lean meat, fish or fowl, about six to eight ounces a day (about two small cans of salmon) and really nothing else. It is obviously not a banquet, but it is almost universally effective and quite safe under medical supervision. It is infinitely preferable to an ordinary low-calorie diet because it utilizes the appetite-appeasing effect of ketosis.

Formula diets of similar composition have been successfully administered by Dr. Victor Vertes of Cleveland and Dr. Robert Linn of Philadelphia. These medically supervised regimens—you eat a prepared formula and nothing else—have both the advantage and disadvantage that they remove eating as we know it from the overweight person's life.

For the majority, weight can be lost without having to resort to these measures. Before undertaking any of these austere diets, where not even salad is allowed, try a diet somewhere between these extremes of quantity where both calories *and* carbohydrates are restricted. Seek out the quantity level that achieves the best balance between satiety and effectiveness.

I prescribe such diets to most of my patients with metabolic resistance. But they may allow for the development of hunger. As a doctor who is also a dieter, I am very disturbed over the prospect of having a patient on a diet that leaves him hungry.

There are several maneuvers that can prevent hunger, however.

THREE LITTLE TRICKS. First, do not wait to eat until you get hungry. Rather, eat a little protein just when the appetite begins to emerge. You will be less ravenous at mealtime and thus able to cut down on quantity.

Second, cut your quantities substantially below the hunger point for several days. After four or five days, your hunger will be less than it was before this maneuver.

Third, remember that the greater the ketosis, the less the hunger. Remember too, that 58 percent of protein can convert into glucose and inhibit ketogenesis to that extent, whereas only 10 percent of fat can do this. Therefore a high-fat, low-protein diet can satisfy hunger better than a high-protein, low-fat diet. Diets high in bacon, cream cheese, mayonnaise, and vegetable oils and low in lean meat, fish, or cottage cheese, may, surpisingly, be better suited to a physically comfortable low-calorie, low-carbohydrate diet. Needless to say, the quantities of these high-fat foods must be exceedingly small.

A SUREFIRE TRICK IF YOU CAN AFFORD IT. Go to Europe. This is not a frivolous suggestion for those who can afford it and who might be planning a trip anyway.

For some strange reason, as yet unexplained, a trip to Europe always seems to help with weight reduction. It may be something in the soil, but more likely the weight gain at home is caused by the fattening hormones which overrun the American meat supply. The best results seem to be achieved in Mediterranean countries: Spain, Greece, Italy, or the south of

France. If you make an honest effort to follow Diet #1, you will find this the most surefire weight loss technique in the book, and the one I use myself.

THE REVERSAL DIET. Another maneuver that often works, but sometimes backfires, is a reversal diet. It is based upon the principle that your new metabolic pathways may have become so efficient that the fuel wastage which at first made you lose weight rapidly diminishes, and the diet becomes less effective. (The one person who *wants* to waste fuel nowadays is a dieter.)

Sometimes if you switch to an all carbohydrate diet for one week, then switch back to your level one diet, the weight loss starts up all over again.

I've used this reversal diet on many patients, and often it works to perfection. But too often it also brings back many of the old problems—the bloat, the water retention, the fatigue, the hunger. In an effort to avoid these symptoms, I have devised a reversal diet which still avoids the major carbohydrate problem foods, sugar and flour.

THE RULES OF THE REVERSAL DIET

Eat all you want of:

Vegetables (including lentils, starchy vegetables, popcorn)
Fruit (except dates, figs, raisins, juice)
Whole grain (but no refined kinds of flour, cereals or breads)
Water, tea, diet soda, club soda
And you may have 4 ounces of whole milk.

Note that there is virtually no protein or fat on this diet, which unfortunately means no meat, and no butter on your corn or baked potato. And there are still no refined carbohydrates.

Such a diet is rarely suitable for long-term use, but if allowed for a week or two, it should set the stage for renewed responsiveness to the first level of Diet #1. Others, such as one of my favorite Hollywood starlets, have discovered such a sense of well-being on this type of vegetarian diet, that they have vowed to remain on a similar diet as a way of life.

IF YOU HAVE A METABOLIC PROBLEM. Failure to lose weight on a diet low in both calories and carbohydrates is strong evidence of a metabolic imbalance, and a medical investigation should be undertaken to find out more about it.

Unfortunately, routine laboratory testing rarely finds the answer for people who have this problem. Often they have consulted several doctors, and the idea that they have a metabolic problem has been scoffed at. Generally, they are told they just eat too much and that they cheat on their diets.

This really disturbs me. A patient struggles to follow the doctor's advice, but does not lose weight, and then his doctor says, "You're cheating." This is double destruction, because not only has the patient failed on the diet, but has been put down by the very person whose help he wanted.

Variations in metabolic responses are important factors in obesity, and any physician should know that he will be seeing many cases of impaired response. If the patient is a sloppy dieter, and the doctor wants to be critical, okay; but a patient who is not losing weight because of his metabolism deserves understanding and sympathy, rather than an attack upon his integrity by a physician who really doesn't understand the condition he's treating.

YOU MAY HAVE A THYROID PROBLEM. Dr. Irving Perlstein in Louisville found that approximately 15 percent of the seriously overweight produced antibodies to their own thyroid hormone. When he gave them large doses of synthetic thyroid, the antibodies were neutralized so that the patients could achieve a normal weight loss when placed on a high-protein, low-carbohydrate, low-fat, frequent-small-feeding diet. The results he found are certainly significant enough to warrant a clinical trial in refractory patients to see whether synthetic thyroid might prove of benefit.

Because tests often don't show up poor thyroid functioning, a clinical trial is sometimes the only sure way to test. Other evidence of poor thyroid function; lethargy, dry skin, prolonged menstrual cycle, and inability to keep warm.

Dr. Perlstein claims that weight reduction and long-term control have been achieved in about 80 percent of his patients receiving thyroid medication plus the diet.

There is one risk involved with thyroid hormones: in a patient who is susceptible to heart disease, there is increased risk of a coronary event. So they are not to be taken lightly.

OTHER APPROACHES. There probably is a place for the drug phenformin in selected cases of obesity associated with diabetic-hypoglycemic disturbances. I have used it upon occasion, with some success, but with unpredictable results. Ask your doctor. I have also used massive doses of vitamin B_6 (1,500 mg.) with success in selected cases. I believe that specific vitamin regimens which promote weight loss will be devised in the future.

THE ONE THING TO REMEMBER. It is worth the effort of trial and error to find your best diet because your best diet will make you feel better than you ever have *and* it will bring you to and keep you at your ideal weight.

If it only makes you feel your best, that is reason enough to stay with it. But with a little attention to the suggestions in this chapter, you should be able to make it do both.

21

Special advice about children

I strongly suggest that anybody who is raising children begin as early as possible to get them on a diet that can promote their future health.

When a tiny infant is born into the world, its first food if it is lucky will be the nourishing milk from its mother's warm, comforting breast; but if it's like most newborns in the United States, its first meal will be water with . . . of all things . . . sugar in it! Right from the first day the infant is conditioned to develop a taste for sugar.

Then, to continue to imprint his brain with the desire for sugar, as a toddler he is rewarded with lollipops at the barbershop or doctor's office (of all places!), is given cookies or candy for being good, and is brought sweets as a symbol of love from grandma and grandpa.

By the time he is a teen-ager he has such a taste for sweets that his diet may be largely made up of soda pop, cakes, candy bars, and pizza, perhaps with a little milk thrown in.

If you want to do your child a big favor, keep him off sugar. Reward him with something else, such as love to sustain him, a steak and fresh salad to nourish him, or a baseball or tennis racket to exercise him. But not with sugar that will set him up for possible poor health the rest of his life.

THE HEALTH PICTURE OF CHILDREN IN THIS COUNTRY IS NOT NEARLY AS GOOD AS WE THINK IT IS. Until recently, severe malnutrition in children was thought to exist only beyond the borders of the United States. Now we know differently. A huge number of our children has deficiencies in vitamins and minerals, and even protein.

The deficiencies often cause apathy in school, growth retardation, and vulnerability to illness. Hundreds of thousands of children make their way listlessly, or perhaps belligerently, through school, failing to reach their inherent potential because teachers, physicians, and parents do not recognize the nutritional cause of their lack of energy.

THE NUTRITION WE GIVE OUR CHILDREN IS BAD BEFORE THEY ARE EVEN BORN. We worry about giving all high school children equal opportunity for development, yet from birth we are not giving our children their full opportunity for optimal health and mental development because we are not providing them necessary nutrition.

Even starting with the prenatal diet we fail them. In the United States, which has the highest material standard of living of the world, an estimated 35,000 newborn babies die every year because their mothers are undernourished during pregnancy. And about 120,000 babies are born malnourished every year.

RICH OR POOR, CITY OR COUNTRY, CHILDREN ARE NOT GETTING A PROPER DIET. A special committee of the American Academy of Pediatrics warns, "Present information should prompt the pediatricians and other physicians caring for children to become increasingly aware, informed and concerned about nutritional problems in a population of growing individuals."

And if you think your kids are getting proper nutrition from the school lunch programs, forget it. A team of scientists from the Rutgers University Food-Science Department surveyed school meals and found inadequacies in almost every area they tested for, including vitamins A and C, the B vitamins, and phosphorus, calcium, and iron.

PROFIT FROM YOUR CHILDREN. One of my pet peeves is the marketing to children of products unnecessarily loaded with sugar. Have you ever watched the commercials on Saturday morning television? In 200 minutes of viewing, a child sees seventy-three brainwashing commercials mostly pushing sugar-laden cereals, candy, cookies, and soda pop. And to make matters worse, the huckstering is frequently worked into the script. Just three of the cereal companies—Kellogg, General Mills, and General Foods—together spend $42 million for television advertising.

The problem of sugar-coated cereals is so bad that the Consumer Sub-Committee of the United States Senate held special hearings on that subject. There Robert B. Choate, chairman of the Council on Children, Media, and Merchandising said, "I believe our children are deliberately being sold the sponsor's less nutritious products over television . . . I have talked to food researchers, the directors of research of major food companies, and have been told time and again they have in their vaults better quality products, and it's the sales policy which dominates whether it will get on the market and how it is sold."

Senator Frank E. Moss, chairman of the Consumer Sub-Committee, said, "I urge the American consumers to take heed. No longer can mothers blithely send their children off to school after serving them a bowl of their favorite cereal confident that they are full of nutritious body-building food. . . . The consumers of this nation have a right to be free from the bombardment of misinformation about the food they buy. They have a right to know about nutrition."

SO WHAT CAN I DO AS A PARENT? You can get your children on the proper diet. In fact, I would have to say that, if you don't allow them their full potential by providing them with proper nutrition, you're being irresponsible as a parent.

YOU SHOULD START YOUR CHILD'S NUTRITION PROGRAM BEFORE HE'S EVEN BORN. Many veterinarians and farmers are decades ahead of some parents and physicians in applying the basic principles of scientific nutrition to pregnancy.

The Society for the Protection of the Unborn Through Nutrition says that the increasing numbers of defective children due to poor nutrition being born to women of all economic classes in our nation is tantamount to a new thalidomide disaster.

MY ADVICE TO POTENTIAL MOTHERS: *Before* you get pregnant, get to your ideal weight. If you are more than ten pounds overweight, go on Diet #1.

Pre-pregnancy fatness definitely means a greater chance of obstetric complications. Obese women have toxemia of pregnancy twenty-five times more often than women who are thin; miscarriages occur twice as often; and need for Cesarean section is nearly three times as great.

And newborn infants of fat mothers have a death rate two and a half times higher than babies born to mothers whose weight is normal.

But do your reducing before pregnancy, your weight *control* during. If you are reducing on Diet #1 and become pregnant, *stop trying to lose,* and adjust your diet to allow you to achieve close to the ideal weight gain of twenty-four pounds total during pregnancy.

EVEN MORE IMPORTANT IS GETTING ENOUGH VITAMINS AND MINERALS. Be sure to keep up your needed vitamin and mineral supplements, and particularly make sure that sufficient calcium is included for the second half of your pregnancy. Vitamins E, C, folic acid, pyridoxine, and the minerals iron and zinc are most important.

THE SINGLE MOST IMPORTANT THING YOU CAN DO AFTER YOUR CHILD IS BORN. That is to breast feed your baby. Babies who feed on breast milk, rather than formula, have been shown to have fewer allergies, fewer colds and other illnesses, miss fewer days in school, and have fewer doctor visits. Also be sure to give him vitamin and mineral supplements that contain adequate amounts of *all* nutrients.

WHEN YOUR CHILD IS READY TO START ON SOLIDS. For heaven's sake don't add sugar. Let him start out appreciating the natural taste of the foods he's being introduced to. Buy baby food that does not have sugar or salt added to it by the manufacturer. Read the labels.

GET SUGAR OUT OF YOUR HOUSE. A lot of my patients, if they go off the diet, give me the excuse, "Well, I ate it because it was there."

And I say, "Why was it there?"

"Oh, for the kids."

The candy, the cakes, the cookies, the Ring Dings, the non-nutritious junk food was in the house for the children!

Now after you have read that sugar is not good for fat people and not good for skinny people, and not good for people with normal weight, who is sugar good for—your loved ones?

Cutting sugar out of your children's diet is one of the most important things you can do for them as a parent because it looks more and more as if the sugar damage causing hypoglycemia, diabetes, and heart attack starts early in childhood.

The Department of Agriculture has found that rats fed a 65 percent sucrose diet just after weaning had much higher blood cholesterol levels in adult life than other rats not fed sugar. In other words, excess sugar in infancy caused high cholesterol levels in adulthood.

Many scientists believe that the same thing is happening to people.

CLEAN YOUR PLATE AND DIE YOUNG—HOW MOTHERS OVERSTUFF THEIR CHILDREN. Help stamp out the clean-the-plate club.

Mothers of America for generations have been taught to believe that children should eat everything on their plates— whether they are hungry or not, that the fat baby is a healthy baby and that a healthy child must eat a set amount of food every day.

Wrong. Wrong on all three counts. Don't make your child eat when he doesn't want to. Children's needs for food vary. Just be sure that when your child *is* hungry you have plenty of nourishing food for him to eat, so that he doesn't fill up on junk.

Once the baby starts on solids, let him cut back on the amount of milk he drinks if he wishes.

BUT WHY SHOULD I WORRY ABOUT FAT IN MY CHILDREN? Because what they have now will probably determine what they have for the rest of their lives.

Baby fat does *not* melt away at puberty. If your child is fat at the age of five, the chances are four out of five that he will be a fat adult.

Obesity, fatigue, and marginal health do not suddenly begin in middle or old age, but begin silently and insidiously early in life. So the best way to make sure your child is a slim and healthy adult is to see that he is a slim and healthy child. Proper nutrition now might mean your child won't have to worry about being fat, tired, and falling apart later.

What I want to see are proper eating patterns established in childhood, making obesity preventable. We have preventive medicine, let's have preventive eating.

EXERCISE IS IMPORTANT TOO. It increases energy, normalizes weight, and builds self-confidence.

HYPOGLYCEMIA IN CHILDREN. If your child has attacks of paleness, limpness, inattention, staring into space, listlessness, headaches, lack of coordination, stupor, convulsions, rapid heartbeats, or sweating, the chances are very great he may have low blood sugar. For low blood sugar can occur in a child. When glucose tolerance tests were done in one group of forty-seven obese children, thirty-four of them had some impairment of glucose metabolism. It is sometimes caused by tumor or hormone imbalances, but after age five, as in adults, it is more likely to be connected with diet.

Those of us who have seen hypoglycemia in children know what deep disturbances low blood sugar can cause. A child may be subject to anxiety attacks, may run away, may be aggressive and destructive, or he may go in the other direction and be lethargic, apathetic, unable to become interested in anything, with few friends and a poor school record.

How many times have you seen a mother standing in the check-out line with a shopping cart piled high with soft drinks, cookies, candies, donuts, and sugar-coated cereal, and right behind her a screaming, uncontrollable child. Is it only coincidence? Or is it really a graphic example of what we are doing to our children with the foods we are giving them?

In addition there are some rather specific problems due to nutritional improprieties. Autistic children, those who interact very poorly with others, underachievers, hyperactive children, those with reading and learning disabilities, those with personality disturbances—all can be helped by nutritional techniques.

This diet, the ketogenic diet, has been known for more than half a century to be invaluable in managing such children. In 1925, Dr. M. G. Peterman of the Mayo Clinic stated: "In all of the children treated with the ketogenic diet, there was a marked change in character, concomitant with the ketosis, a decrease in irritability, and an increased interest and alertness; the children slept better and were more easily disciplined."

And Dr. Ben Feingold of the Kaiser-Permanente Foundation has discovered that many such children respond to the simple technique of removing all food additives and chemical flavoring agents from their diets.

SYMPTOMS IN OLDER CHILDREN. If your teen-ager needs extraordinary amounts of sleep, seems depressed, or is undergoing behavior changes, consider the possibility that he too may have hypoglycemia. Body changes plus the turmoil of growing up put many stresses upon the teen-ager that he never had before, stresses that affect the carbohydrate metabolism greatly. In addition, the teen-ager at this time is also likely to be adding caffeine, alcohol, and perhaps cigarettes to his body stresses.

The almost universal complaint of parents about their teen-age children is their lethargy and lack of energy. Teen-agers seem to sleep forever and wake up only to find a place to sit down and rest. How much of this teen-age fatigue syndrome is due to hypoglycemia from a thoughtless diet remains to be seen. But I think you'll find some pretty astounding changes in your teen-ager's energy level if you put him on our diet program. When I review the history of a tired adult and ask when it first began, the most frequent answer is "in my teens." And that's just when you should look for hypoglycemia to be most likely to appear in your child.

IF YOU THINK YOUR CHILD HAS HYPOGLYCEMIA. Do the same kind of careful diet and medical history on your child as you did on yourself, including the at-home glucose tolerance test. Then take him for the six-hour glucose tolerance test to your family doctor or to someone who specializes in hypoglycemia, nutrition, or metabolism.

If no other physical causes are found for his symptoms, then do try the changes in his diet. Start with the diet most suitable to his body weight. You may find that simply eliminating candy, cookies, cake, and soft drinks in addition to giving him the vitamin and mineral supplements will do the trick.

A child can easily learn to watch for the signs that his sugar level is dropping. He may find himself aimlessly staring into space, or grinding his teeth, clenching his fists, or feeling anger without due cause. A teen-ager may crave a cigarette or a Coke.

Help him avoid cheating by not having soda pop and sweets around the house. Instead keep the refrigerator loaded with ready-to-eat salads, cheeses, diet sodas, and nutritious leftovers.

Do not ignore a child's symptoms if they persist! They can have serious repercussions in his development, in his school life, and even carry through with complications in adulthood.

Your child depends on you. It is your responsibility to see that whatever is causing these symptoms is treated.

22

In defense of the egg

Contemporary medicine has come to the point where, if a person were to call a doctor and say, "Doctor, I can't move my legs, I am feverish, my body is racked with pain, I'm spitting blood, and my cholesterol is high," the doctor will say, "Well, don't eat any eggs."

The No. 1 medical fear-provoker in America today seems to be an elevated cholesterol level. I must conclude that the emphasis is grossly misplaced. I am not saying that cholesterol elevation has no significance as a risk factor for heart attacks, but it is certainly not the major cause of heart attacks, as we are being rather emphatically led to believe.

Millions of advertising dollars are being spent each year urging us to consume margarine and egg substitutes and to cut down on eggs and saturated fats.

IS CHOLESTEROL ALL BAD? The lay person, exposed to this massive advertising barrage, may think so. But cholesterol is a complex chemical that is absolutely essential to life. It is the basic molecular building block, from which adrenal hormones, sex hormones, vitamin D, and the bile acids necessary to digestion are formed.

Cholesterol forms part of the membranes that surround every cell in our bodies. It is part of the protective covering of the nerve fibers; it makes up a large part of the brain. It combines with various proteins to form lipoproteins, needed to transport fats used as energy. Recent findings indicate that cholesterol may be essential to normal growth, longevity, and resistance to infection and toxicity.

NOT GETTING ENOUGH FAT AND CHOLESTEROL CAN CAUSE BIG PROBLEMS. Many of my patients who have been on low-fat low-cholesterol diets have very dry skin. I have seen women with cholesterol levels so low they don't menstruate, probably because their bodies do not contain enough cholesterol to form the sterol ring, the basic structure of the sex hormones. Some women may develop menstrual irregularities, lack of sex drive, painful intercourse or poor bust development from the systematic exclusion of fats from the diet. By eating eggs and high nutrient diets, many have resumed a regular menstrual pattern.

IT'S TIME TO EXAMINE THE REAL FACTS BEHIND THE CHOLESTEROL CONTROVERSY. Fact One: Dietary cholesterol as found in egg yolks, shellfish, and other food provides only 20 to 30 percent of the cholesterol in your body. Most is manufactured within your body by your liver and intestines from the metabolism of either proteins, fats, or carbohydrates. In fact, in people eating a *high*-carbohydrate diet, the source of most cholesterol is the dietary carbohydrate.

Fact Two: A complicated feedback mechanism operates which means that the more cholesterol you eat, the less you manufacture; the less you eat, the more you manufacture.

Fact Three: There is a limit to the amount of cholesterol that can be absorbed through your digestive tract, particularly beyond the cholesterol contained in two eggs per day (500 mg.).

THE NET RESULT. For every 100 milligrams of cholesterol removed from the daily diet, the blood level falls only three points. Eliminating two eggs a day from your diet could only be expected to lower your cholesterol 15 points at most.

And, if the latest study by Dr. Roslyn Alfin-Slater of UCLA is any indication, there may be very little effect. Her research group fed two extra eggs daily to fifty-two young and middle-aged men for eight weeks. *There was no significant increase in their cholesterol level.*

"We, like everyone else, had been convinced that when you eat cholesterol, you get cholesterol," Dr. Alfin-Slater said in an interview. "But when we stopped to think that all of the studies in the past never tested the normal diet in relation to egg eating, we decided to see what happens. Our findings surprised us as much as anyone else."

THE AMERICAN HEART ASSOCIATION'S BIG POINT. Their major argument seems to be that blood cholesterol levels are valuable in predicting heart problems. And they are—I'll agree to that readily. But there is a difference between the level of cholesterol in your *blood* and the level of cholesterol in your *diet*. And there is a difference between a prediction and a cause. For example, many arthritics say they can *predict* weather changes by their rheumatism; this does not mean their rheumatism *causes* weather changes.

As Dr. George Mann, professor of medicine at Vanderbilt's School of Medicine, has stated, the Heart Association has "committed the nutritional disaster of the century by confusing association with causation, to the endless delight and profit of food companies that employ cholesterol-scare tactics in the advertising."

The highly respected Framingham study failed to show any correlation between cholesterol in the diet and heart attack rates, nor did the survey of over four thousand people in Tecumseh, Michigan.

The several clinical trials that do show where a fat, low-cholesterol diet lowered the frequency of heart attacks have been criticized in numerous ways, as when items such as sugar were also restricted.

THERE ARE MANY EXCEPTIONS. In Japan, for example, during the period when there was a 14 percent *decrease* in deaths from heart attacks, the consumption of eggs went *up* by 300 percent.

Dr. Michael DeBakey, the well-known Houston heart surgeon, says, "About 80 percent of my sickest patients have cholesterol levels of normal people." He observed in seventeen hundred patients that there was no correlation between serum cholesterol levels and the nature and extent of atherosclerotic disease.

ANIMAL EXPERIMENTS SHOW THE SAME RESULTS. In one experiment, Dr. G. Sperling fed rats high-cholesterol diets over a long period and found the rats whose diets were supplemented with eggs every day lived longer than the others. Dr. T. C. Huang of Canton, Ohio, showed cholesterol supplements and saturated fats both prolonged the life-span of rats.

BUT EVEN IF CHOLESTEROL IS LOWERED, THERE IS NO ASSURANCE THAT THE DEATH RATE FROM HEART DISEASE IS LOWERED. Between 1960 and 1969, the Medical Research Council in England followed a group of 393 men who had had heart attacks. A test group was fed a diet that succeeded in dropping mean cholesterol levels, but there was *no decrease in cardiovascular deaths*. A similar English study on a low-fat diet involving 264 men was so disappointing that the researchers concluded: "A low-fat diet has no place in the treatment of myocardial infarction."

And more recently, the Minnesota Coronary Survey studied over nine thousand subjects for over four years, comparing a low-cholesterol, high-polyunsaturated-fat diet with a normal one. Although the cholesterol levels dropped, "There was not the slightest hint of benefit" in lowering the frequency of death or of heart attacks.

THE CORONARY DISEASE PREVENTION STUDY. The government did an eight-year study on 8,000 people in fifty-three cities, testing drugs used to lower cholesterol to see if people who had had a heart attack could avoid the second attack. The drugs *did* lower cholesterol level, but did *not* prevent the second coronary.

THE BRITISH STATEMENT. In Great Britain the most recent government report on diet and coronary heart disease points a very accusing finger at the amount of sugar in the diet, but not at cholesterol.

They say, "There is no certainty that the reduction of cholesterol intake diminishes the susceptibility to heart disease. . . . We have found no evidence which relates the number of eggs to a risk of heart disease."

The panel also points out that the higher the national consumption of sucrose, the higher the death rate from heart attacks. They recommend that elimination of sugar should begin in childhood.

SUGAR APPEARS TO BE A BIGGER CAUSE OF HEART DISEASE THAN EITHER CHOLESTEROL OR FAT. In Yemenites, heart disease (and diabetes) increased distinctly with increased intake of sugar, while the intake of eggs and fats remained nearly the same.

Heart disease (and diabetes) was unheard of in Iceland until the 1930s, but is quite prevalent now. Sugar was brought to the Icelandic diet in the 1920s. The development of a heart disease epidemic in Poland and Yugoslavia was concomitant with a quadrupling of the sugar intake, despite a fall in animal fat intake.

The Eskimos never had heart disease when they lived on a high-fat Eskimo diet, but have it now that they eat sugar. The Masai and Samburu tribes in Africa are noted for their very low blood cholesterol levels even though they have a high cholesterol and fat diet. They eat no sugar.

Drs. Daniela Gsell and Jean Mayer studied a group of Swiss Alpine villagers who consume more animal fat and cholesterol than their urban counterparts, but have much lower cholesterol levels. In their diet, however, "desserts are extreme rarities."

Ethiopia, which has one of the world's lowest intakes of sugar, has virtually no heart disease, whether blood cholesterol levels are high or low.

TO ME IT IS HISTORICAL EVIDENCE THAT IS MOST CONVINCING. There is one extremely important fact to bear in mind. Coronary heart attacks have not always been a part of our lives—and deaths. The very first mention of them in the scientific literature was in 1896 and the second in 1912. Since then, the condition has skyrocketed to the point where half our population must expect to die of coronary heart disease.

THIS FACT DEMANDS AN EXPLANATION. How can a population change from total resistance to heart disease to susceptibility in just a few generations? To blame it only on stress or lack of exercise is illogical. Many people in the nineteenth century were indolent or excitable.

If the prime cause is dietary, as most experts believe it is, then there must be dietary factors which are common now, but which were very rare then.

LET'S EXAMINE THE HISTORY OF OUR FOOD SUPPLY. Bearing in mind that heart disease takes twenty to fifty years to develop, we must examine changes in food supply which precede the escalation of heart disease by that many years. Since the incidence of heart disease has been climbing since 1920, our study of food habits should begin around the year 1890. Drs. Antar, Ohlson, and Hodges have done just that.

They found we eat approximately the same quantities of protein, fats, and carbohydrates as we did at the turn of the century. However, the *types* of these foods have changed dramatically. We now consume considerably more sugar and refined starches, and significantly *less* animal fat and *more* vegetable fat than we did then. For instance, between 1940 and 1970, our consumption of animal fats has *halved,* while our consumption of vegetable oils has *more than doubled.*

HOW IMPORTANT ARE REFINED CARBOHYDRATES? Consider the study by Dr. S. L. Malhotra, who analyzed railroad workers in both the north and south of India. In the south, only 3½ percent of the calories are supplied by fat (45 percent of which are polyunsaturated), the bulk coming from a *refined* form of rice. The diet in the north is 23 percent fat, and almost all saturated animal fats, but the major carbohydrates are *unrefined* wheat and maize. The result? Coronary disease is seven times more common in the low-fat south than in the north!

THERE'S ANOTHER HALF TO THE CHOLESTEROL STORY. No consideration of lipids (blood fats) and coronary heart disease could be remotely complete without an understanding of the importance of triglyceride, the substance that fills our fat cells.

And triglyceride levels, like cholesterol, are important in predicting the likelihood of developing heart attacks. Many authorities believe that triglyceride may be even *more* important than cholesterol.

Drs. Lars Carlson and L. E. Böttiger in Stockholm found that both cholesterol and triglyceride are independent predictors of heart disease and neither one is better than the other.

The important consideration for you is not to know that triglycerides are worse than cholesterol, or vice versa, but to know that lipid patterns can be quite different in different people. Two people eating exactly the same diet can have completely different patterns: one may have high triglyceride and low cholesterol (called the type IV pattern), and the other may have high cholesterol, but low triglyceride (the type II pattern).

WHAT DOES THIS MEAN TO YOU? Simply this: You must find out from your doctor what *your* pattern, *your* lipid profile is. More importantly you must know your response to different diets.

It appears that there are some who respond to a high fat or high cholesterol intake with an elevation of cholesterol levels. There is no reason to penalize those who do *not* respond in such a way and deny them the nutritional advantages or the enjoyment of eggs, shellfish, and marbled cuts of meat.

WHY ARE TRIGLYCERIDES SO IMPORTANT? One recent study shows how important triglycerides can be. In a midwest hospital, 500 patients who had had coronaries at a particularly young age were analyzed. For every *one* person stricken with heart disease in the prime of life who had cholesterol elevation, there were *three* afflicted in association with high levels of triglyceride. Triglycerides increase in your bloodstream, not when you eat fats or eggs or meat, but when you eat carbohydrates.

Many studies show a dramatic lowering of triglyceride on a low-carbohydrate diet. Dr. George Bray and his associates demonstrated that triglyceride levels in obese subjects fell after just two weeks on a 60-gram carbohydrate diet. The readings dropped from 184 to 85. The insulin level, another forecaster of heart disease, dropped also. Dr. Y. Fujita of Dallas, Texas, also reports that insulin levels and triglyceride levels are much lower on a 10-gram carbohydrate diet. In my obesity studies, the average triglyceride level when a patient came to me was a rather high 180 mg. percent. After a month or two on my diet, the average reading was 115 mg. percent, a perfectly normal reading. And Dr. Raymond Watten of San Diego Naval Station, studying two thousand overweight subjects on a high-fat, low-carbohydrate diet, reports almost exactly the same results.

A LOW-CARBOHYDRATE DIET USUALLY LOWERS BOTH CHOLESTEROL AND TRIGLYCERIDE. Many studies have shown the dramatic lowering of blood fats on a low-carbohydrate diet. Dr. Willard Krehl's study showed it; seven obese women all decreased their cholesterol on a diet very similar to mine.

A group at Harvard used a 26-gram low-carbohydrate diet to treat a group of patients with high triglycerides. In a few weeks, the triglycerides fell from 1628 to 286 and the cholesterol from 470 to 290. Several other studies have shown similar results.

THE ESTABLISHMENT TRIED TO REFUTE THESE FACTS. They cite a Harvard study in which cholesterol levels were measured before beginning a strict low-carbohydrate diet and were remeasured a week later. Now it is well known that any strict diet will cause an initial elevation of the cholesterol level. Dr. Norman Ende of Vanderbilt University demonstrated this when he showed that, on the third and fourth days of fasting, the cholesterol levels would always go up. Presumably the cholesterol is leaving its storage places, being mobilized into the bloodstream so that it can be used as fuel. Many diets effective in lowering the cholesterol show this phenomenon during the first week. The Harvard group studied Dr. Stillman's Quick Weight Loss Diet, and—to no one's surprise—found that in one week the cholesterol levels went up. Very few subjects were observed for much longer than one week. Their conclusion that the diet provided "potential risk" for the long term was obviously unwarranted.

The study casts doubt upon itself by calling the diet "rich in fat" after tabulating that the diet contained only 73 grams of fat, compared to the national average of 115 grams. If anything, the study actually proved that cholesterol levels may go up if the intake of fat is reduced.

MANY SCIENTISTS AGREE WITH ME. Arthur Blumenfeld, in seeking support for his personal view that a low-fat diet *is preferable,* sent a questionnaire to over one hundred "eminent medical scientists." The question was: Which of two diets, one a low-carbohydrate, the other a low-fat, is more anticoronary? To his chagrin and surprise, more than 90 percent of these acknowledged experts in the field of lipid metabolism expressed a preference for a low-carbohydrate diet.

THE OTHER CONTROVERSY—POLYUNSATURATES. A diet high in polyunsaturates causes a depletion of vitamin E in the body, and without sufficient vitamin E even red blood cells can be destroyed.

One plastic surgeon reports that 78 percent of his patients on high polyunsaturated diets showed signs of premature aging and a high frequency of precancerous or cancerous skin lesions. A study done at the Mayo Clinic found breast cancer patients had high concentrations of polyunsaturated fats in their blood and in the diseased tissue. A study at the Veteran's Hospital in Los Angeles showed that patients fed a high polyunsaturated diet developed 60 percent more cancers than a control group. A study by Dr. Hans Kaunitz showed the development of cirrhosis of the liver in laboratory animals fed diets high in polyunsaturates.

Dr. Fred A. Kummerow and a research team from the University of Illinois reported in 1974 that margarine caused more atherosclerosis than cholesterol-rich beef fat, butter, and eggs. Sugar was second in causing damage.

And polyunsaturates may increase blood pressure. Dr. Denham Harman, of the University of Nebraska, concludes from animal studies that the concentrated use of polyunsaturates can shorten a person's life by fifteen years.

And when a polyunsaturated fat is heated, it becomes more dangerous. When such heated oil was fed to animals, breast cancer increased by 127 percent. Some animals develop cancers if fed more than 10 percent unsaturates, which is less than the American Heart Association recommends.

Dr. Kurt Oster, of Bridgeport, Connecticut, calls the recommendations of limiting cholesterol and saturated fats, a "simplistic, naive solution not based on any scientific facts. This is

biologically unsound and is possibly dangerous to the consumer's health." But, as Dr. George Mann said in an interview,
"It sells a hell of a lot of margarine, doesn't it?"

MANY FACTORS. We have concentrated so much on cholesterol that very little attention has been paid to other theories of
coronary risk factors, such as too much sugar, lack of trace minerals, softness of water, lack of exercise, smoking, impaired glucose tolerance curves, The Pill, all of which have been
significantly related to heart attacks.

We must look at all of these factors as well as obesity,
stress, aggressiveness, high blood pressure, diabetes, triglyceride elevations, and an abnormal level of certain hormones,
especially insulin. All of these, not just cholesterol, are important.

I DO NOT BELIEVE THAT HIGH BLOOD CHOLESTEROL IS THE
ONLY FACTOR IN HEART DISEASE. Nor do I believe that decreasing eggs or fat in the diet is the best way to prevent heart
disease.

Further, I believe you get better results by eliminating
sugar in your diet and supplementing your diet with vitamins
and minerals.

For I believe that elevations of cholesterol are a reflection
of a nutritional imbalance, and it is that nutritional imbalance,
rather than the cholesterol itself, that truly causes heart disease.

One of the best sources of key nutrients is the egg. If you
don't eat eggs for breakfast, what are you going to have?
Presweetened cereal? A donut? Black coffee and a cigarette?
No one can make me believe those are healthier than an ome-
lette.

Eggs are an important source of protein, of the sulfur-containing amino acids, of vitamins, especially those in the B complex, and of important trace minerals such as selenium.

What I believe, and so do many others, is that unless you
have demonstrated specific inability to handle cholesterol, consumption of cholesterol-containing foods is safe *as long as the
rest of the diet is good.*

This has been shown in both animal and human studies.
Rats fed an average diet with very large amounts of fat get

atherosclerosis. But give them high quality protein, vitamins, and minerals, and they can eat a diet of 62 to 65 percent fat and not get atherosclerosis. Drs. L. D. Greenberg and J. F. Rinehart showed that when monkeys were made deficient in vitamin B_6, they developed atherosclerosis rapidly. When they were given vitamin B_6, *even when they had high cholesterol diets* their cholesterol levels went down.

Dr. Constance Spittle, a British pathologist, found vitamin C mobilized cholesterol from the arteries of patients with atherosclerosis. And Dr. Boris Sokoloff, with 1 to 3 grams of vitamin C per day, found "moderate to impressive" improvement in atherosclerotic patients.

Yes, I believe your cholesterol (and your triglycerides) should be as close to the ideal as possible. Not because they *cause* heart disease, but because they reflect an ideal state of good health.

Dean of nutritionists Dr. Roger Williams agrees. He says, "Even if prevailing views are to be contrary, I think that the evidence points strongly toward the conclusion that the nutritional environment of the body cells—involving minerals, amino acids and vitamins—is crucial, and that the amount of fat or cholesterol is relatively inconsequential."

THERE ARE MANY THINGS YOU CAN DO TO IMPROVE YOUR HEALTH AND LOWER YOUR CHOLESTEROL, AND NONE OF THESE REQUIRE THAT YOU STOP EATING EGGS. Tens of thousands of cholesterol determinations have been done in my office, many patients getting as many as ten different readings. The low-carbohydrate diet usually produces favorable results. For most people a diet need not restrict fat if it restricts carbohydrates and if it supplies the proper vitamins and minerals. I have long felt that a portion of the success my patients have with their lipids is due to the liberal usage of nutrition supplements.

Among the nutrients that have been reported to lower cholesterol levels are vitamin A, vitamins B_3 and B_6, vitamin C, lecithin, choline, inositol, calcium and magnesium orotates, B_{15} (pangamic acid), chromium, and manganese.

All of these are an integral part of the Superenergy Diet. And if you are one of the rare people who need still further help, plant sterols, bran, pectin, and guar gum may serve to lower cholesterol.

So too will exercise.

If you are overweight, reducing your weight will usually reduce your cholesterol and triglycerides no matter how many eggs you eat.

So will reducing stress. If you are anxious or tense, your cholesterol can change by as much as 100 percent.

So will eliminating sugar in your diet. In tests at Brookhaven National Laboratory, triglyceride deposits in patients on a high-sugar but low-fat diet were two to five times greater than in patients on a low-sugar high-fat diet. Dr. John Yudkin showed about one-third of people responded to sugar with increase in triglycerides, insulin, and stickiness of blood platelets. And Dr. Ancel Keys, Dr. J. T. Anderson, and Dr. F. Grande found when men ate simple sugars, serum cholesterol levels were high. When the sugar was replaced by complex carbohydrates derived from fruits and vegetables, the serum cholesterol levels went down.

THE IMPORTANT FINAL DETERMINANT IS YOUR OWN BLOOD PICTURE. The most important measure you can take is to obtain a base line cholesterol and triglyceride level before embarking on any dietary regimen, and *then see your response* to the diet.

You must find out your own individual lipid profile. Nobody else's cholesterol is important to you, only yours. Cholesterol is highly unpredictable. I can have two new patients sitting in the waiting room, both consuming similar diets, and one will have a normal cholesterol of 190 and the other a high cholesterol of 390. It's no surprise that they may respond so differently to a new diet.

In my patients, cholesterol and triglyceride are checked at the first visit; if they are elevated, we recheck in about three weeks; if not, we check in four to eight weeks. Then if the patient is on the low-carbohydrate diet and both cholesterol and triglycerides are down, as they usually are, we check again in three or four months. At any time that the blood levels are not satisfactory, we make the appropriate dietary modification and recheck in three or four weeks. When a patient finishes a course of dietary counseling, he has developed about the best balance between cholesterol, triglycerides, and blood sugar that we can possibly work out.

In our patients on the Superenergy Diet, we find that 63 percent show a lower cholesterol, in some the cholesterol level falling to less than half what it was before; and 94 percent have a lowered level of triglycerides.

Many of my patients even eat three or four eggs a day and still drop their cholesterol levels a hundred points or more.

As it looks now, one of the more promising ways to avoid heart attacks would be to go back to the diet of the preheart-disease era when people ate eggs but did not eat large amounts of sugar.

23
Bonus benefits

When I began working with these diets, I soon learned that overweight, fatigue, depression, and hunger would all recede when patients adopted the new eating patterns. But I was frequently surprised to hear my patients report that a wide variety of other symptoms seemed to clear up at the same time. Headaches, intestinal complaints, sleep problems, menopausal troubles, emotional problems, heart symptoms, dizzy spells—all these, and more, seemed to improve unexpectedly in many, many cases.

In fact, this experience gave form to my belief that nutritional therapies will one day prove to be much more effective than drug treatments for *most* of our common medical problems.

My patients had lived with these symptoms so long that they accepted them as normal, sometimes not even mentioning them on their first visit. But they told me when they came back: "You know, Doc, my headaches [or dizzy spells or whatever] have gone!"

YOU MIGHT CALL THESE BONUS BENEFITS. They come mainly as a result of four facets of the diet: elimination of sugar, proper use of vitamins and minerals, correction of hypoglycemia, and the benefits of being in ketosis. Sometimes these benefits come about because of one small feature of the regimen, such as the correction of a zinc or folic acid deficiency, or elimination of a food causing an allergic reaction; but usually the benefit results from all parts of the diet working together.

Let me make it quite clear that I'm not claiming that *all* of these conditions clear up in *all* patients—that would be ridiculous. There can be many causes of ailments besides the nutritional. But the above problems clear up in enough patients to be of real significance.

THE DIET AND YOUR HEART. Since my specialty in medicine immediately prior to my interest in nutrition was cardiology, the bonus benefits relating to heart disease were the first that I observed.

I found the diet benefits heart patients in the following ways: it combats water retention, and thereby combats heart failure; it lowers high blood pressure; it relieves the chest pain called angina pectoris; it decreases many disturbances in heart rhythm (palpitations); and it lowers cholesterol and triglycerides.

Let's take these points, one by one.

THERE IS A WATER LOSS WHEN CARBOHYDRATES ARE RESTRICTED. All studies have shown this phenomenon. The water loss is especially beneficial in congestive heart failure, in which there is swelling of the feet and ankles from excess fluid and, frequently, shortness of breath because of fluid backup in the lungs. A low-carbohydrate diet is safer and more effective than medications to get the extra water out of the body. I have had hospitalized patients in congestive failure lose forty pounds of fluid in just two weeks, with just bedrest and the ketogenic diet!

THIS DIURETIC EFFECT OF THE DIET HAS OTHER APPLICATIONS, TOO. Many women have a condition called idiopathic or cyclical edema. If you have it, you may notice puffiness and tightness in your hands so you are unable to remove your rings, or your face may be puffy when you wake up, or your shoes tight at the end of the day. Or you may have a tense and bloated abdomen, or have headache, irritability, weakness, mental confusion, inertia, anxiety, depression, or light-headedness on changing position. When women with this syndrome were studied by Drs. Ralph A. Shaw and Leonard J. Kryston at Hahnemann Medical College, and by Dr. Ethan Allen Sims in Vermont, four out of five showed abnormalities in their glucose tolerance tests, approximately half being diabetic and half being hypoglycemic. In my own experience, when this disturbance is treated with carbohydrate restriction, the results are dramatic. I have treated hundreds of such patients just in my own practice and have seen the majority of them improve.

AND WHAT ABOUT BLOOD PRESSURE? Because of this water loss, the weight loss, and the curtailment of sugar intake, the blood pressure drops on this diet, improving in about 80 percent of my patients. If a patient's elevation is mild, I usually do not have to do anything else except to put him on the diet. In more extreme cases of hypertension, severe sodium restriction can produce a further response. In about 20 percent of the patients, we must continue pills for high blood pressure, but, in almost all of these, the dosage can be reduced considerably when the diet is followed.

Critics of the Diet Revolution make note of this in a roundabout way, saying that the diet causes postural hypotension (low blood pressure), making some people feel faint and dizzy when they stand up suddenly. Yet every *drug* that they would recommend to lower the blood pressure does the very same thing. If you have hypertension, make sure both you and your doctor find out promptly what your new diet does for your blood pressure. If you are on medications, chances are that the dosage can be reduced. If you get dizzy spells, have your doctor find out whether your blood pressure has gone too low. The symptom is not very serious and can be avoided by liberalizing the diet just a little.

ANGINA PECTORIS. When a heart patient overexerts himself and is not slowed down by shortness of breath, he may be halted by a pressure, tightness, or pain across his chest. This symptom, called angina pectoris, implies that the blood supply that serves the heart is not sufficient. The cause of this symptom is inadequate circulation through the coronary arteries, the ones that supply the heart muscle itself.

Early in my career, I learned that when my angina patients

went on the ketogenic diet, their angina lessened. And when they cheated by adding some carbohydrate to their diets, the pain would come back.

This fact is not well known, and the explanation for it is somewhat of a mystery. But I am not the first one to discover it. Drs. D. Adlersberg and O. Porges mentioned this effect in a paper written in 1933. In 1942, Dr. Tinsley Harrison pointed out that a sharp fall in glucose to hypoglycemic levels could be the cause of many anginal attacks, and Dr. Benjamin P. Sandler showed that angina pectoris and heart attacks themselves can usually be prevented by maintaining heart patients on a sugar-free, low-carbohydrate, high-protein and fat diet to stabilize blood glucose levels.

Dr. H. J. Roberts of West Palm Beach, Florida, points out that anginal chest pains with onset in the middle of the night that awaken the patient from his sleep are almost invariably linked to low blood sugar and respond to an antihypoglycemic diet.

I have made the following observation on patients with angina pectoris: of those who require nitroglycerine to relieve angina, 80 percent of the ones who go on the ketogenic diet will report improvement and also a reduction in the frequency of need for medication.

PALPITATIONS OF THE HEART. The most frequent disturbances in the rhythm of the heartbeat come on suddenly and are called paroxysmal atrial tachycardia (very rapid regular heartbeat) and paroxysmal atrial fibrillation (chaotic irregularity). A common, less serious rhythm upset is premature (or skipped) beats.

You would be astounded to learn just how often these rhythm irregularities are triggered by falling blood sugar, and how often they are correctable by a dietary program.

I learned about this when my first head nurse was constantly reporting to the hospital emergency room with attacks of paroxysmal tachycardia. I noted that she was a four-teaspoons-of-sugar-in-her-coffee person and made her take a glucose tolerance test. Her curve showed the typical diabetic-hypoglycemic pattern. When we finally got her to avoid sweets, she stopped having the attacks.

More than half the patients who consult me for upsets in

heart rhythm have reported vast improvement after going on the diet.

If you are subject to any of these heart rhythm disturbances, no medical investigation of your case could be considered thorough unless a five- or six-hour glucose tolerance test is performed. If the results suggest an unstable sugar response, then an antihypoglycemic diet might just solve the problem.

YOUR HEART BENEFITS IN OTHER WAYS. Other bonus benefits derive from the vitamins and minerals you will be taking. Drs. Mildred Seelig and Alexander Hettgviet were able to collect 228 references prior to 1973 on research projects confirming the value of just one of these minerals, magnesium, on coronary artery disease. We have already discussed how the diet usually lowers cholesterol and triglyceride levels.

THE KETOGENIC DIET AND DIGESTIVE DISORDERS. These diets will be exceedingly useful also to the gastroenterologist, who deals in problems of the digestive system.

Peptic ulcer, hiatal hernia, esophagitis, gastritis, heartburn, or "nervous stomach" tend to have one common feature: an excess of stomach acid and secretions.

There's plenty of evidence that diets high in refined carbohydrates are a prerequisite for this type of digestive disorder. Dr. Denis P. Burkitt, in a classic essay, pointed out the rarity of conditions such as hiatal hernia and peptic ulcer in societies that don't eat refined carbohydrates the way we do in westernized countries. The refined carbohydrates are responsible for higher insulin levels. And insulin causes increased amounts of gastric acids and enzymes.

As you would expect, you often find abnormal glucose tolerance tests associated with these gastric disorders. Every medical workup for a stomach complaint of this nature should include a glucose tolerance test. I find abnormal curves in 60 percent of my patients with stomach disorders. Dr. Benjamin Sandler first described this same finding in 1940 and I have never seen it refuted.

If insulin is indeed behind these stomach problems, then an anti-insulin diet such as this one should relieve it. Dr. John Yudkin has published several studies, showing that 70 percent of patients with dyspepsia will improve on his version of a low-carbohydrate diet. Again, I find very similar results.

Conclusion: The bland milk-cereal-mashed potatoes high-carbohydrate diet that is frequently prescribed for stomach ailments may not be as effective as a low-carbohydrate diet.

THE LARGE AND SMALL INTESTINE. Conditions such as colitis (ulcerative or mucous colitis, irritable colon), diverticulitis, or ileitis respond quite favorably to the low-carbohydrate program. It probably works by slowing the overly rapid movement of the intestinal tract. Although some textbooks state that a colitis patient should not be placed on a reducing diet, I disagree very strongly. In fact, I have never had a colitis patient who did not show at least some degree of improvement when placed on the ketogenic diet.

WHAT ABOUT GALLBLADDER DISEASE? Critics believe this diet might make gallbladder conditions worse, but I have not found it so. The fact that gallbladder disease is definitely associated with obesity, with diets containing refined carbohydrates, and with diabetes suggests an antisugar regimen might indeed be beneficial in its prevention. It was shown to be so in animals.

Liver diseases do not seem to be either improved or worsened by a ketogenic diet, except for liver disease associated with alcoholism, which improves along with the alcoholism.

THE NEUROLOGIST SHOULD KNOW THIS DIET TOO. The first clinical application of the ketogenic diet in anything besides diabetes was in the purview of the neurologist. Dating back to 1920, neurologists at Mayo Clinic found that a high-fat, low-carbohydrate diet, similar to this version that you are now studying, was exceedingly effective in the treatment of seizure disorders in children. In fact, the diet served as the mainstay of treatment for epilepsy until the discovery of the drug dilantin some fifteen years later. I still use the diet with good results in my patients with seizure disorders, many being able to get off the antiseizure drugs. One word of caution here: Folic acid combats these drugs and must be used sparingly.

MÉNIÈRE'S SYNDROME. This common disorder with attacks of dizziness and ringing in the ears usually will clear up on the diet.

THE COMMONEST SYMPTOM FOR THE NEUROLOGIST TO DEAL WITH—HEADACHE. Headache can come from a variety of causes, some of them serious, most of them benign—and unexplained. Unexplained because too few doctors order a glucose tolerance test as part of the routine investigation of headaches, which can often be caused by hypoglycemia.

Dr. H. J. Roberts described hundreds of hypoglycemic patients, most of whom were obese, who suffered from attacks of overwhelming sleepiness, called narcolepsy. The majority of these people also complained of headache. He found that low blood sugar brought on the headache attacks, and a low-carbohydrate diet "promptly abolished or minimized" the headaches.

OTHER NEUROLOGICAL SYMPTOMS. An involuntary twitching called the Gilles La Tourette syndrome seems to be improved by the diet. So, too, are many cases of peripheral neuritis, which may produce burning or sharp pains or cramps in the legs. Symptoms such as muscle twitching, muscle cramps, shakiness and dizziness often respond to the diet.

THE ALLERGIST WOULD BE WELL ADVISED TO KNOW HOW TO USE THESE DIETS. Asthma, hay fever, hives, all common conditions that have been associated with hypoglycemia, are often improved with the low-carbohydrate diet and vitamin therapy.

Drs. Seale Harris and E. M. Abrahamson have both described the coexistence of asthma and abnormal glucose tolerance tests. Dr. Theron G. Randolph, well-known allergist, has implicated sugar as a factor in allergy symptoms. And the fact that asthma in children would sometimes respond to the ketogenic diet was published as far back as 1930.

In addition, there are specific food allergies, caused especially by wheat, corn, and milk, that often clear up on a diet such as this.

In my experience, the diet has helped many patients with allergies, and in those patients who must be on steroid (cortisone, prednisone) therapy, I have found in most cases that the dosage can be reduced. Should the patients cheat and go off their diet, the symptoms come back promptly.

IF YOUR DOCTOR'S SPECIALTY IS OBSTETRICS AND GYNECOLOGY. He should do routine glucose tolerance tests on all women with premenstrual tension and edema, dysmenorrhea (painful menses), and weight gains following pregnancy. Women with these symptoms should be careful about taking estrogen, since it has a profound effect upon carbohydrate metabolism. I do not believe a woman should be placed on these hormones unless her glucose tolerance results are quite normal, or unless there is no alternative.

Your gynecologist should also be aware that birth control pills have an adverse effect on folic acid, B_2, B_6, B_{12} and perhaps B_1 and A. And they produce an increase in copper levels and a decrease in zinc levels. Between the vitamin-mineral regimen and the diet, these gynecologic complaints often clear up promptly. In fact, I have never found a treatment more effective for premenstrual problems.

THE UROLOGIST, TOO, SHOULD KNOW THIS DIET. The ketogenic diet was used in the treatment of a variety of urinary tract infections back in the 1930s, in the days before there were antibiotics. The results were quite good.

And Dr. H. J. Roberts made a rather convincing case for linking disorders of the prostate gland with diabetic hypoglycemia. If he is right, then even this most common of all urologic problems can be benefited by this diet.

There has been an allegation that kidney problems spring up in association with a low-carbohydrate diet. Yet I have followed my patients closely in this regard and have never found such a case. Nor have I found any case reports in a search of the medical literature. The exception is that a patient with far-advanced kidney disease cannot tolerate a high-protein diet. Such a person should not go on this diet. Beginning the diet only after a thorough medical checkup automatically prevents this unlikely possibility.

IMPOTENCY. Loss of sexual drive is seen in hypoglycemia and in vitamin and mineral deficiencies. It obviously stands a very good chance of being corrected by this regimen, which treats both hypoglycemia and nutritional deficiencies. Most patients will report some improvement.

INFECTIOUS DISEASES. The first studies linking excessive carbohydrate consumption to "colds" dates back to the 1930s.

Abrahamson showed that rheumatic fever recurs less frequently on a low-carbohydrate diet. And Sandler used it successfully to help treat tuberculosis.

Since then many workers found low-carbohydrate diets, plus nutritional supplements, to be effective in reducing the severity of systemic infections. Infectious disease has long been known to improve with good nutrition.

Some of the infection-fighting benefits are due to the decreased hypoglycemia or to the vitamins and minerals, but a major factor also is the elimination of sugar.

Dr. U. D. Register, chairman of the department of nutrition at Loma Linda University in California, found that there may be as much as a 50 percent temporary decrease in the ability of white blood cells to destroy bacteria after a person eats eighteen to twenty teaspoons of sugar. This may explain why children who eat a lot of sweet food are particularly vulnerable to infections.

Dr. Cleave, in his book *The Saccharine Disease*, says a massive dose of sugar could cause so great a proliferation of intestinal organisms such as E. coli that appendicitis (especially in children) could occur in hours.

In fact, Dr. Cleave claims that not only appendicitis, but also cholecystitis (inflammation of the gallbladder) and diverticulitis all arise from the proliferation of bacteria from people eating too much sugar and refined flour. "Hardly any of these conditions are seen in those races who do not eat white flour and sugar," he says.

NOTE TO DERMATOLOGISTS. Many conditions of the skin clear up on this diet, especially abscesses and boils. If one takes the time to do glucose tolerance tests on acne patients he will find a large percentage have glucose abnormalities. Vitamins may be very valuable in skin conditions. My dieting patients frequently report cessation of hair loss and improved hair texture.

THE EYE SPECIALIST KNOWS. Blurred vision is extremely common in hypoglycemia, and many cases of episodic blurred vision are due to hypoglycemia. Interestingly enough, if a hypoglycemic person wears glasses, the new diet can often change the refraction. There was one woman who after two weeks on the diet said, "Something terrible is happening to my vision." It turned out that her vision was improving, thus making her eyeglasses too strong.

THE ORTHOPEDIST, TOO. Backaches, painful feet, swollen and painful joints, stiff neck, tense muscles—all these may be improved by the program. These benefits are more likely derived from loss of weight or from vitamins B3, B6, PABA, pantothenic acid, folic acid, and the minerals zinc and manganese, all of which have been described as valuable in the treatment of arthritis.

YOUR PSYCHIATRIST WILL SEE A CHANGE IN YOUR MENTAL HEALTH. If your problem involves poor memory, inability to concentrate or to make decisions, mood swings, hostility, irritability, lack of initiative, fears and phobias, worry, apathy, disinterest or restlessness, expect that this nutrition program will probably cause a benefit you can see readily.

The diet is remarkably beneficial in the learning and behavior disorders of children and adolescents. It should be tried on every schoolchild who is considered an underachiever.

There are many who believe that much of the hostility and violence that threatens our society is partly due to an epidemic of blood sugar upsets caused by our diet.

I can certainly attest that I have watched many persons undergo a drastic personality change, from hostility to tranquillity, upon changing to this diet. Further, I have seen dozens of patients enter a rage during their glucose tolerance test at the time their blood sugar was dropping rapidly. How much crime must be committed at times of similar blood sugar change!

DRINKING PROBLEMS. Every medical investigator who has reported on hypoglycemia has discussed its prevalence in alcoholism. Cause and effect are so intertwined that they cannot be separated. The conditions worsen together and they improve together; alcohol intake produces hypoglycemia, and hypoglycemia leads to increased alcohol intake. Attack one and you attack the other.

THERE ARE MANY REASONS TO CONNECT ALCOHOLISM WITH HYPOGLYCEMIA. Almost any alcoholic, still drinking or "on the wagon," will show an abnormal glucose tolerance curve, with both diabetes and hypoglycemia being common and the combination of both most common.

The low-carbohydrate, megavitamin regimen that is so successful in correcting hypoglycemia is exceedingly useful in treating alcoholics. Most heavy drinkers, after a brief period on the diet, report that their cravings for a drink are substantially less and that they are better able to stay "on the wagon."

Furthermore, alcohol intolerance and alcoholism run in families. Careful history-taking reveals that diabetes, hypoglycemia, and weight problems also run in these same families.

And many alcoholics will gravitate toward diets that are high in sugar, coffee, and other carbohydrates. All of these, plus alcohol itself, are the substances that cause a temporary elevation of the blood sugar.

Many reformed alcoholics are troubled by a syndrome called the "dry jitters," an adrenalinlike reaction involving clamminess, dryness of the mouth, and shakiness, the exact symptom-complex produced by hypoglycemia. It, too, can be transiently relieved by taking in sugar.

THE DIET WORKS. Doctors connected with Alcoholics Anonymous and Al-Anon groups are beginning to use low blood sugar treatment. As one of these doctors said: "Many members were unable to stay sober until they were placed on a sugar-free diet with megavitamins." In one alcoholic rest home megavitamins and hypoglycemic diets resulted in an overall recovery rate of 86 percent in long-time alcoholics who had failed in all other treatment. They have remained sober for two years or more as a result of the diet.

People who get drunk on just a few drinks, by the way, often have hypoglycemia. Apparently some people with low blood sugar are extra sensitive to alcohol, especially on an empty stomach, and after only a drink or two may be drunk.

THE THEORY THAT MAKES THE MOST SENSE TO ME GOES SOMETHING LIKE THIS. A person whose genetic background shows a susceptibility to sugar is given a nutritionally improper diet, high in sugar and refined carbohydrates as a child. In later years he develops hypoglycemia and at the same time is exposed to social drinking. The alcohol which relieves his low blood sugar symptoms seems to have an extra benefit for him, providing him a "lift" beyond the mere inhibition-suppressing effect of alcohol itself. He finds himself turning to alcohol more and more. The increased alcohol intake further impairs the nutritional protection of the drinker, and the low blood sugar response becomes *more* established. Thus, the alcohol–low-blood-sugar–alcohol cycle becomes more vicious.

The cycle even seems to be present in animals. Laboratory rats fed a nutritionally inadequate diet will consume alcohol, in contrast to those given a nutritionally adequate diet, who will drink water. Through a mechanism not too different, addiction to drugs, too, can arise out of hypoglycemia and can be helped by this diet. Perhaps the best example is "speed" (amphetamine) which has a direct effect on blood sugar.

YOUR DENTIST KNOWS ANY LOW SUGAR DIET WILL IMPROVE DENTAL HEALTH. There have been several surveys showing significantly increased dental caries in Eskimos and African tribesmen as they switched from primitive foods to modern refined foods, particularly sugars. Natives of the island Tristan da Cunha in 1938 who ate potatoes and fish, but no sugar, had no dental problems. In 1962, they were consuming an average of one pound of sugar per week per person and 50 percent of their molars had cavities.

Many studies in many countries demonstrated that the less sugar intake, the lower the dental caries.

THE DOCTOR WHO WILL OBSERVE THE GREATEST VARIETY OF BONUS BENEFITS FROM THE DIET—YOUR FAMILY PHYSICIAN. So many conditions just categorized as "complaints" will improve on the diet: symptoms like cold hands and feet, leg cramps, restless legs, blurred vision, excessive thirst, dry mouth, moist palms, fainting spells, insomnia. All these stand a strong chance of clearing up on this diet.

What medical specialist could *not* benefit from learning how to use this diet?

24

The biggest benefit of all— stopping the diabetes cycle

When I was a medical student at Cornell Medical College, one of my brightest classmates was Edwin L. Bierman. As we shared the tribulations of acquiring a good medical education, neither of us dreamed that our separate paths would lead us to become protagonists in what promises to be one of the major medical controversies of the next decade. The important question to be resolved: "What should the diabetic eat?"

The increase in diabetes is becoming one of the gravest of medical problems. It now ranks behind only heart disease and cancer as our leading cause of death. Six million Americans are now estimated to be diabetic, and with the documented rate at which the disease is increasing, that number will be ten million within just a few years.

Dr. Bierman, as chairman of the dietary recommendations committee of the American Diabetes Association, has been largely responsible for the official recommendation that the diabetic's diet be unrestricted in carbohydrates—encouraging diabetics to eat as much as 45 percent of their calories in the form of carbohydrates.

The more I study my data on diabetes, the more convinced I am that the American Diabetic Association is moving in exactly the wrong direction. The diabetic's diet should be sharply *restricted* in its carbohydrate content.

Now, the Bierman group's data, as far as they went, are

quite valid. The 45 percent carbohydrate level, from the standpoint of the major complication, heart disease, is probably better than the 35 percent carbohydrate diet against which it was compared.

But what Dr. Bierman and his colleagues *failed* to do was compare it with the less than 5 percent carbohydrate diet—the one in this book—the one that makes diabetic manifestations *go away*, not just fail to get worse.

DIABETES IS A PROGRESSIVE DISEASE. The longer a person is diabetic, the higher will his blood sugars be and the greater the deterioration of his blood vessels—unless there is a major change in his diet pattern. My data clearly show that a very low carbohydrate diet will not only prevent this progression, but will, in most cases, render the diabetes nearly undetectable. It will, in other words, cause the condition to go "into remission." Equally important, it will drastically reduce the triglyceride levels, which are so commonly elevated in diabetes. And the cholesterol level, which is less commonly elevated in diabetes, will behave favorably more often than not. Further, when a patient is using insulin or oral medications, the dosage necessary for blood sugar control can be reduced in more than 90 percent of the cases. More than half the patients on these drugs who come to me have been able to get off medication entirely.

Since a doctor in private practice can't hold back care for his patients to be used as "control" subjects, which would be necessary to prove a point in medicine, I, personally, am not in the position to *prove* this point, but others are.

THIS IS WHAT SHOULD BE DONE: The federal agencies interested in this vital health matter should appoint a task force to review the data of physicians like me who are working with carbohydrate-restricted diets, to verify that the vast majority of these diabetic subjects do, in fact, demonstrate the improvements I have just described. The design of a federally funded study to compare the low-carbohydrate diet with the "balanced" one currently in favor would be simple and relatively inexpensive. Within a year, the public could learn which diet is superior for the short term; and within several years, the long-term benefits would begin to be apparent. Who would not agree that failure to investigate this lead would constitute criminal neglect on the part of our public health agencies?

THERE ARE TWO KINDS OF DIABETES. The far more common kind is the one I am talking about. It is called "stable, adult-onset diabetes." It seems to be an outgrowth of a highly refined carbohydrate diet, hyperinsulinism, hypoglycemia, and obesity. The other kind, "juvenile, insulin-dependent diabetes," may even be a different disease. One of the chief differences is that those afflicted with this type tend to *lose* weight, whereas the adult-onset type tends to *gain*. A low-carbohydrate diet can be treacherous when applied to the juvenile type, and it takes a physician with a good deal of experience to manage it correctly. When I treat such patients, I use a *somewhat* restricted carbohydrate diet, which seems to help stabilize the "brittle" diabetic, the one who is forever fluctuating between the symptoms of high blood sugar and insulin reactions.

THE KETOGENIC DIET WORKS WELL IN ADULT DIABETES. Remember that hypoglycemia is not the opposite of diabetes, but rather the forerunner of it, an early warning sign to look out for the full-blown symptoms of diabetes in the future.

This was shown effectively by Dr. Henry T. Ricketts of the University of Chicago, who studied twenty-five young adults whose parents both had diabetes. This made them almost certain candidates for diabetes in later life and they were considered to be prediabetic. Dr. Ricketts did five-hour glucose tolerance tests and found that half these subjects had measurable low blood sugar (readings below fifty) compared to only one out of every twelve control subjects. Further, almost all of the eight prediabetics who were also overweight showed low blood sugar.

So one way to counteract diabetes is to counteract hypoglycemia. This is what Dr. Leon S. Smelo demonstrated when he showed that treating the disease in its hypoglycemia stage by diet can arrest the course of the diabetes so it never reaches its overt stage.

The effectiveness of a very low carbohydrate diet in preventing excess insulin production has also been reported by

Drs. Walter A. Muller, Gerald R. Faloona, and Roger H. Unger and by Drs. E. F. Pfeiffer, and H. Laube of Ulm, West Germany.

WHAT COULD I SHOW A RESEARCH TASK FORCE? If a medical team were to review my case records on diabetic patients, this is what they would find:

1. After following the ketogenic diet, the majority of patients reported feeling better, and virtually all had lost weight.

2. Ninety percent of patients showed either a significant lowering of blood sugar or a reduction of antidiabetic drug dosage, and 10 percent remained approximately the same.

3. The majority of those whose fasting blood sugars were moderately elevated (115 to 200 range) showed fasting blood sugars completely within the normal range.

4. Virtually *none*, despite the absence of dietary carbohydrates, consistently showed a blood sugar *below* the normal range.

5. Ninety percent showed an improvement in triglycerides if they were elevated, and the majority showed an improvement in cholesterol levels.

What other diet can treat diabetes so well?

WHAT ABOUT KETOSIS? Perhaps you were told a diabetic should avoid ketosis. It is essential that you (and your doctor) make some very important distinctions here. *Ketosis is a risk only when it represents an insulin-dependent diabetic who is out of control.* It is not a risk in the normal person on a low-carbohydrate diet for reducing, nor is it a risk in the stable noninsulin-dependent diabetic who, with regard to developing ketosis, behaves almost the same as the nondiabetic. The only possible exception is a theoretical one, that is, the newly developed insulin-dependent diabetic who does not know he has this condition. And since every patient gets a thorough blood sugar evaluation *before* he begins the diet, this would not happen.

WHAT ABOUT MEDICATIONS? IF I'M TAKING ANTIDIABETIC MEDICATIONS, SHOULD I STOP THEM? In this instance, I tend to agree with the current teaching that any diabetic who can keep his blood sugars within or near the normal range with diet alone should do so, and medications should not be used. Fortunately, the great majority of diabetics fall into this category. Approximately half of the overweight patients who were controlling their diabetes with a "balanced" diet plus oral medication will find that Diet #1 without medication provides effective control. The other half will find that a lessened dose will be necessary. Obviously, changes in medication such as this can only be accomplished with the awareness and approval of your doctor. My personal preference is not to use the sulfonylurea medications (orinase, diabinese, tolinase, dymelor) because they promote further increase in the already excessive insulin levels and tend to increase weight. Despite its many problems, I prefer to use phenformin when it can be tolerated, if only because insulin levels are decreased and there is some tendency to aid in weight loss.

INSULIN IS ANOTHER PROBLEM. Many people taking insulin are insulin-dependent and cannot be taken off. However, some insulin-takers are *not* insulin-dependent and may find that the new diet is sufficient to bring their insulin requirement to zero. Self-regulation of a problem involving reduction of insulin dosage is hazardous. Therefore, I will not be too specific lest I encourage self-experimentation. If your doctor is working closely with you, I offer him these suggestions: When the diet is changed from the 160-gram carbohydrate level to a 40-gram level, a useful starting point, it should be accompanied by a reduction of insulin dose by approximately 40 percent of the previous optimal level. Urines should be collected four times daily and blood sugars at frequent intervals. Regular insulin should be available as a supplement if the insulin reduction appears to have been too drastic. If, on the other hand, the urines run sugar-free, a further gradual decrease in insulin dose is in order. If the patient has done well, but is not losing the desired weight, level one of Diet #1 might be used, along with another slight decrease in insulin dosage. A good percentage of obese insulin-takers will end up on no insulin at all.

WHAT ABOUT EARLY OR MILD DIABETICS? Are any special precautions needed? Most of my diabetic patients fall into this category, the diagnosis having been made merely because the glucose tolerance test is done routinely on all my new patients. I have found that these patients are virtually no different from my nondiabetic patients. They respond to the diet with just about the same weight loss, ketone levels, and energy increase as the "normals." They soon, in fact, do themselves become "normals," even their blood sugars, after following the diet. The main consideration is that they must understand the axiom "Once a diabetic, always a diabetic." In these cases, that means knowing that they never again can return to the old eating pattern that brought out their diabetic predisposition in the first place.

WHAT ARE THE SYMPTOMS OF EARLY DIABETES? There may be none, or, since diabetes is an outgrowth of hypoglycemia, there may be any of the myriad of symptoms deriving from low blood sugar. The tendency to gain weight eating foods on which others stay slim implies diabetes, as does a disturbance in appetite with hunger recurring soon after a full meal. Gross childhood obesity is usually the forerunner of diabetes. So, too, are high birthweights or giving birth to babies of high birthweights (ten pounds or so); especially predictive is the phenomenon where each baby weighs more than the previous one. Women who get symptoms on The Pill or estrogen therapy often are early diabetics. When unexplained weight gains turn into spontaneous weight loss, it usually means diabetes has progressed *beyond* the early stage. So too, does an increased urinary output and increased thirst.

THIRST IS AN INTERESTING SYMPTOM. Excessive thirst very commonly *precedes* diabetes by years. I do not know the mechanism, but I am quite impressed with the high number of very thirsty people whose glucose tolerance tests show low blood sugar, or the high-low curve. This symptom usually improves a good deal on the low-carbohydrate diet.

WHY DON'T OTHER DOCTORS RECOMMEND THIS DIET FOR DIABETICS? There is no real reason except that the concept is too new to have yet gained general acceptance. But Dr. George Blackburn, using a very strict zero carbohydrate diet, has been able to get every one of a selected group of obese insulin-taking diabetic patients off insulin. More and more doctors are becoming aware of results of this type, and I predict that in the near future scientists will be revamping their thinking about diabetic management. The goal will be improvement or remission, not merely slowing down its progression.

But there is no need to wait until then. The bonus benefit of stopping the diabetes cycle is available to you—now!

25

We must discuss the controversial aspects

Whether you are one of my boosters or knockers, or simply are curious, I think you will be interested in what has happened to me since I wrote my first book.

The book came out in October 1972, and soon became the fastest-selling book in the entire history of publishing. At one time David McKay Company had five printers working full time to turn out 100,000 copies ordered in *a week*, more than most books sell in a lifetime!

The diet stormed the country. Letters poured in by the thousands. Phone calls came in all day. There were radio and TV shows. Restaurants carried "Dr. Atkins' Specials." Ketostix sales boomed.

I was not surprised that the book was a success because for years patients had been coming to me saying that this was the best reducing diet there ever had been. But what did surprise me, because I was totally naive about medical politics, was that the diet would be attacked so bitterly by medical groups.

I had always respected my own organization, the American Medical Association. I was confident when I wrote the book that the knowledge that a large number of people were success-fully following a low-carbohydrate diet would be welcomed by practicing physicians as something they could use to help their patients. I felt that the AMA would react similarly.

I felt they would give it their support, if only as a way to solve the embarrassing problem of amphetamine-dispensing for weight reduction.

INSTEAD THE AMA RESPONDED WITH A PEARL HARBOR SNEAK ATTACK. I was speaking in Houston. I had no advance notice that there would be any criticism. A press release was issued by the AMA to all newspapers, magazines, wire services, radio and television calling the book and diet "unscientific and potentially dangerous to health."

I knew nothing about it until I saw the front-page headlines in the newspaper.

They had released the 16-page report without ever talking to me about the diet, without ever asking to see case histories and laboratory data, without ever investigating the results of the diet on patients.

It was beyond credibility. My emotions were a mixture of outrage, frustration, and total disillusionment about the integrity of American medical institutions. While they were screaming it couldn't be done, more than one million Americans were doing it—following the diet, losing weight, and feeling rejuvenated.

DAYS LATER, CAME THE NEXT SNEAK BOMB. My own county medical society—the one representing New York City physicians—decided to hold a major press conference about my diet under the auspices of their Committee on Public Health, which committee, incidentally, does not even have the constitutional authority to hold such a conference; they have only the authority to hold hearings. When I read the day before that there was to be a press conference, my attorneys called and told them I would like to be present, but they conveniently neglected to answer the call.

This was the press conference where the most unsubstantiated charges of all were leveled upon my research— claims such as the one that my diet caused kidney problems, when not one of the panelists had ever seen or even read about a bona fide case of kidney complications induced by the diet. A similar diet since the 1930s has been recommended as a *treatment* for urinary tract infections.

Shortly thereafter the same county medical society attempted to censure me for appearing on radio and television shows for interviews about the book.

I FOUGHT THEIR CENSURE—AND WON. *The appellate court threw out all of their censure motions.* The censure was ruled improper.

THE NEXT PEARL HARBOR BOMB CAME FROM THE MAGAZINES. It takes a magazine months to prepare an article, yet several one-sided attacks upon my book appeared within weeks of that AMA press release. The writers had not even been curious enough to interview me or look at my files.

In fact in all these years, no one has ever taken me up on my still open offer to review all my case histories, including charts and laboratory work.

AND FINALLY . . . LAWSUITS. In this country anyone who wants to get some free publicity for around $250 can sue a public figure; there need not be a real case. And since defending these nuisance actions can run up a bundle in lawyer's fees, it is a technique whereby a big organization can bankrupt the little man and defeat him.

If, as I believe, the AMA or the food industry was in reality behind the series of lawsuits which I had to defend, they succeeded, in part at least, in getting major publicity directed against me. And unfortunately, most newspapers don't print the fact that a suit has been dropped.

WHAT REALLY HAPPENED. Three of the suits that made the headlines were either dropped, thrown out of court, or I won the case. These include the ones you may have heard about in Ohio on behalf of people I had never seen, who couldn't even demonstrate any ill effects. It is because the language of their brief included the verbatim wording of the AMA press release less than a day after it was issued that I suspect these suits really came out of the AMA's own "bag of dirty tricks."

The other suits that are pending were all instituted by a single attorney. The cases are so flimsy that my state medical society, upon reviewing them, renewed my malpractice premiums at the same rate as before these suits. In fact, the chief attorney for the medical society thereupon became my patient. Recently a special committee of doctors who review these claims officially issued the unanimous verdict that I had no liability whatsoever.

MY DAY IN WASHINGTON. Shortly after all this excitement, I was in the news again when on April 12, 1973, I appeared before the Senate Committee on Nutrition and Human Needs, chaired by Senator George McGovern. If you saw the film clips on the news, it looked as though I had been subpoenaed to appear there for investigation of fraud. The truth of the matter is that I had written a letter to the preceding commission, under Senator Gaylord Nelson of Wisconsin, at the time hearings were being conducted on amphetamines and their abuse and *requested* to be a witness before the committee. I felt I had a great deal to say about amphetamines because I had been working with a diet that had totally circumvented the need for them. In fact, you'll find in the transcript of the hearing that McGovern says, "Dr. Atkins, you're not under criticism." But most of the network news coverage somehow managed to make it appear as if I were being investigated as a possible diet fraud.

I only wish the networks had shown the entire hearing. My statement to the Senate Committee included a point-by-point rebuttal to the AMA critique upon my diet. (This statement appears in the back of all Bantam soft-cover editions of *Diet Revolution.*)

THE AMA REQUEST: When the AMA issued their press release attacking my diet, they told all physicians in America that "observations on patients who suffer adverse effects from this regimen should be reported." After three years of waiting for these cases to be reported the AMA had to concede that their file was empty—*no adverse cases had been reported that could be directly attributed to my diet.*

I TRIED TO FIGHT BACK. How much I wanted to tell the public that every issue the AMA raised to cloud the picture was contrary to the real bottom line: that the diet had been tested and had been proved safe—and that the AMA had made their entire case without any firsthand investigation of the results the diet was achieving.

But there was a brick wall of media resistance. My detractors were given free rein on the most important of network talk shows, but I was consistently shut out from the very shows that claim to thrive on controversy.

More than a year after my book was published, I got a chance to appear on the Mike Douglas show only because Tony Curtis, who has gone on the diet himself and *knew* it worked, insisted that I be on while he was co-host.

Another glimmer of light was the Merv Griffin Show. Merv too knew the diet was great because he had gone on it, and he also has courage enough to let the nation know our nutrition is alarmingly bad. He not only gave me a chance to be heard, but he has also introduced the public to the true nutrition prophets, people like Linus Pauling, Roger Williams, and others who have been developing the science of nutrition medicine.

Perhaps some of you saw the exciting show in which I appeared with Jean Nidetch, the Weight Watcher lady, and the late Dr. Irwin Stillman and Adelle Davis. Ms. Davis, a grand and gracious lady I had never met before, gave me her enthusiastic support and told millions of viewers that she had used my diet successfully to lower her cholesterol and lose weight.

THERE WERE MANY STRANGE EXPERIENCES. On one Washington, D.C., talk show, I was to appear with several doctors, one of whom was Dr. J. P. Hutchins, the president of the International College of Applied Nutrition, who had been invited from California just to make this appearance. He was scheduled for a twelve-minute segment on the show as shown on the program outline. Just before the show, one of the staff members interviewed Dr. Hutchins and asked what he had to say against the Atkins diet. Dr. Hutchins said, "Nothing at all. I approve of it heartily, and I've been using it to treat my patients."

"You don't have any criticism of Dr. Atkins?"

He had not.

A few minutes later, Dr. Hutchins received word that there would be no time for him to appear on the show. The other two doctors who were against my diet were kept on the show and given as much time as they wanted.

BUT ALL WAS NOT DISAPPOINTMENT. Legions of people out there were obviously getting the same successful results that my office patients recorded. On an all-night talk show in Boston, there were over fifty calls from people I had never met, all of whom had followed the diet in the book, and all of whom reported they had done well.

And whenever I give a lecture, there is always at least one person in the audience asking me to autograph a copy of my book, who shyly but proudly informs me, "You know, Dr. Atkins, I lost over a hundred pounds on your diet."

Many people say to me, "I don't know where you get all your courage."

If anybody has ever gone through something like this, he knows it is not courage that impels him to go on, but rather, there is something about knowing that he is right that gives the illusion of courage. I could never live with myself if I backed down or compromised on a position that I know to be true.

Is Robert Atkins really a nut, a hoax? Then what about the tens of thousands of people writing and calling saying how much better they feel? Are they after me because I didn't publish in a medical journal first? Hardly reason enough for this much flak. Is it jealousy that my book was so successful and they think I'm getting rich? I would have made more per hour collecting old Captain Marvel comic books. Or do the leaders of the American Medical Association, the FDA, major drug companies, and the food industry do their best to repress advances that are unorthodox or that involve nutrition or that threaten their profit picture?

THE FUTURE. Chances are that this book, just like my first one, will become the storm center of a violent controversy. Not only do I expect it to draw tens of thousands of enthusiastic supporters who will have learned firsthand what the diet program can do for their everyday well-being, but I expect it to draw critics.

WHOM CAN YOU BELIEVE? I want to tell you something that will help you understand *all* nutrition controversies, whether they involve megavitamins in psychiatry, vitamin C against the common cold, or *any* claim about nutrition therapies.

To know whom you can believe, remember this principle: *Nutrition thinking in our country emanates from the food industry, and medical thinking derives from the drug industry.*

And the very food industry that is responsible for the food supply that threatens our health is the food industry that is playing the role of our nutrition advisor.

The more you look into this, the more you will see how widespread is this conflict of interest.

FOR EXAMPLE. Some of our most respected university nutrition leaders, giants of influence in medical circles, serve as consultants to the food industry, receiving large financial stipends.

One Harvard nutritionist has actually testified that cereal with sugar and milk is more nutritious for children than a protein breakfast of bacon and eggs. He admitted to an incredulous reporter that he received fees from cereal makers—more than $50,000 that year. And his Harvard School of Nutrition has received millions of dollars in grants from the purveyors of flour and sugar.

This same man serves on influential policy-making medical committees both at the AMA and in government and he uses his syndicated newspaper column to reach the public with further biased advice and to serve as hatchetman against the legitimate nutrition crusaders questioning industry practices. This is a conflict of interest of major proportions!

THIS IS NOT AN ISOLATED EXAMPLE. At one meeting on Sugar in the Diet of Man leading nutritionists from Harvard, Columbia, the University of Minnesota, the University of Pittsburgh, and the University of Washington issued such statements as:

"It might be worthwhile to increase sugar calories from an average of 15–20 percent of total calories to one of 20–25 percent," or "That the eating of sugars and starches is especially apt to produce excess body weight . . . is nonsense," or "A cereal breakfast is better than ham and eggs."

One document that "says it all" was a special issue of the journal called *Nutrition Reviews* in which articles stated vitamin C should not be used for the common cold; vitamin E is ineffective; hypoglycemia is rare; nutrition-oriented orthomolecular psychiatry is of "low credibility"; the Atkins diet is "potentially harmful" and many nutritionists including Adelle Davis, Carlton Fredericks, Jerome Rodale and myself were dispensers of "hogwash." In short, it was a broadside attack against all the major nutritional advances.

Nutrition Reviews, the most influential journal on nutrition read by doctors, just happens to be published by the Nutrition Foundation, an organization by its own statement "created and supported by leading companies in the food and allied industries." On its roster of trustees are officers from over two dozen carbohydrate-manufacturing giants.

HOW TO SPOT A BOUGHT-OFF NUTRITIONIST. One of the food industry nutritionists tells people they can spot nutrition "quacks" with a checklist.

Why then should you not have a set of guidelines to help you tell when information is coming from the food industry?

I have prepared a checklist. You can recognize readily the nutrition spokesmen who serve the food industry by the following:

1. They will claim that nothing is wrong with the American diet, that nothing is incorrect or missing in our diet, that there is no need to eliminate food additives or overprocessing techniques.

2. They will claim that supplementary vitamins or minerals are generally useless, and that a "balanced diet" provides all the nutrients we need.

3. They will claim that "there is no good evidence that . . ." when you know very well there is at least some scientific evidence to support the contrary view.

4. They will claim that a heretofore safe nutritional concept is dangerous, suddenly finding danger in vitamin B or vitamin C or even a low-carbohydrate eating pattern.

5. They will make personal attacks on the proponents of the nutritional concept, such as "Dr. A. is senile; or Dr. B is dishonest; Dr. C. is self-aggrandizing; Dr. D. does not have proper credentials; Dr. E. just wants to make money."

6. They will use quotations and opinions by others *rather than scientific data.* Groups that quote one another often are the AMA, the Nutrition Foundation, the Food and Drug Administration, the National Academy of Sciences—National Research Council, to name a few.

7. They will reach an illogical conclusion. Example: folic

acid supplements are dangerous to everyone because folic acid supplements can cover up a rare disorder related to pernicious anemia.

8. They will indicate that drugs or medications constitute better therapy than nutrition.

9. Their "logic" will be a construction of fragments, but will scrupulously avoid "bottom lines." Example: Is this a high-fat diet and do high-fat diets raise cholesterol levels and are high cholesterol levels associated with heart disease? rather than the direct issue: Does this diet cause heart disease?

10. They will raise a howl about cholesterol, but will soft pedal the dangers of sugar. Remember that the egg industry consists of a group of small businessmen with little capital, whereas the economic power of sugar, cereal, and vegetable oil interests is staggering.

11. They will state and restate the theory that "a calorie is a calorie is a calorie," despite all the evidence of differences in metabolic pathways. This protects the economic interests of *all* segments of this food industry.

12. Occasionally there is less subterfuge and one may actually spot the words, "based on a grant from the Cereal Institute or the Sugar Research Council."

Keep in mind that the food industry feels threatened by the growing number of voices speaking out about the hazards of refined carbohydrates and about our needs for vitamins and trace minerals, because this implies that the food industry is providing us with an inadequate diet. Inherent in the statement that our diet is inadequate is the need for nutritional reforms, which in turn pose a financial threat to the food industry.

PLEASE DON'T ACCEPT MY GUIDELINES ALONE. Always depend most on your most reliable advisor: yourself. Prove things to yourself, carry out a personal trial. If a proposal seems reasonable and involves sound nutritional suggestions such as taking vitamins and minerals or protein or restricting junk foods, try it. If the recommendations seem to be working, either making you feel better or making you lose or gain weight as you desire, or helping you overcome an illness which has been troubling you, then you will know for yourself.

In the case of this book and the controversy it will surely arouse, the truest way to judge whom you can believe is to try out the recommendations the book has provided, and base your conclusions on your own firsthand experience.

Be aware that there will be controversy, keep an open mind, try it for yourself, and if it works . . . believe.

26
What the future holds

I believe that the public will play a very important role in changing the concepts of nutrition in this country.

The consumer need not be the innocent victim of the food industry's self-interest. Instead the consumer can be a powerful force in restoring the adequacy of our nutrition.

WHAT CAN CONSUMERS DO? As individuals you can eliminate sugar from your diet. You can avoid junk foods and drinks that are mostly water, sugar, and chemicals. You can refuse to buy those foods that have been refined to the point where their nutritional value is incomplete.

Instead, you can buy unrefined wholesome products. You can buy protein foods as well as fresh fruits and vegetables. You can learn the correct use of vitamin and mineral supplements.

You can urge congressional leaders not to let the FDA limit the dosage of vitamins and minerals we can buy and to reinstate those they have limited on the basis of flimsy evidence. Write your congressman, work through your professional organization, let your voice be heard wherever you have influence.

OUR FOOD SUPPLIERS WILL SUPPLY US WHAT WE DEMAND. The one advantage of a free enterprise economy is that the consumer can create the demand. We've allowed poor nutrition to get the best of us because we've allowed the merchandiser to tell us what we wanted. There is no reason why food manufacturers have to refine the products. There's no reason why they have to add sugar to everything. There's no compelling reason why they must include so many chemical additives in our food supply. They will change the food, but only if we demand uncontaminated, unrefined, unsugared, unflavored wholesome foods and threaten to boycott the junk products.

SO MANY THINGS NEED TO BE ACCOMPLISHED. The consumer is vital to bringing them about.

These are some of the things that I would like to see happen:

Decreased consumption of refined sugar and bleached flour in our total diet.

A greater awareness of the prevalence of hypoglycemia and of the spectrum of conditions it can cause.

Recognition that the glucose tolerance test should be done on virtually every new patient evaluated by a physician, with a better understanding of how to interpret it.

Increased use of vitamins and minerals in conformity with the true nutritional picture in each individual.

A total enrichment program that puts back *all* the nutrients that are removed from foods, not merely a selection of them.

Elimination of nitrites and dyes and hormones from our foods, but the restoration of a good sugar substitute.

Food product labeling required to list all ingredients. This should include the listing of sugar when it is part of a *medication* and accurate labeling of so-called "diet" products.

Use of warning labels on candy, chewing gum, and soft drinks that excessive consumption of sugar involves health hazards.

Willingness of the media to air controversial nutrition viewpoints that may prove to be at odds with their sponsors.

Elimination of advertising of sugar products on children's TV shows. Also, banning of advertising that suggests nutritional benefit for products when that is not proven.

Development by food manufacturers of new products based on nutrition instead of just palatability.

Publication of federal or other official evaluation of actual data from the case histories of patients of doctors like myself working with high-nutrient, carbohydrate-restricted diets.

Cessation of *speculative* comments by official agencies about what a diet might do when *real* data are available.

A federally funded, long-term study of the preventive aspects of these diets against diabetes, heart disease, and shortened life-span.

I would like to see more meaningful teaching of nutrition in medical school. Particularly would I like to see a faculty of the great nutrition scientists brought into one great entity devoted to integrating our now disjointed knowledge of nutrition medicine.

And finally, I would like to see the influence of the food industry totally withdrawn from nutritional teaching.

MANY SERVICES ARE NEEDED. For those who are interested in nutritional help there are so many more services that must be provided.

As I learn of more and more doctors who are in sympathy with nutrition medicine, I plan to operate a referral service and will be able to pass names of qualified nutrition-oriented physicians on to anyone who needs such a doctor in his area.

The nation could well do with a series of nutrition centers where people in different cities could be seen by a nutrition-knowledgeable doctor and be given dietary counseling.

And how about Diet Revolution diet clubs where you could get the moral support of weekly meetings with fellow dieters and proper nutritional counseling?

And, we need a line of Diet Revolution foods to be available in supermarkets, in gourmet diet restaurants, and in low-carbohydrate fast-food eateries across our nation.

One of my all-time favorite ideas would be a vacation health spa where guests could go to get themselves in shape in the shortest possible time. No refined carbohydrates would be allowed on the premises, but the management would serve Diet Revolution foods at a marvelous buffet.

And why shouldn't there be a children's summer camp for those who are overweight or those who have learning disabilities due to faulty nutrition? For many, it would be the only time when parents and doctors could be certain their children are eating 100 percent correctly.

And to keep you informed of the rapid scientific progress being made in this exciting field of nutrition, there should be a newsletter you could subscribe to. A syndicated newspaper column would also help make the public aware.

WHY ALL THE ABOVE? All these ideas, even if you don't participate, will help *you* in a very real way. Dieting, no matter how easy the diet, is made a hundred times easier if your diet foods are handy to you and if the people around you know that you are one of *many* dieters. Then your local luncheonette may offer menus where bread, crackers, potatoes, or grits don't automatically come with every meal. Or your dinner party hostess will provide something besides a sugar dessert for guests. And when you do your grocery shopping you would find that there are new appropriate products created to serve the burgeoning high-nutrient, low-carbohydrate eaters.

WHAT CAN YOU DO? You can be a Diet Revolutionary. This does not mean merely following your diet. It means actively fighting the fraud and self-interest that is suppressing the advances in nutrition that I see being developed every day. It means convincing others—people who give incorrect advice and people who follow it.

And—very important—you can complete the questionnaire in this book. Only then can sufficient information be obtained to convince the powers that be of the effect of the diet regimen—good or bad.

Appendix A.
Carbohydrate counter

As you plan your menus and choose brands, do not be concerned with small differences in carbohydrates since these differences can be caused by differences in sampling or measuring techniques.

Also keep in mind that product ingredients change. Learn to read labels on the products you buy. Use those that have no sugar added. Use those with whole grain rather than refined flour.

The values are averaged from data compiled by the United States Department of Agriculture or from data supplied by manufacturers.

Food	*Quantity*	*Carbohydrate (grams)*
A		
Apple	1 med.	20
Apple Cider	6 fl. oz.	19
Applesauce, unsweetened	½ cup (4.3 oz.)	13
Apricot, fresh	1 cup	20
Apricot Nectar, low cal.	½ cup	5
Asparagus	1 cup	6
Asparagus Soup, with milk	1 cup	16
Avocado	½ cup	5

Food	Quantity	Carbohydrate (grams)

B

Food	Quantity	Carbohydrate (grams)
Bamboo Shoots	½ lb.	3
Banana, med.	8¾″ long	26
Barley	¼ cup	39
Beans, green	½ cup	4
Beans, kidney	½ cup	20
Beans, lima	½ cup	17
Beef	4 oz.	0
Beer, regular 4.5% alcohol	12 fl. oz.	14
Beet Greens	½ cup	2
Beets	½ cup	7
Bitter Lemon, soft drink	6 fl. oz.	23
Bitters (Angostura)	½ tsp.	1
Blackberry	4 oz.	14
Blueberry	½ cup	11
Bran Breakfast Cereal	1 cup	27-45
Brazil Nuts	½ cup	7
Bread		
cracked wheat	.8 oz. slice	12
date-nut loaf	1 slice	19
Finn-Crisp	1 piece	5
flat, Norwegian	1 double wafer	5
Glutogen Gluten	1 slice	6
oatmeal	.8 oz. slice	11
Profile	1 slice	10
Protogen Protein	1 slice	9
whole wheat	.8 oz. slice	11
Breadfruit	4 oz.	30
Broccoli	½ cup	4
Brussels Sprouts	½ cup	6
Butter	1 T.	.1

C

Food	Quantity	Carbohydrate (grams)
Cabbage	½ cup	3
Cabbage, Chinese	½ cup	1
Cantaloupe	½ med. melon	14
Carrot	½ cup	5
Casaba Melon	4 oz.	7
Cauliflower	½ cup	2

Food	Quantity	Carbohydrate (grams)
Caviar	1 oz.	1
Celery	½ cup	2
Celery Soup, cream of	1 cup	15
Chard, Swiss	½ cup	3
Cheese		
American, Cheddar, Bleu, Brick, Camembert, Caraway, Chantelle, Colby, Edam, Gouda, Gruyere, Liederkranz, Limburger, Monterey Jack, Mozzarella, Muenster, Roquefort	1 oz.	1
Cottage	1 cup	6
Cream cheese	1 oz.	.6
Gjetost	1 oz.	13
Cherries		
Sour	½ cup	8
Sweet	½ cup	12
Cherries, Maraschino	1 avg.	2
Chestnuts	4 oz.	48
Chicken	4 oz.	0
Chicken Soup, cream of, with milk	1 cup	14
Chick-Pea or Garbanzos	1 cup	122
Chicory Greens	4 oz.	2
Chocolate Syrup, low cal.	1 T.	3
Club Soda	6 fl. oz.	0
Corn	1 cup	26
Corn Chips	1 oz.	15
Cornbread	4 oz.	33
Crab	4 oz.	1
Cranberry	1 cup	12
Cranberry Juice	½ cup	23
Cream	1 T.	1
Cucumber	7½″ x 2″ pared	7

D

Food	Quantity	Carbohydrate (grams)
Dandelion Greens	½ cup	6
Date	1	6
Duck	4 oz.	0

Food	Quantity	Carbohydrate (grams)

E

Food	Quantity	Carbohydrate (grams)
Eel	4 oz.	0
Egg	1	.4
Eggnog	½ cup	16
Eggplant	1 cup	8
Endive	1 cup	3
Escarole	1 cup	3

F

Food	Quantity	Carbohydrate (grams)
Fat	1 cup	0
Fish	4 oz.	0
Flour		
buckwheat	1 oz.	20
corn	1 oz.	21
wheat, whole	1 oz.	20
Frankfurter	1	.7
Fresca	6 fl. oz.	.1
Frog Legs	4 oz.	0
Fruit Cocktail, unsweetened or dietetic	½ cup	8

G

Food	Quantity	Carbohydrate (grams)
Gelatin, dietetic	½ cup	0
Grape		
Concord, Delaware, Niagara, Catawba, and Scuppernong	½ cup	7
Malaga, Muscat, Thompson seedless, Emperor, and Flame Tokay	½ cup	15
Grape Juice, unsweetened	4 oz.	17
Grape-Nuts, cereal	¼ cup	23
Grapefruit	½ med.	14
Grapefruit Juice, unsweetened	½ cup	12

H

Food	Quantity	Carbohydrate (grams)
Ham	1 oz.	0
Honey	1 T.	17
Honeydew	2″ x 7″ wedge	13

Food	Quantity	Carbohydrate (grams)

K

| Kale | ½ cup | 2 |

L

Lamb	4 oz.	0
Lemon Juice	1 T.	1
Lettuce	1 cup	2
Lime Juice	1 T.	1
Liqueur	1 fl. oz.	8-15
Liquor		
brandy, bourbon, Canadian whiskey, gin, Irish whiskey, rum, rye, Scotch, tequila, and vodka.	1 fl. oz.	Trace
Liver	4 oz.	5
Liver Sausage	1 oz.	.5
Lobster	4 oz.	.4

M

Macadamia Nuts	1 oz.	4
Manhattan Cocktail	3 fl. oz.	2
Margarine	4 oz. (1 stick)	.5
Martini Cocktail	3 fl. oz.	Trace
Mayonnaise	1 T.	.3
Melba Toast	1 piece	1.5
Milk	1 cup	12
Muffin		
bran	1	20
corn	1	20
Mushroom	½ cup	1
Mushroom Soup, with milk	1 cup	15
Mussels	4 oz.	4
Mustard Greens	1 cup	9

N

| Nectarine | 4 oz. | 19 |
| Nutrament | 1 can | 47 |

Food	Quantity	Carbohydrate (grams)
O		
Oat Flakes, cereal	1 cup	29
Oatmeal	1 cup	25
Octopus	4 oz.	0
Oil, salad or cooking	1 T.	0
Okra	½ cup	5
Olive	1 med. size	.1
Onion	1 (2½" dia.)	9.6
Onion Soup	1 cup	5
Orange	3" dia.	19
Orange Juice	½ cup	13
Oysters	13-19 med.	8
P		
Papaya	1 cup	18
Pea	½ cup	10
Pea Soup	1 cup	22
Peach	2" dia.	10
dried	½ cup	60
frozen	½ cup	22
Peach Nectar	1 cup	29
Peanuts	½ cup	13
Peanut Butter	1 T.	3
Pear	3" x 2½"	25
Pecan	½ cup	8
Pepper	1 med.	3
Pernod	1 fl. oz.	1
Pineapple	½ cup	11
Pistachio Nuts	½ cup	12
Popcorn	1 cup	8
Pork	4 oz.	0
Potato	1 med.	21
Potato Chips	10	10
Potato Salad	4 oz.	15
Q		
Quinine or Tonic Water low cal.	6 fl. oz.	18

Food	Quantity	Carbohydrate (grams)
R		
Raisins	½ cup	55
Raspberries	½ cup	10
Rhubarb	½ cup	2
Rice, brown	4 oz.	29
Roe	4 oz.	2
Rolaids	1	1
S		
Saccharin	1 tablet	0
Salad Dressing	1 T.	1-4
Sauerkraut	1 cup	6
Shredded Oats, cereal	1 oz.	20
Shredded Wheat	1 cup	28
Spam	12 oz.	5
Spinach	1 cup	1
Strawberries	1 cup	12
Sugar, unrefined	1 cup	194
Sweet Potato	1 med.	36
T		
Tangerine	2½" dia.	10
Tea	8 fl. oz.	Trace
Tomato	1 med.	7
Tomato Juice	½ cup	5
Tom Collins	6 fl. oz.	16
Tongue	4 oz.	1
Turkey	4 oz.	0
Turnip Greens	½ cup	3
V		
Veal	4 oz.	0
W		
Walnut	½ cup	9
Watermelon	1 cup	10
Wheat Flakes, cereal	1 oz.	23

Food	Quantity	Carbohydrate (grams)
Wheat Germ	¼ cup (1 oz.)	13
Whitefish	4 oz.	0
Wild Rice, cooked	½ cup	22
Wines	3 fl. oz.	.1-22
Y		
Yam	4 oz.	26
Yeast	1 oz.	3
Yogurt		
plain	8 oz.	13
flavored	8 oz.	40-50
Z		
Zwieback	1 oz.	21

Appendix B.
A special note to physicians

In 1972 I published a book for the layman concerning my experiences treating 10,000 overweight subjects using a ketogenic, low-carbohydrate, free usage of protein and fat, reducing diet.[1] In it I stated that I had observed some degree of weight loss on this regimen in nearly 100 percent of cases, and that the program was usually associated with an improvement in energy level, improved mood level sometimes approaching euphoria, and a marked elimination of appetite or hunger. I described cases in which losses of up to eighty-five pounds in seventeen weeks were achieved using a diet of 3,000 calories per day, when carbohydrates were virtually eliminated.

In the following year the Council of Food and Nutrition of the American Medical Association issued a denunciation of the diet based on a review of the medical literature, but not upon any directly performed studies or observations on the diet itself.[2]

There is substantial evidence that the AMA critique is one-sided, biased, and not representative of the academic tradition of medical reviews in which an effort is made to present all reports pertinent to the subject.

THE EARLY LITERATURE

In fact, the medical literature reveals just the opposite—a rather impressive series of reports highly favorable to the use of the low-carbohydrate diet.

The principle of carbohydrate restriction for the management of obesity was first brought to public attention by Dr. William Harvey a century ago.[3] A similar diet had been developed in 1797 by John Rollo, the English Surgeon-General, and was widely advocated in the century before insulin was discovered as the treatment of choice in the management of diabetes.[4] In 1928, the Arctic explorer Vilhjalmur Stefansson, impressed with the excellent health of Eskimos on their all-meat diet, volunteered with another subject to be observed for one year on the metabolic ward of Bellevue Hospital on such a diet. Edward Tolstoi, in his paper concerning this study, noted that the chemical composition of the blood was "very little affected."[5]

Of note is that the cholesterol level of one of these subjects dropped, even though the AMA report states, inaccurately, that both "rose to high levels."[2]

THE PREOBESITY APPLICATIONS

All through the 1920s, the ketogenic diet was widely used at major medical centers for the treatment of children with epilepsy.[6] M. G. Peterman of Mayo Clinic reported on the successful treatment of thirty-seven epileptic children.[7] Many other reports followed, expanding the applications to adult epilepsy[8] as well as to other pediatric problems such as asthma.[9] Its usefulness in a variety of genitourinary infections was described.[10] It was named as an aid to resistance against all infections.[11]

By 1934, Eugene Foldes reported that a low-carbohydrate diet provided "good effect in epilepsy, eclampsia, migraine, angina pectoris, bronchial asthma and other allergy, hypertension, polycythemia, pernicious anemia, acne, gout, and nervous and psychiatric disturbances."[12]

Blake Donaldson found an extraordinary range of applications of a low-carbohydrate, mainly meat diet.[13]

In a series of papers in the 1940s, Benjamin P. Sandler wrote that a low-carbohydrate diet was helpful in the control of such widely disparate conditions as peptic ulcer,[14] tuberculosis,[15] and the chest pain of coronary artery disease.[16]

ITS FIRST MODERN USE IN OBESITY

In the next decade, Alfred W. Pennington described his success in getting executives of the duPont Company to lose an average of twenty-two pounds in three weeks on a ketogenic low-carbohydrate diet similar to Diet #1. He stressed his clinical observation that the dieters felt well and were never hungry.[17,18] And in England, Richard Mackarness wrote the first popular book recommending carbohydrate restriction alone for the purpose of losing weight.[19]

THE UNDERLYING BASIC SCIENCE

One of the first demonstrations of the rationale behind carbohydrate restriction was presented by Alan Kekwick and Gaston L. S. Pawan, in London.

First they showed that animals would lose weight on an all-fat or all-protein diet, but not on an all-carbohydrate diet of the same number of calories. This was an important step in demonstrating the fallacy that all calories are degraded equally within the body under all conditions. But these findings were disputed with the claim that weight loss was water, not fat. Kekwick and Pawan showed later that the animals on the no-carbohydrate diets actually excreted significantly more calorie-containing carbon compounds, confirming that the extra weight loss was indeed adipose tissue.[20,21]

Kekwick and Pawan, along with T. M. Chalmers, also found another key to explain weight loss on a low-carbohydrate diet by recovering the now well-established Fat Mobilizing Substance (FMS or FMH) from animals and people on diets containing less than 80 grams of carbohydrate.[22] Recently, FMS has been isolated and can be injected into human volunteers to cause a loss of weight.[23]

A promising lead evolved from the observations by Garfield Duncan of Philadelphia that fasting patients lose all sense of hunger after forty-eight hours without food.[24] Hunger went away when ketones began to appear in the urine. Walter Bloom and Gordon Azar of Atlanta showed the same remarkable disappearance of hunger with production of ketone bodies on a diet without carbohydrates.[25]

These observations provided the rationale for the use of the ketogenic diet in the management of obesity—it suppressed appetite and led to a decreased food intake. This was confirmed by the surveys of Yudkin and Stock who demonstrated that both the total caloric and total fat intakes of overweight subjects placed on an unrestricted protein and fat, low-carbohydrate diet was significantly reduced.[26]

KETONES

Although diets which promote ketone bodies have been decried by some, their presence in the bloodstream has long been known to be a "perfectly natural mechanism for utilizing fatty acids."[27]

Ketone bodies have been shown to be normal constituents of blood and urine in the fed as well as the fasted state.[28,29,30,31] They not only are used as an effective fuel for metabolic energy needs, but have been shown to be a "preferred fuel" used in preference to glucose in tissues such as the myocardium[32] and skeletal muscle.[33] Owen, Cahill, and associates have shown that ketone bodies provide the major source of fuel for brain metabolism in man subjected to prolonged caloric deprivation.[34]

Moreover, as a major metabolic fuel, ketone bodies do not accumulate, but achieve a steady state on a given diet, being derived from free fatty acids only as the metabolic requirements of the body demand.[35] They were recently shown not to be neurotoxic even in the concentrations found in diabetic coma[36] or in starvation,[37] and they have been administered by intravenous infusion in man with no adverse effects.[38] In short, ketone bodies are the principal metabolic fuel involved in providing the energy derived from stored fat to tissues such as the brain.[39]

IS THERE A METABOLIC ADVANTAGE?

One question remains open, because no definitive studies have ever been reported, pro or con. That concerns whether the calorie theory is, as has been suggested, irrefutable, or whether by changing the composition of the diet, one can create a metabolic advantage, so that more weight may be lost on one of two equicaloric diets.

The theoretical background to explain how this is possible is presented by Edgar S. Gordon, who showed that different pathways of metabolism are utilized with different levels of thermogenic efficiency.[40] One would expect a diet in which almost all metabolic fuel is stored fat to take these inefficient, heat-wasting pathways.

Overfeeding studies, by Sims,[41] Bray,[42] and Kasper[43] demonstrate "Luxusconsumption" with nearly half the ingested calories being unaccounted for.

The metabolic advantage of low-carbohydrate diets has

been demonstrated and redemonstrated by Kekwick and Pawan[20-21] and by the body composition studies of Benoit, Watten, and Martin.[44] In the latter, a very low carbohydrate diet of 1,000 calories produced a greater fat loss than did fasting.

COMPARATIVE STUDIES

Yet the AMA Council, in considering the calorie theory irrefutable, has cited studies which purport to show that no metabolic advantage exists. Most of these studies are done at such a low level of caloric intake that the advantages of carbohydrate restriction are obscured. The proper way to demonstrate this phenomenon is at the 2,000 calorie or more level, and this has never been done.

The Kinsell[45] and Werner[46] studies are not applicable, using far too high a carbohydrate intake level. The Pilkington[47] work is seriously flawed by the elimination of the all-important first twelve days on the diet. The other study, by Olesen and Quaade, presents data favorable to the low-carbohydrate diet, with seven of eight subjects losing rapidly on it, and the eighth maintaining a weight loss despite a 900 calorie increase in intake.[48]

There is a surprisingly high incidence of conclusions not deriving from the data, which leads one to suspect that the calorie theory is being underwritten by nonscientific interests. For instance, Willard Krehl and his associates found that a diet almost identical to the Diet Revolution program took thirty-two pounds off a group of women in ten weeks, lowered their cholesterol and triglycerides, and produced a high level of appetite satiation. Yet they dismissed this achievement as "commensurate with caloric restriction" and went on to warn us of "the increased hazards of such diets."[49]

A comparative study was done at Cornell University by Charlotte Young and her associates. They compared 1,200-calorie diets containing 30, 60, and 104 grams of carbohydrate. Despite their conclusion that a higher carbohydrate diet should be recommended, their data clearly showed quite the opposite. The lower the carbohydrate intake, the more the subjects lost, and most importantly, on the 30-gram diet almost all of the weight lost was body fat, in contrast to the higher carbohydrate diets, where a significant portion of the lost weight was lean body mass, and not fat.[50]

However, there have been several published studies in Germany in which *both* the data *and* the conclusions support the thesis that a very low carbohydrate diet produces a metabolic advantage.[51-53] At the University of Wurzburg, in Germany, Rabast, Kasper, and Schönborn studied forty-five hospitalized patients for thirty-five days, the most comprehensive study done to date. The low-carbohydrate diet of the same number of calories significantly produced greater weight loss than the "balanced" version. The same workers demonstrated that the rate of metabolism was increased by the low-carbohydrate diet.[53]

CLINICAL RESULTS

Clinical success with the ketogenic diet in obesity has been reported uniformly since Pennington's work. Herman Taller compared the weight loss of patients on his low-carbohydrate diet with patients treated with a low-calorie diet. At the end of a year, the mean weight loss of patients on the high-fat, low-carbohydrate diet was sixty-three pounds, while the corresponding loss among the other patients was only twenty-three pounds.[54]

Robert Kemp, in Liverpool, England, using a 60-gram carbohydrate diet, reported that 707 out of 1,450 patients (49 percent) were able to lose at least 60 percent of their surplus weight.[55]

One of the largest series was gathered by Raymond H. Watten, who followed 2,000 patients at the San Diego Naval Station, using a 5 percent carbohydrate, 1,000-calorie, 80 percent fat diet. Weight loss was rapid and despite the high fat intake, subjects showed a slight drop in the mean cholesterol, and a 40 percent drop in their triglycerides.[56]

THE DIET'S SAFETY

There were no reports of adverse side effects in all the early studies on the ketogenic diet. The AMA report cites a study by Kark,[57] in which pemmican was administered to soldiers during an Arctic bivouac, and by Bloom and Azar,[58] where three subjects complained of fatigue. But these are studies of nonobese individuals. More definitive is the Kekwick and Pawan study which showed that whereas the majority of *nonobese* subjects developed symptoms and low fasting blood sugar on the ketogenic diet, only one of fourteen *obese* subjects developed these side effects.[59]

George Blackburn, using a diet with *no* carbohydrates which produces a maximal state of ketosis, states: "We have found no ill effect from this physiologic state."[60,61]

For long term use, the paucity of side effects has been annotated in several studies, in addition to my own.[1,8,13,17,18,19,39,43,44,49,51,53,54,55,56,62,63,64,65] Its beneficial effect on lipid metabolism has already been discussed.

In summary: There is ample documentation of the safety and efficacy of a ketogenic low-carbohydrate diet in obesity, diabetes, and a variety of other conditions.

I hope that a number of uncommitted, truth-seeking medical scientists will conduct a fair clinical trial of some of the book's nutritional principles, to evaluate for themselves the role that diet can play in helping patients.

When these precepts are put to the test, then physicians will see what I have been seeing and learn what I have learned—that many common symptoms and chronic illnesses respond rather dramatically to dietary and nutritional manipulation, and without pharmacological side effects.

The physician can do so much for his patients in this new area of nutrition medicine by simply guiding the patient in his eating pattern.

Try a dietary approach on a few patients who keep returning with the same symptoms and see if it helps those symptoms clear up.

I would like to quote Dr. Robert H. Moser, JAMA editor (March 24, 1975)—on a completely different subject, unrelated to my diet. But the philosophy is related to any controversy, to any new idea in science.

"Each of us must practice medicine on the basis of his own best judgment. . . . As new information becomes available, it will be placed on the scales. . . . Just remember, neither package insert, nor governmental 'approval,' nor journal article, nor pronouncements of scientific societies has the imprimatur of a divine revelation. All data must be weighed before a therapeutic decision is made . . . each of us must make up his own mind about what is best for his patient."

That is my one desire: for truth to prevail.

1. Atkins, R. C., *Dr. Atkins Diet Revolution*. New York: McKay, 1972
2. AMA Council on Foods and Nutrition, "A critique of low-carbohydrate reducing regimens," *JAMA* 224:1415, 1973.
3. Harvey, W., *On Corpulence in Relation to Disease*. London: H. Censhaw, 1872.
4. Wood, F. C., and Bierman, E. L., "New Concepts in Diabetic Diets," *Nutrition Today* 7:4, 1972.
5. Tolstoi, E., "The Effect of an Exclusive Meat Diet on the Chemical Constituents of the Blood," *J. Biol. Chem.* 83:753, 1929.
6. Ellis, R. W. B., "Some Effects of the Ketogenic Diet," *Arch. Dis. Child.* 6:285, 1931.
7. Peterman, M. G., "The Ketogenic Diet in Epilepsy," *JAMA* S4:1979, 1925.
8. Helmholz, H. F., "Ten Years Experience in Treatment of Epilepsy with the Ketogenic Diet," *Arch. Neurol. Psych.* 29:808, 1933.
9. Peshkin M. M., and Fineman, A. H., "Asthma in Children: Role of Ketogenic and Low Carbohydrate Diets in the Treatment of a Selected Group of Patients," *Am. J. Dis. Child.* 39:1240, 1930.
10. Nesbitt, R. M., and McDonald, C. H., "Low Calory, Low Fat Ketogenic Diet for Treatment of Infections of the Urinary Tract," *JAMA* 105:1183, 1935.
11. Hoelzel, F., "Diet and Resistance to Colds," *Science* 86:399, 1937.
12. Foldes, E., "Dehydrating Action of the Low Carbohydrate Diet and Its Therapeutic Applications," *Klin. Wochenschrift* 13:261, 1934.
13. Donaldson, B., *Strong Medicine*, London: Cassell, 1963.
14. Sandler, B. P., "Carbohydrate Metabolism in Ulcer Patients," *JAMA* 134:1120, 1947.
15. Sandler, B. P., and Berke, R., "Treatment of Tuberculosis with a Low Carbohydrate Diet," *Amer. Rev. Tuberculosis* 46:238, 1942.
16. Sandler, B. P., "The Control of the Anginal Syndrome with a Low Carbohydrate Diet," *Med. Annals Dist. of Col.* 10:371, 1941.
17. Pennington, A. W., "An Alternate Approach to the Problem of Obesity," *J. Clinical Nutrition* 1:100, 1953.
18. Pennington, A. W., "Treatment of Obesity with Calorically Unrestricted Diets," *J. Clinical Nutrition* 1:100, 1953.
19. Mackarness, R., *Eat Fat and Grow Slim*. New York: Doubleday, 1958.
20. Kekwick, A., and Pawan, G. L. S., "Calorie Intake in Relation to Body Weight Changes in the Obese," *Lancet* 1:155, 1956.
21. Kekwick, A., and Pawan, G. L. S., "Metabolic Study in Human Obesity with Isocaloric Diets High in Protein, Fat, or Carbohydrates," *Metabolism* 6:447, 1957.
22. Chalmers, T. M., Kekwick, A., and Pawan, G. L. S., "On the Fat-Mobilising Activity of Human Urine," *Lancet* 1:866, 1958.
23. Kroc, R. P., et al., American Chemical Society meeting, June 6, 1973.
24. Duncan, G., "Intermittent Fasts in Correction and Control of Intractable Obesity," *Am. J. Med. Sciences* 245:515, 1963.

25. Bloom, W. L., and Azar, G. J., "Similarities of Carbohydrate Deficiency and Fasting," *Archives Int. Med.* 112:333, 1963.

26. Stock, A. L., and Yudkin, J., "Nutrient Intake of Subjects on Low Carbohydrate Diet Used in Treatment of Obesity," *Am. J. Clin. Nutr.* 23:948, 1970.

27. Wick, A. N., and Drury, D. R., "The Effect of Concentration on the Rate of Beta-Hydroxy Batyric Acid in the Rabbit," *J. Biol. Chem.* 138:129, 1941.

28. Williamson, D. H., and Hems, R., "Metabolism and Function of Ketone Bodies" in *Essays in Cell Metabolism.* New York: Wiley-Interscience, 1970.

29. McKay, E. M., "The Significance of Ketosis," *J. Clinical Endoc.* 3:101, 1943.

30. Wieland, O., "Ketogenesis and Its Regulation," *Advances in Metabolic Dis.* 3:1, 1968.

31. Cahill, G. F., Jr., et al., "Hormone-Fuel Interrelationships During Fasting," *J. Clinical Invest.* 45:1951, 1966.

32. Williamson, J. R., and Krebs, H. A., "Acetoacetate as a Fuel of Respiration in the Perfused Rat Heart," *Biochem J.* 80:540, 1961.

33. Owen, O. E., and Reichard, G. A., Jr., "Substrate Extraction and/or Production by Forearm During Progressive Starvation, *Clin. Research* 18:2, 1970.

34. Owen, O. E., et al., "Brain Metabolism During Fasting," *J. Clin. Invest.* 46:159, 1967.

35. Cahill, G. F., Jr., and Aoki, T. T., "How Metabolism Affects Clinical Problems," *Medical Times* 98(10):106, 1970.

36. Ohman, J. L., et al., "The Cerebrospinal Fluid in Diabetic Ketoacidosis," *New Eng. J. Med.* 284:283, 1971.

37. Owen, O. E., et al., "Comparative Measurements of Glucose, Beta Hydroxybutyrate, Acetoacetate, and Insulin in Blood and Cerebrospinal Fluid During Starvation," *Metabolism* 23:7, 1974.

38. Cahill, G. F., Jr., Marliss, E. B., and Aoki, T. T., "Fat and Nitrogen Metabolism in Fasting Man," *Hormone and Metabolic Res., Suppl.* 1:181, 1970.

39. Blackburn, G. L., et al., "Preservation of the Physiological Responses in a Protein Sparing Modified Fast," *Clinical Research* 22:461A, 1974.

40. Gordon, E. S., "Metabolic Aspects of Obesity," *Advances in Metabolic Disorders* 4:229, 1970.

41. Sims, E. A. H., et al., Experimental Obesity in Man," *Transactions Assoc. American Physicians* 81:153, 1968.

42. Bray, G. A., "Lipogenesis in Human Adipose Tissue: Some Effects of Nibbling and Gorging," *J. Clin. Invest.* 51:537, 1972.

43. Kasper, A., Thiel, H., and Ehl, M., "Response of Body Weight to a Low Carbohydrate, High Fat Diet in Normal and Obese Subjects," *Amer. J. Clin. Nutr.* 26:197, 1973.

44. Benoit, F. L., Martin, R. L., and Watten, R. H., "Changes in Body Com-

position During Weight Reduction in Obesity Balance Studies Comparing Effects of Fasting and a Ketogenic Diet," *Annals Int. Med.* 63:604, 1965.

45. Kinsell, L. W., et al., "Calories Do Count," *Metabolism* 13:195, 1964.

46. Werner, S. C., "Comparison Between Weight Reduction on a High Calorie, High Fat Diet and on an Isocaloric Regimen High in Carbohydrate," *New Eng. J. Med.* 252:661, 1955.

47. Pilkington, T. R. E., et al., "Diet and Weight Reduction in the Obese," *Lancet* 1:856, 1960.

48. Olesen, E. S., and Quaade, F., "Fatty Food and Obesity," *Lancet* 1:1048, 1960.

49. Krehl, W. H., et al., "Some Metabolic Changes Induced by Low Carbohydrate Diets, *Am. J. Clin. Nutr.* 20:139, 1967.

50. Young, C. M., et al., "Effect on Body Composition and Other Parameters on Obese Young Men of Carbohydrate Level of Reduction Diet," *Am. J. Clin. Nutr.* 24:290, 1971.

51. Knick, B., and Grebe, H. V., "Dietary Carbohydrate Restriction," *Med. Ernährung* 6:233, 1965.

52. Wessels, M., et al., "Metabolic Consequences of Carbohydrate Poor Diet in Normal Persons," *Deutsch Med. Wschr.* 95:382, 1970.

53. Rabast, V., et al., "Treatment of Obesity with Low Carbohydrate Diets," *Med. Klin.* 70:653, 1975.

54. Taller, H., "Dietary Management of Obesity," *Am. J. Obs. Gyn.* 83:62, 1962.

55. Kemp, R., "The Overall Picture of Obesity," *Practitioner* 209:654, 1972.

56. Watten, R. H., Personal communication.

57. Kark, R. M., et al., "Defects of Pemmican as an Emergency Ration for Infantry Troops," *War Medicine* 7:345, 1945.

58. Bloom, W. L., and Azar, G. J., "Similarities of Carbohydrate Deficiency and Fasting," *Arch. Internal Med.* 112:333, 1963.

59. Kekwick, A., and Pawan, G. L. S., "Resistance to Ketosis in Obese Subjects," *Lancet* 2:1157, 1959.

60. Blackburn, G. L., Letter, *J. Amer. Diet. Assoc.* 15:194, 1974.

61. Flatt, J. P., and Blackburn, G. L., "The Metabolic Fuel Regulatory System: Implications for Protein-Sparing Therapies During Caloric Deprivation and Disease," *Am. J. Clin. Nutr.* 27:175, 1974.

62. Piscatelli, R. L., et al., "The Ketogenic Diet" in *Obesity,* F. A. Davis, 1969.

63. Khurani, R. C., "Modified Ketogenic Diet in Obesity," *Current Med. Dialog.* 40:528, 1973.

64. Evans, E., et al., "The Absence of Undesirable Changes During Consumption of the Low Carbohydrate Diet," *Nutrition and Metabolism* 17:360, 1974.

65. Weiss, H., "A Treatment for Diabetes," in *New Dynamics of Preventive Medicine,* 4:101, 1976.

References

Page Line

9 5   Gortner, W., Council for the Advancement of Science Writing, Brookhaven, 1971.

9 27   Klinger, A. D., *Medical Tribune*, August 14, 1974.

13 32   Anthony, D., and Forsham, P., *Diabetes*, volume 22, 1973.

16 5   Faludi, G., Bendersky, G., and Gerber, P., *Annals of the New York Academy of Science*, volume 148, March 26, 1968.

16 7   Harper, C. R., United Airlines, quoted in *New Dynamics of Preventive Medicine*, Stratton–New York, volume 3, 1975.

16 37   Special Report: Statement on Hypoglycemia, *Diabetes*, volume 22, 1973.

17 28   Special report: Sugar conspiracy. *Drug Therapy*, October, 1976.

23 25   Special report: Sugar conspiracy. *Drug Therapy*, October, 1976.

24 5   Ahrens, R. A., *American Journal of Clinical Nutrition*, volume 27, 1974.

26 31   Ahrens, R. A., *American Journal of Clinical Nutrition*, volume 27, 1974.

16 37   Special Report: Statement on Hypoglycemia, *Diabetes*, volume 22, 1973.

25 20   Hodges, R. E., and Krehl, W. A., *American Journal of Clinical Nutrition*, volume 17, 1965.

26 21   Paton, J. H. P., *British Medical Journal*, volume 1, 1933.

26 36   United States Senate Select Committee on Nutrition and Human Needs: "Sugar in the Diet, Diabetes and Heart Disease." Hearing April 30–May 2, 1973.

28 19   Masironi, P., *Bulletin of World Health Organization*, volume 42, 1970.

28 25   Lopez, A., Hodges, R. E., and Krehl, W. A., *American Journal of Clinical Nutrition*, February, 1966.

28 33   Gigon A., *Zeitschrift ges. exp. Med.*, volume 40, 1924.

28 35   Davis, R. H., et al., *Experientia*, volume 30, 1974.

29 10   Yudkin, J., Senate hearings, May 1, 1973.

Page Line
29 11   Cohen, A. M., Senate hearings, April 30, 1973.
30 24   Naismith, D. J., *Nutrition and Metabolism,* volume 16, 1974.
30 25   Winitz, M., Graff, J., and Seedman, D. A., *Archives Biochemistry and Biophysics,* volume 108, 1964.
30 25   MacDonald, I., and Braithwaite, D. M., *Clinical Science,* volume 27, 1964.
30 28   Rifkind, B. M., et al., *Lancet,* volume 2, 1966.
30 34   Yudkin, J., and Morland, J., *American Journal of Clinical Nutrition,* volume 20, 1967.
31 18   Jung, Y., et al., *Diabetes,* volume 20, 1971.
34 12   Proxmire, Senator William, quoted in *Prevention,* September, 1974.
34 24   United States Senate Select Committee on Nutrition and Human Needs, hearings, April 12, 1973.
35 3   United States Department of Health, Education, and Welfare publication numbers 72–8130 through 72–8134, 1972.
35 15   Klinger, A., *Medical Tribune,* August 7, 1964.
35 20   "Nutrition Canada," in *Nutrition Today,* January, 1974.
35 27   Zee, P., *Journal of the American Medical Association,* volume 213, 1970.
35 27   Third Western Hemisphere Nutrition Congress, Bal Harbour, Florida.
38 9   Schweicker, Senator Richard, United States Senate hearings, April 30, 1973.
38 30   Mertz, W., United States Senate hearings, April 30, 1973.
39 5   Pfeiffer, C. C., *Mental and Elemental Nutrients* (New Canaan: Keats, 1975).
39 12   Schroeder, H., *The Trace Elements and Man* (Old Greenwich: Devin-Adair, 1973).
41 15   White, P. S., editorial in *Journal of American Medical Association,* August 11, 1975.
60 14   Lincoln, J. E., *American Journal of Clinical Nutrition,* volume 25, 1972.
61 27   Cohen, A. M., Senate hearings, April 30, 1973.
62 17   Merimee, T. J., *New England Journal of Medicine,* volume 285, 1971.
62 17   Genuth, S. M., *Annals of Internal Medicine,* volume 79, 1973.
62 37   Cleave, T. L., and Campbell, G. D., *Diabetes, Coronary Thrombosis, and the Saccharine Disease* (Bristol: John Wright and Sons, 1969).
64 1   Sussman, K. E., et al., *Diabetes,* volume 15, 1966.
64 4   Faludi, G., Bendersky, G., and Gerber, P., *Annals of the New York Academy of Science,* volume 148, March 26, 1968.
64 5, 29 Kryston, L. J., *Endocrinology and Diabetes* (New York: Grune & Stratton, 1975).
64 17   Wapnick, S., et al., *Lancet,* 1972.

Page Line

64 32   Duncan, G., et al., *Annals of the New York Academy of Sciences,* volume 148, 1968.

64 31   Perlstein, I. B., *Internist Observer,* 1974.

64 32   Dumitrescu, C., et al., *Rev. Roumaine de Medecine Interne,* volume 10, 1973.

65 22   Seltzer, H., Fajans, S. S., and Conn, J. W., *Diabetes,* 1956.

65 30   Ricketts, H. T., et al., *Diabetes,* volume 15, 1966.

66 20   Smelo, L. S., *Modern Treatment,* volume 3, 1966.

67 11   Faludi, G., Bendersky, G., and Gerber, P., *Annals of the New York Academy of Science,* volume 148, March 26, 1968.

67 24   Muller, W. A., et al., *New England Journal of Medicine,* volume 285, 1971.

67 26   Pfeiffer, E. F., and Laube, H., *Advances in Metabolic Disorders,* volume 7, 1974.

71 8   Conn, J. W., *Journal of Clinical Investigation,* volume 15, 1936.

71 16   Conn, J. W., and Seltzer, H. S., *American Journal of Medicine,* volume 19, 1955.

71 32   Portis, S. A., and Zetman, I. H., *Journal of the American Medical Association,* volume 121, 1943.

71 32   Fabrykant, M., *Metabolism,* volume 4, 1955.

71 32   Gyland, S. P., *Journal of the American Medical Association,* volume 163, 1957.

71 32   Salzer, H. M., *Journal of the National Medical Association,* volume 58, 1966.

71 32   Beuhler, M. S., *Lancet* (Minneapolis), volume 82, 1962.

75 28   Danowski, T. S., et al., *Diabetes,* volume 19, 1970.

80 29   Hawkins, D., and Pauling, L., *Orthomolecular Psychiatry* (San Francisco: W. H. Freeman and Company, 1973).

103 26   Yudkin, J., *Postgraduate Medicine,* volume 51, 1972.

112 26   Owen, O. E., et al., *Journal of Clinical Investigation,* volume 46, 1967.

114 9   Yudkin, J., *Lancet,* October 29, 1960.

114 9   Theologides, A., *American Journal of Clinical Nutrition,* volume 29, 1976.

114 26   Blackburn, G. L., *Journal of the American Dietetic Association,* volume 65, 1974.

114 27   Sapir, O. G., et al., *Journal of Clinical Investigation,* volume 51, 1972.

114 35   Grey, N., and Kipnis, D. M., *New England Journal of Medicine,* volume 285, 1971.

114 37   Cahill, G., and Aoki, T. T., *Medical Times,* volume 98, 1970.

114 37   Flatt, J. P., and Blackburn, G. L., *American Journal of Clinical Nutrition,* volume 27, 1974.

115 2   Sims, E. A., et al., *Hormone and Metabolic Research,* volume 4, 1974.

Page Line

115 3   Yudkin, J., *Nature*, volume 239, 1972.

115 26 Sassoon, H., *American Journal of Clinical Nutrition*, volume 26, 1973.

115 36 Flatt, J. P., et al., *Metabolism*, volume 23, 1974.

116 21 Benoit, F. L., Martin, R. L., and Watten, R. H., *Annals of Internal Medicine*, volume 63, 1965.

116 33 Grande, F., *Annals of Internal Medicine*, volume 68, 1968.

117 4   Sims, E. A., *Recent Progress in Human Research*, volume 29, 1973.

117 6   Bray, G. L., *Journal of Clinical Investigation*, volume 51, 1972.

131 9   Kunin, R. A., *Journal of Orthomolecular Psychiatry*, volume 5, 1976.

139 36 "Nutrition Canada," in *Nutrition Today*, January, 1974.

142 17 Yew, M. S., *Science News*, May 5, 1973.

144 25 Harper, A. E., *Journal of the American Dietetic Association*, February, 1974.

147 7   Altschule, M., *Preventive Medicine*, volume 3, June, 1974.

147 11 Williams, R. J., *Biochemical Individuality* (New York: John Wiley and Sons, 1956).

147 36 Hoffer, A., and Osmond, H., *International Journal of Neuropsychiatry*, volume 2, 1966.

147 36 Cott, A., *Schizophrenia*, volume 1, 1969.

147 36 Hawkins D., and Pauling, L., *Orthomolecular Psychiatry* (San Francisco: W. H. Freeman and Company, 1973).

148 12 Newbold, H. L., *Meganutrients for Your Nerves* (New York: Wyden, 1975).

148 19 Green, R. G., *Schizophrenia*, volume 2, 1970.

150 21 Regnier, E., *Review of Allergy*, October, 1968.

150 22 Wood, H. C., Jr., *Overfed but Undernourished* (New York: Tower Publications, Inc., 1971).

151 5   Wilson, C. W. M., et al., *Journal of Clinical Pharmacology*, volume 15, 1975.

151 5   Anderson, T. W., et al., *Canadian Medical Association Journal*, volume 107, 1972.

151 5   Coulehan, J., et al., *New England Journal of Medicine*, volume 290, 1974.

151 5   Charleston, S. S., and Clegg, S. M., *Lancet*, volume 1, 1972.

151 5   Pauling, L., *Medical Tribune*, April 7, 1976.

151 14 Klenner, F. R., *Journal of the International Academy of Preventive Medicine*, Spring, 1974.

151 22 Cameron, E., and Pauling, L., *Proceedings of the National Academy of Sciences*, October, 1976.

151 7   Hawkins, D., and Pauling, L., *Orthomolecular Psychiatry* (San Francisco: W. H. Freeman and Company, 1973.

152 7   Ginter, E., et al., *Clinical Nutrition and Metabolism*, volume 12, 1970.

152 9   Spittle, C. R., *Lancet*, volume 2, 1971.

Page Line

152 9   Sokoloff, B., et al., *Journal of American Geriatric Society,* volume 14, 1966.

152 16   Verangieri, A., *Rutgers University News,* June 18, 1975.

152 22   Greenwood, J. C., *Medical Annals of the District of Columbia,* volume 33, 1964.

152 28   Riccitelli, M. L., *Journal of American Geriatric Society,* January, 1972.

152 34   Passwater, R. A., *Supernutrition* (New York: Dial Press, 1975).

152 37   Schlegel, J. E., *Transactions of Association of Genito-Urinary Physicians,* volume 61, 1967.

152 39   Mirvish, S. S.; Raineri, R., et al.; Kamm, J. J., et al., *Annals of the New York Academy of Sciences,* volume 258, 1975.

153 4   Newbold, H. L., *Meganutrients for Your Nerves* (New York: Wyden, 1975).

153 6   Pfeiffer, C. C., *Mental and Elemental Nutrients* (New Canaan: Keats, 1975).

153 33   Hawkins, D., and Pauling, L., *Orthomolecular Psychiatry* (San Francisco: W. H. Freeman and Company, 1973).

154 8   Osmond, H., and Hoffer, A., *Lancet,* volume 1, 1962.

154 16   Spies, T., *Annals of Internal Medicine,* volume 26, 1947.

155 22   Ellis, John M., and Presley, J., *Vitamin B₆: The Doctor's Report* (New York: Harper and Row, 1973).

155 29   Collipp, P. J., *Annals of Allergy,* volume 35, 1975.

155 31   Cochrane, W. A., Ninth International Congress of Pediatrics, 1959.

155 33   Coursin, David B., *Annals of New York Academy of Science,* September 30, 1969.

156 7   Pfeiffer, C. C., *Mental and Elemental Nutrients* (New Canaan:
160 21   Keats, 1975).

156 18   Williams, R. J., *Nutrition against Disease* (New York: Bantam, 1973).

157 12   Sobota, S., and Bialecki, M., *Proceedings European Rheumatology Congress,* 1964.

157 13   Thomas, A. M., and Freedman, B., *Transactions of Royal Society of Tropical Medicine and Hygiene,* volume 40, 1947.

157 14   Day, P. S., and Sydenstricker, L., *Archives of Opthalmology,* volume 65, 1967.

157 37   Ralli, E., *Vitamins and Hormones,* volume 11, 1953.

158 18   Leinwand, I., and Moore, H., *American Heart Journal,* volume 38, 1949.

158 34   Morrison, L. M., and Gonzales, W. F., *Proceedings of Society for Experimental Biology and Medicine,* volume 73, 1950.

159 11   Kets, K. N., and Novoselova, N. A., *Soviet Medicine,* April, 1971.

159 34   United States Department of Health, Education, and Welfare publication numbers 72–8130 through 72–8134, 1972.

159 38   Sullivan, L., and Herbert, V., *Journal of Clinical Nutrition,* volume 43, 1964.

Page *Line*

160 2   Baker, H., et al., *American Journal of Clinical Nutrition,* volume 28, 1975.

160 4   Ahmed, F., et al., *American Journal of Clinical Nutrition,* volume 28, 1975.

160 4   Daniel, W. A., Jr., *American Journal of Clinical Nutrition,* volume 28, 1975.

160 20   Herbert, V., *Proceedings of the XIV International Congress of Haematology,* São Paulo, Brazil, 1972.

161 3   Ellis, F. R., and Nasser, S., *British Journal of Nutrition,* volume 30, 1973.

161 16   Ahmed, F., et al., *American Journal of Clinical Nutrition,* volume 28, 1975.

161 18   Herbert, V., in *Modern Nutrition in Health and Disease* (Philadelphia: Lea and Febiger, 1973).

161 25   Fitzpatrick, W. H., *Nutrition Research in the USSR,* United States Department of HEW publication number 72:57, 1972.

161 25   McNaughton Foundation, *Vitamin B₁₅,* 1967.

162 6   Houston, R., *American Journal of Clinical Nutrition,* volume 26, 1973.

163 7   Williams, H. T. G., Fenna, D., and MacBeth, R. A., *Surgery, Gynecology and Obstetrics,* volume 132, 1971.

163 7   Haeger, K., *Vascular Disease,* volume 5, 1968.

163 7   Boyd, A. M., and Marks, J., *Angiology,* volume 14, 1963.

163 8   Hodges, R. E., *Cardiac Rehabilitation,* volume 4, 1974.

163 8   Toone, W. M., *New England Journal of Medicine,* November 1, 1973.

163 8   Ochsner, A., *New England Medical Journal,* volume 271, 1964.

163 11   Ayers, S., Jr., *California Medicine,* October, 1973.

163 11   Abrams, A., *Medical World News,* Annual Review, 1966.

163 11   Shute, W. E., and Taub, H. J., *Vitamin E for Ailing and Healthy Hearts* (New York: Pyramid Publications, 1972).

164 5   Underwood, B., *Science,* December 27, 1974.

164 18   *Pediatric Herald,* January–February, 1969.

164 21   Seifter, E., American Chemical Society annual meeting, Chicago, August 29, 1975.

164 24   Chernov, M. S.; Hale, H. W., Jr.; and Wood, M., *American Journal of Surgery,* volume 122, 1972.

164 33   Bauernfeind, J. C., et al., *American Journal of Clinical Nutrition,* March, 1974.

166 32   Jones, J. E., et al., *Annals New York Academy of Sciences,* volume 62, 1969.

167 13   Bersohn, T., and Oelofse, P. J., *Lancet,* volume 1, 1957.

167 18   Seelig, M. S., and Heggtveit, H. A., *American Journal of Clinical Nutrition,* January, 1974.

169 4   Halsted, J. A., and Smith, J. C., Jr., *Lancet,* volume 1, 1970.

169 4   Vallee, B. L., et al., *New England Journal of Medicine,* volume 255, 1956.

Page Line

169 7   Hassey, H. H., *Journal of the American Medical Association*, volume 228, 1974.

169 11   Smith, J. C., Jr., et al., *Science*, September 7, 1973.

169 15   *Time* magazine, November 19, 1965.

169 33   Pfeiffer, C. C., and Iliev, V., *International Review of Neurobiology*, Supplement 1, 1972.

170 30   Wolff, J., *American Journal of Medicine*, volume 47, 1969.

171 18   Schroeder, H., *Trace Elements and Man* (Old Greenwich: Devin-Adair, 1973).

171 26   Mertz, W., *Physiological Reviews*, volume 49, 1969.

171 26   Bonner, E. M., et al., American Institute of Nutrition Conference, August 8, 1976.

172 13   Ershoff, B. H., *Proceedings of the Society of Experimental Biology and Medicine*, July, 1951.

187 9   Veech, R. L., *Drug Therapy*, October, 1976.

190 16   Greden, J. F., *American Journal of Psychology*, volume 131, 1974.

190 24   Burg, A. W., *Tea and Coffee Trade Journal*, January, 1975.

190 24   *Medical World News*, January 26, 1976.

190 34   Frienkel, N., et al., *Diabetes*, volume 14, 1965.

190 36   McLaughlan, V. M., et al., *Nutrition Reports International*, volume 8, 1973.

196 37   *Medical World News*, January 11, 1974.

197 33   Hofeldt, F. D., *Metabolism*, September, 1975.

199 10   Philpott, W., *New Dynamics of Preventive Medicine*, volume 1, 1974.

200 28   Beck, P., *Metabolism*, volume 22, 1973.

201 6   Rivers, J. M., *American Journal of Clinical Nutrition*, volume 28, 1975.

201 7   Ahmed, F., et al., *American Journal of Clinical Nutrition*, volume 28, 1975.

201 7   Prasad, A. S., et al., *American Journal of Clinical Nutrition*, volume 28, 1975.

201 7   Smith, J. L., et al., *American Journal of Clinical Nutrition*, volume 28, 1975.

206 31   Blackburn, G. L., et al., *Federation Proceedings*, volume 72, 1973.

209 29   Perlstein, I. B., *Internist Observer*, 1974.

212 23   *Medical World News*, January 5, 1973.

212 37   Lachance, P. A.; Miskimin, D.; and Powers, J., *Food Technology*, February, 1974.

214 9   Peckham, C. H., and Christianson, R. E., *American Journal of Obstetrics and Gynecology*, volume 111, 1971.

215 22   Golubjatnikov, R., *Modern Medicine*, December 25, 1972.

216 9   Parra, A., et. al., *Pediatrics Research*, volume 5, 1971.

216 22   Dunn, P. J., *New Dynamics of Preventive Medicine*, volume 2 (New York: Stratton, 1974).

216 25   Court, J. M., et al., *Archives of Diseases of Children*, volume 46, 1971.

Page Line

217 14   Peterman, M. J., *Journal of the American Medical Association,* volume 84, 1925.

217 17   Feingold, B. F., *Introduction to Clinical Allergy* (Springfield, Illinois: C. C. Thomas, 1973).

220 4   Huang, T. C., et al., American Chemical Society Annual Meeting, Chicago, 1973.

220 16   Passwater, R. A., *American Laboratory,* September, 1972.

220 25   Bhattathiry, E., and Siperstein, M., *Journal of Clinical Investigation,* volume 43, 1963.

220 28   Wilson, J., and Lindsay, C., *Journal of Clinical Investigation,* volume 44, 1965.

220 34   Svacha, A. J., et al., *Federation Proceedings,* volume 33, 1974.
Takeuchi, N., et al., *Clinical Pharmacology and Therapeutics,* volume 16, 1974.

220 37   Alfin-Slater, R., et al., Tenth International Congress of Nutrition, Kyoto, Japan, August, 1975.

221 21   Mann, G. V., Fourth Annual Food Writers Conference, Chicago, 1974.

221 23   Kannel, W. B., *Annals of Internal Medicine,* volume 74, 1971.

221 25   Nichols, A. B., et al., *Journal of the American Medical Association,* volume 236, 1976.

221 29   Pearce, M. L., and Dayton, S., *Journal of the American Medical Association,* volume 214, 1970.

221 29   Pinckney, E. R., *Medical Counterpoint,* May, 1971.

221 29   Reiser, R., *American Journal of Clinical Nutrition,* volume 26, 1973.

221 29   Jacobson, N. L., *BioScience,* volume 24, March, 1974.

221 29   Altshule, M. D., *Medical Counterpoint,* November, 1970.

221 37   DeBakey, M., et al., *Journal of the American Medical Association,* volume 189, August 31, 1964.

222 4   Sperling, G., *Journal of Nutrition,* volume 55, 1965.

222 6   Huang, T. C., American Chemical Society Annual Meeting, 1975.

222 12   Report of a research committee, *Lancet,* volume 2, 1968.

222 16   Report of a research committee, *Lancet,* volume 2, 1965.

222 22   Frantz, I. D., et al., *Internal Medicine News,* volume 9, 1976.

222 28   Coronary Drug Project, *Journal of the American Medical Association,* volume 231, January 27, 1975.

223 4   Report of the British Advisory Panel, *Nutrition Today,* January, 1975.

223 15   Masironi, P., *Bulletin of World Health Organization,* volume 42, 1970.

223 20   Cleave, T. L., The Saccharine Disease (Bristol: Wright & Sons Ltd., 1974).

223 24   Gsell, D., and Mayer, J., *American Journal of Clinical Nutrition,* volume 10, 1962.

223 27   Loginon, A. S., *Kardiologiya,* 1962.

Page Line
224 18   Antar, M. A.; Ohlson, M. A.; and Hodges, R. E., *American Journal of Clinical Nutrition*, volume 14, 1964.
224 21   American Health Foundation, position statement. *Preventive Medicine*, volume 1, 1972.
224 27   Malhotra, S. L., *American Journal of Clinical Nutrition*, volume 20, 1967.
225 2   Kuo, P. T., *Transactions of the Association of American Physicians*, volume 78, 1965.
225 2   Albrink, M. J., *Postgraduate Medicine*, volume 55, 1974.
225 5   Carlson, L., and Böttiger, L. E., *Lancet*, volume 1, 1972.
225 27   Goldstein, J. L., et al., *Journal of Clinical Investigation*, volume 52, 1973.
225 34   Bray, G., et al., *Diabetes*, volume 23, 1974.
225 38   Fujita, Y., *Diabetes*, volume 23, 1974.
226 6   Watten, R. H., personal communication.
226 9   Albrink, M., *Progress in Biochemical Pharmacology*, volume 8, 1973.
226 11   Krehl, W., *American Journal of Clinical Nutrition*, volume 20, 1967.
226 16   Reissell, P. K., et al., *American Journal of Clinical Nutrition*, volume 19, 1966.
226 16   Galbraith, W. B.; Connor, W. E.; and Stone, D. B., *Annals of Internal Medicine*, volume 64, 1966.
226 24   Ende, N., *American Journal of Clinical Nutrition*, volume 11, 1962.
226 38   Rickman, F., et al., *Journal of the American Medical Association*, volume 228, 1974.
227 8   Blumenfeld, A., *Obesity and Bariatric Medicine*, volume 3, 1974.
227 9   Pinckney, E. R., and Pinckney, C., *Cholesterol Controversy* (Los Angeles: Sherbourne Press, 1973).
227 13   Griffiths, C. O., Jr., quoted in Pinckney, *Cholesterol Controversy.*
227 23   Kaunitz, H., and Johnson, R. E., *Lipids*, volume 8, 1973.
227 27   Kummerow, F. A., et al., Federation of American Societies for Experimental Biology meeting, 1974.
227 31   Harman, D., *Journal of Gerontology*, volume 26, 1971.
228 2   Oster, K., *Medical Counterpoint*, January, 1974.
228 3   Mann, G. V., *Moneysworth*, November, 1975.
228 9   Mirkin, G., *Journal of the American Medical Association*, March 26, 1973.
228 9   Fabrykant, M., and Gelfand, M., *American Journal of Medical Science*, volume 247, 1964.
228 13   Tzagournis, M., et al., *Annals of Internal Medicine*, volume 67, 1967.
229 3   Barboriak, J. J., *Journal of Nutrition*, volume 64, 1958.
229 3   Naimi, S., *Journal of Nutrition*, volume 86, 1965.

Page Line
229 7   Greenberg, L. D., and Rinehart, J. F., *Proceedings of the Society for Experimental Biology and Medicine,* volume 76, 1951.
229 10   Spittle, C., *Lancet,* volume 2, December 11, 1971.
229 13   Sokoloff, B., *Journal of the American Geriatrics Society,* volume 14, 1966.
229 23   Williams, R., *Nutrition against Disease* (New York: Bantam Books, Inc., 1973).
229 38   Bersohn, I., *Lancet,* volume 1, 1957.
229 38   Morrison, L. M., and Gonzales, W. F., *Geriatrics,* volume 13, 1958.
230 2   Riccardi, B. A., and Fahrenbach, M. J., *Proceedings for the Society for Experimental Biology and Medicine,* volume 124, 1967.
230 3   Wing, H., and Fletcher, A. D., Federation of American Societies for Experimental Biology, 1972.
230 12   Shreeve, W., et al., *Metabolism,* volumes 23 and 24, 1974 and 1975.
230 14   Yudkin, J., *Nature,* volume 239, 1972.
230 19   Anderson, J. T., et al., *Journal of Nutrition,* volume 79, 1963.
234 6   Shaw, R. A., et al., *American Journal of Cardiology,* volume 21, 1968.
234 6   Sims, E. A. H., et al., *Annals of Internal Medicine,* volume 63, 1965.
235 7   Adlersberg, D., and Porges, O., *Klinische Wochenschrift,* volume 12, 1933.
235 9   Harrison, T., *American Heart Journal,* volume 26, 1943.
235 13   Sandler, B. P., International College of Angiology annual meeting, Montreal, 1974.
235 18   Roberts, H. J., *Journal of the American Geriatrics Society,* volume 14, 1966.
236 13   Seelig, M., and Hettgviet, A., *American Journal of Clinical Nutrition,* volume 27, 1974.
236 26   Burkitt, D. P., et al., *Journal of the American Medical Association,* volume 229, 1974.
237 31   Peterman, M. J., *Journal of the American Medical Association,* volume 84, 1925.
237 2   Yudkin, J., *British Medical Journal,* June 17, 1972.
237 8   Martini, G. A., *Klinische Wochenschrift,* volume 54, 1976.
237 21   Heaton, K. W., Ninth Advanced Medicine Symposium, Pitman, London, 1973.
237 32   Livingston, S., *Comprehensive Management of Epilepsy in Infancy, Childhood and Adolescence* (Springfield, Illinois: C. C. Thomas, 1972).
238 9   Dalessio, D. J., *Journal of the American Medical Association,* volume 232, 1975.
238 15   Roberts, H. J., *Journal of the American Geriatrics Society,* volume 15, 1967.
238 29   Harris, S., *Annals of Internal Medicine,* volume 16, 1936.

Page Line
238 29   Abrahamson, E. M., *Journal of Clinical Endocrinology*, volume 1, 1941.
238 30   Randolph, T. G., et al., *Journal of Laboratory Clinical Medicine*, volume 16, 1950.
238 32   Peshkin, M. M., and Fineman, A. H., *American Journal of Diseases of Children*, volume 39, 1930.
239 22   Nesbitt, R. M., *Journal of the American Medical Association*, volume 105, 1935.
239 25   Roberts, H. J., *Journal of the American Geriatrics Society*, volume 14, 1966.
240 4   Spiesman, I. G., and Arnold, L., *American Journal of Digestive Diseases*, volume 1, 1937.
240 4   Hoelzel, F., *Science*, volume 86, 1937.
240 4   Paton, J. H. P., *British Medical Journal*, volume 1, 1933.
240 6   Abrahamson, E. M., *Journal of Clinical Endocrinology*, volume 4, 1944.
240 7   Sandler, B. P., *Diseases of the Chest*, volume 17, 1950.
240 11   *Science*, May 9, 1975.
240 11   Latham, M. C., *Science*, 1975.
240 11   Scrimshaw, N. S.; Taylor, C. E.; and Gordon, J. E., *World Health Association*, Series Number 57, Geneva, 1968.
241 37   Adams, R., and Murray, F., *Megavitamin Therapy* (New York: Larchmont Books, 1973).
242 34   Smith, R. L., quoted in *Psychodietetics*, by Cheraskin and Ringsdorf (New York: Stein and Day, 1974).
243 17   Register, U. D., et al., *Journal of the American Dietetic Association*, volume 61, 1972.
243 29   Cleave, T. L., *The Saccharine Disease* (Bristol: John Wright and Sons, 1974).
246 30   Ricketts, H. T., et al., *Diabetes*, volume 15, 1966.
246 35   Smelo, L. S., *Modern Treatment*, volume 3, 1966.
247 1   Muller, W. A., et al., *New England Journal of Medicine*, volume 285, 1971.
247 2   Pfeiffer, E. F., and Laube, H., *Advances in Metabolic Disorders*, volume 7, 1974.
250 2   Bristrian, B. R., and Blackburn, G. L., et al., *Clinical Research*, volume 23, 1975.
254 29   White, P. L., *Journal of the American Medical Association*, volume 224, June 4, 1973.
257 5   Adams, R., *Did You Ever See a Fat Squirrel* (Emmaus, Pennsylvania: Rodale Books Inc., 1972).
257 32   Stare, F. J., editor, *World Review of Nutrition and Diabetes*, volume 22, 1975.
258 2   "Nutrition Misinformation and Food Faddism," *Nutrition Reviews*, Special Supplement, July, 1974.

Index

National Diet Study

By filling in the following questionnaire you will become a participant in a novel experiment that will test nationwide the effect of a new diet on tens of thousands of people. If you participate, I promise to send you the national results of what I hope will be the largest, most worthwhile experiment of its kind ever conducted!

REGISTRATION CARD (To be filled out and mailed before you start the diet)

- -

Dr. Atkins: Yes, I want to participate in your nationwide test of a new diet program. Please register my name and "benchmark" information immediately. As I progress, I will fill in the questionnaire and complete and mail it to you in eight weeks.

BASIC DATA

Mr. ☐
Mrs. ☐ _____
Ms. ☐

AGE _____

ADDRESS _____

SEX _____

A)

CITY _____

HEIGHT _____
feet   inches

STATE _____ ZIP_____

WEIGHT _____

B) Have you consulted your doctor?   ☐ Yes   ☐ No
(If "no," skip next question)

C) Were laboratory tests done?   ☐ Yes   ☐ No
(If so, please submit results in
Part A, subdivision C of Participation Questionnaire)

D) Your weight goal: ☐ Lose   ☐ Gain   ☐ Stay the same

FOLD HERE -   FOLD HERE   - - - - -

NAME _____
ADDRESS _____
CITY _____
STATE _____ ZIP_____

AFFIX
POSTAGE
STAMP

DR. ROBERT C. ATKINS
6 COMMERCIAL STREET
HICKSVILLE, NEW YORK 11801

FASTEN HERE

Participation Questionnaire

By filling in the following questionnaire you will become a participant in a novel experiment that will test nationwide the effect of a new diet on tens of thousands of people. If you participate, I promise to send you the national results of what I hope will be the largest, most worthwhile experiment of its kind ever conducted!

Note that Part A should be filled in *before* you start the diet, Part B after you have been on the diet one week, Part C after three weeks, Part D after eight or more weeks.

PART A. TO BE FILLED IN <u>BEFORE</u> YOU BEGIN THE SUPERENERGY DIET

A. AGE _____ SEX M F HEIGHT _____ WEIGHT _____
                                    ft. in.   lbs.

B. Have you consulted your doctor? Yes ☐ No ☐
   (In case you did not, go to Part E)

C. Were laboratory tests done? Yes ☐ No ☐

D. Please list your glucose tolerance results:
   Fasting sugar _____   Highest reading _____
   Lowest reading _____   GTT was a _____ hour test.
   Your cholesterol reading _____   Triglyceride _____
   Uric acid _____   Blood pressure _____
   Abnormalities on any other tests _____
   _____

   Known diagnoses (example, high blood pressure). List.
   _____
   _____

E. Your weight goal: To maintain same ☐ To lose _____ lbs. To gain _____ lbs.
   Your energy score (see p. 53) _____   Your mood score (see p. 56) _____
   List your three major symptoms, if you have any, and their scores (see p. 57)
   (in these, 100 is the absence of symptom; 0 is the symptom at its worst)

   _____   _____
                                                        score
   _____   _____

   _____   _____

PART B. TO BE FILLED IN AFTER BEING ON THE DIET FOR ONE WEEK

Did you follow the diet? 100% ☐ Almost 100% ☐ Fairly well ☐ Not really ☐
List any new symptoms _____
Average energy score on the last 2 days _____
Average mood score on the last 2 days _____
Score for symptom 1 _____
Score for symptom 2 _____
Score for symptom 3 _____
List any other symptoms that worsened _____
List any other symptoms that improved _____
Weight gain of _____ lbs. or weight loss of _____ lbs.

PART C. TO BE FILLED OUT AFTER BEING ON THE DIET FOR THREE WEEKS

Did you follow your diet? 100% ☐ Almost 100% ☐ Fairly well ☐ Not really ☐

List any new symptoms _____

Energy score during third week _____

Mood score during third week _____

Score for symptom 1 _____

Score for symptom 2 _____

Score for symptom 3 _____

List any other symptoms that worsened _____

List any other symptoms that improved _____

Weight gain (since the beginning of diet) of _____ lbs. or weight loss of _____ lbs.

PART D. TO BE FILLED IN AFTER BEING ON THE DIET FOR EIGHT WEEKS

Did you follow your diet? 100% ☐ Almost 100% ☐ Fairly well ☐ Not really ☐

List any new symptoms _____

Energy score during eighth week _____

Mood score during eighth week _____ FOLD HERE

Score for symptom 1 _____

Score for symptom 2 _____

Score for symptom 3 _____

List any other symptoms that worsened _____

List any other symptoms that improved _____

Weight gain of _____ lbs. or weight loss of _____ lbs.

Which diet are you on now? _____

Do you take vitamin supplements?

Yes, as in book ☐ More than in book ☐ Yes, but less than in book ☐ No ☐

Do you plan to stay on a version of this diet?

Yes, always ☐ For a limited time ☐ From time to time ☐ No ☐

If you have seen your physician since diet, what are the test results now for:

Fasting blood sugar _____   Cholesterol _____

Triglyceride _____   Uric acid _____

Blood pressure _____

Other abnormality or special comments _____

_____

FOLD HERE

AFFIX
POSTAGE
STAMP

NAME _____

ADDRESS _____

CITY _____

STATE _____ ZIP _____

DR. ROBERT C. ATKINS
6 COMMERCIAL STREET
HICKSVILLE, NEW YORK 11801

FASTEN HERE